The purpose of this book is to help practicing an̲... ...and grading and *to do* it. Chapters, illustrations, and ... ...ᵤ aı nelping readers to (a) see how grades function in schools and schooling, and (b) develop skills in assigning grades to student work and combining grades into marks for student report cards. Grades are a major means of communicating about student work to students, parents, future teachers, and other schools, so it is important that they convey information as clearly and accurately as possible. Grades also evoke many emotional responses and can cause difficulties for teachers, parents, and students if they are not handled carefully; therefore, it is important for teachers to understand their function in the process of schooling.

The theoretical principles on which the recommendations in this book are based come from the research literature. The reference list is lengthy, and I encourage readers to research their areas of interest. The practical applications of measurement and instructional theories to teaching come from my years of experience, first as a classroom teacher and then as a college professor, working with teachers and school administrators about the thorny issues of measuring school achievement. My bias is explicitly stated as a theme of the book: In a perfect world there would be no grades—at least, not as we know them now.

Assessment in general, and grading in particular, is the part of their work that many teachers like the least. Since we tend to do best the things we like and know, one of the goals of this book is to serve as a resource that will help teachers begin to see themselves as competent graders. Because most teachers' professional practice will require them to grade papers and assign report card grades, it is important to learn how to do these things well. At the same time, it is important to learn how to advocate for changes in student assessment practices that will serve students even better than present practices do.

CHANGES IN THE SECOND EDITION

This text has been improved based on feedback from reviewers and users, and it has been updated to reflect current events in educational assessment. Chapters 6 and 7 from the first edition have been merged into one chapter (Chapter 6), making the book one chapter shorter. The section on legal issues in grading has been rewritten. The contents of several of the chapters have been changed to reflect the current interest in standards-based report cards, a movement that was in its infancy at the time of the first edition but that has grown considerably since that time. And finally, references have been updated. The result is a book that should help today's readers understand grading.

TEXT ORGANIZATION AND SPECIAL FEATURES

The text is characterized by clear explanations, lots of stories and illustrations, samples of student work, sample report cards and other artifacts, and references for further study. Each chapter begins with a list of key concepts. Each chapter ends with a set of questions or practice exercises designed to assess understanding of the chapter's contents. Since one of the main goals of the book is skill development, some of these exercises are aimed at practical skill development (e.g., assign a grade and write feedback for a sample of work). Each major part of the book ends with a more comprehensive assignment designed to assess synthesis of major concepts and applications of readers' understanding to their future work as educators. The material is organized into three parts.

Part 1, Understanding Grading, introduces the subject of grading and its importance, defines terms, and sets grading in its historical, social, legal, and psychological contexts. Because of the huge impact of grading practices on both learning and motivation, an entire chapter is devoted to the educational psychology of grades. Self-reflection is encouraged, at the outset and throughout readers' progress through this book.

Part 2, Integrating Assessment and Instruction, discusses the grading of individual assignments. Chapters 4 and 5 present instruction and assessment concepts, whereas Chapter 6 is more skill oriented. When teachers talk about "grading" papers, they usually refer to both assigning a grade or score *and* writing formative feedback to students on those papers. Assigning valid and reliable scores and writing helpful feedback are different skills, although both are crucial to the teaching-learning process.

Part 3, Combining Grades Into Marks for Report Cards, discusses how to move from a set of individual assignments or observations to a report card grade. Different methods of arriving at composite grades are demonstrated, and readers will learn how to select the method that best suits their particular grading purpose. Sample report cards are shown. Aspiring teachers sometimes assume that all report cards are like the ones they had in school. Because report cards seem so "official," it's odd at first to realize that there can be so much variation among them. Chapter 10 summarizes other ways to communicate information about student achievement.

WAYS TO USE THIS BOOK

Practicing teachers may wish to read this book in order to polish their skills at grading and enrich their understanding of grading's underlying concepts. Aspiring teachers or their professors may wish to read this book as a supplemental text, in conjunction with a text on educational psychology, instructional methods, or educational measurement, depending on the focus of the course. This book does not attempt to be a general textbook on classroom assessment, but rather to project a clear and detailed picture of a currently important teaching function—grading.

ACKNOWLEDGMENTS

Many people have helped me in developing my thoughts and opinions about grading, with the ideas and examples presented in this book, and with the task of writing the text itself. Permit me to name some of them here.

I would like to thank all of the authors on whose work I have drawn and who are named in the reference section at the end of this text. Some of these scholars are friends with whom I have had interesting conversations about classroom assessment in general and grading in particular. Others are scholars whom I have not met, but whose work has enriched my thinking. Some, indeed, are no longer living, but their ideas are still with us. Two colleagues whom I would like to thank by name are Tony Nitko and Rick Stiggins, both measurement scholars who have inspired me by their keen grasp of the tension between classroom realities and measurement principles and their equally keen insistence that both must be served at a high level in order to serve children.

I am particularly grateful to the superintendents, principals, teachers, and students who so graciously shared their work with me so that I can share it with you in this book. As a teacher, I know the power of an example, and I know that this book without the examples would have been a much weaker offering.

For steadfast love and personal support, during the writing of this book and always, thanks go to my husband, Frank. He cheerfully puts up with my long hours at the word processor, piles of papers on the floor, and all the other inconveniences of writing. I would not be who I am without him.

Thanks also to Kevin Davis, Assistant Vice President and Publisher, and the staff at Merrill. Special thanks to S. E. Phillips for advice about the section on legal issues in grading.

Thanks to the reviewers for their helpful comments: Cynthia Campbell, Northern Illinois University; Sarah Huyvaert, Eastern Michigan University; Kimberly Knesting, University of Northern Iowa; and Stewart Wood, Madonna University.

I hope that this book helps readers to reflect on their own thoughts and feelings about grading, and to carefully consider how their grading practices influence the students they serve. I would welcome comments and feedback from interested readers. Any errors or omissions in this work, of course, remain my responsibility.

BRIEF CONTENTS

CONTENTS

Note: Every effort has been made to provide accurate and current Internet information in this book. However, the Internet and information posted on it are constantly changing, so it is inevitable that some of the Internet addresses listed in this textbook will change.

Part 1

Understanding Grading

CHAPTER

1

Introduction

KEY CONCEPTS

- In a perfect world there would be no grades—at least, not as we know them now.
- Since most teachers' professional practice will require them to grade papers and assign report card grades, it is important to learn how to do these things well. At the same time, it is important to learn how to advocate for changes in student assessment practices that will serve students even better than present practices do.
- The primary purpose for grading—for both individual assignment grades and report card grades—should be to communicate with students and parents about their achievement of learning goals. Grades are only one way to communicate student achievement and should be used with additional feedback methods.
- Grades and other communication about student achievement should be based on solid, high-quality evidence. Teachers should be able to describe that evidence and explain how they arrived at any judgments about the quality of student work.
- Whether an individual grade for an assignment or a term grade on a report card, grades should convey interpretable, appropriate information about the particular achievement in question. This quality of meaningfulness and appropriateness is called *validity*.
- Whether an individual grade for an assignment or a term grade on a report card, grades should convey accurate information about achievement and not just chance variation in performance. This quality of accuracy and consistency is called *reliability*.
- Grading practices are inextricably tied to instructional practices and classroom management practices.
- Teachers' beliefs about learning will affect grading decisions. Ongoing reflection will help teachers articulate their thoughts, feelings, and beliefs and understand their relationship to grading decisions.

When Ann was in high school, she regarded grades as a mixed blessing. On the one hand, she was a good student, and it was nice to have her work affirmed by receiving good grades. On the other hand, it was not always easy to be a good student. Sometimes her classmates didn't seem to like the fact that she did so well. But in her high school, there were lots of other good students, and she usually hung out with them. Carla was an especially close friend. Both of them were in the chorus, and they always sat together. Grades didn't make a difference with Ann and Carla. Both girls' grade point averages (GPAs) were always exactly the same—a perfect 4.0.

Senior year, there was room in the schedule for an elective. Ann took elementary French, which was easy for her since she had already studied other languages. Carla took a course called Biology II, a challenging, college-level biology course with a lab. Ann got an A in French, and Carla got a B in biology. So, Ann graduated from high school in first place with three other students, and Carla dropped to fifth place. Carla tried to pretend it didn't matter, but Ann thought it wasn't fair that her friend had worked harder that year than she had, and learned more, but graduated at a lower rank. What sense did it make to average Carla's biology grade and her French grade as if they held equal weight?

In college, Ann found that her classmates talked about grades frequently. In her sophomore year, Ann was pretty sure that she might get the Dean's Prize for the sophomore with the highest grade point average, and she thought of her friend Carla. She wrote a letter to the Dean's office and declined the award, which made her feel really good. She carried that feeling with her until the end of her junior year, when another hapless sophomore got the Dean's Prize—and with it a check for $50.

Ann hadn't realized there was money involved! When senior year came, Ann still carried a GPA of 4.0. There was a prize for the senior with the highest average, and this time Ann didn't write a letter. On graduation day, honors were read, and Ann received an envelope containing a certificate—and a check for $50. With chagrin, she thought to herself, "They say everyone has a price. I guess I just found out mine." Grades may not mean much in their own right, but they are important for what they can "get" you, she concluded.

Grades and grading practices connect with all sorts of emotions. For adults like Ann, they often trigger memories of school events that were important for growth and development. For children, grades and grading practices are still an active part of the context of their growth and development. Grades send messages about what is considered important in school and how children measure up to those expectations. School children use this information as they develop their understanding of their own capabilities and interests as learners. They also use this information as they develop their understanding of the nature of learning itself.

People's feelings about grades tend to be longstanding, based on their school experiences over many years. As you read this book, it will be important for you to acknowledge your feelings about grades and reflect upon how those feelings influence your grading philosophy. For the sake of the students whom *you* will grade as a teacher, it will be important for you to learn as much as you can about the topic.

WHY GRADING

In a perfect world, there would be no need for the kind of grades we use in school today. Grades on individual assignments would be replaced by discussions with peers and with teachers who would go over our individual strengths and weaknesses, affirming what we do well and coaching us on how to improve. There would be no "failure" because we would simply continue with additional problems or tasks until we mastered a concept or skill. There would be no "top" grade because any performance could always be improved. We wouldn't all be doing the same assignments, anyway. Each of us would be doing assignments we helped design ourselves.

But the demands of schooling as we know it have kept us from reaching that utopia. Most of you who read this book will become teachers in schools or districts that require you to grade papers and assign report card grades. Therefore, it is important to learn how to grade well. As you learn the basic concepts and develop grading skills, you will also learn how you can apply these principles to improve grading policies and practices in your schools and districts.

What are some of these demands? Most school districts issue report cards, and providing students and parents with grades is part of a teacher's job. Surveys of parents have found that most of them expect, and want, grades for their children so they know how they are doing in school. They consider other kinds of feedback, like conferences or narrative descriptions, good additions to grades, but by and large they don't see them as replacements for grades.

Another perceived source of demand for grades is the progress of students through grade levels in school and from school to school—middle school to high school, high school to college, even college to graduate school. Narrative descriptions are harder to compare and interpret from school to school than grades, even grades that come from different classes, teachers, and schools.

This book will try to stand the middle ground. Grades are not going to disappear from schools any time soon. Therefore, teachers need to base their grading practices on sound instructional and assessment principles to send clear and helpful messages about student learning to the students, their parents, and other teachers. Teacher education students need to learn how to do the job as best they can and how to apply assessment concepts to help improve the system at every opportunity.

PURPOSES FOR GRADING

The primary purpose for grading—for both individual assignment grades and report card grades—should be to communicate with students and parents about students achievement of learning goals. Grades are only one way to communicate student achievement and should be used with additional feedback methods. A letter or number grade can convey one piece of information: a level of achievement, a judgment of quality. As you will learn in Chapter 3, descriptive feedback that conveys information students can use for improvement is more useful than evaluative (judgment) feedback alone. In Chapter 6 we will discuss ways to provide descriptive feedback on individual assignments, and in Chapter 10 we will discuss ways to provide descriptive feedback on work for a report period or other term or unit of instruction. The primary purpose of all of these efforts is clear communication about student achievement of important learning goals.

Secondary purposes for grading include providing teachers with information for instructional planning, providing teachers and administrators with information for evaluation of school programs, and providing teachers, administrators, parents, and students with information for selection and placement of students (Figure 1-1). Grades do not serve all of these purposes equally well, however. Although information resulting from the grading system can be useful for these secondary purposes, the best use for the grading system is the communication purpose for which it was designed and for which it should provide just the right information. Grades have only *some* of the right information for these other purposes.

Consider, for example, what would happen if a district looked at students' math grades alone to determine whether a newly adopted math program was satisfactory.

FIGURE 1-1

Some purposes for grading

Grades Communicate Information About Student Achievement, Which Tells:	Primary Users of Information			
	Students	Parents	Teachers	Administrators
How Students are Learning	*	*	*	
Information for Instructional Decisions			*	
Information for Program Evaluation			*	*
Information for Student Selection or Placement	*	*	*	*
Information for Other Administrative Decisions				*

If students' grades were lower than expected, it could be that the program was not as good as the one it replaced. But it could also mean that teachers were still adjusting to the new material, or that the new program presented more challenging material, or that this year's classes of students were not as able as previous classes. To find out which of these conclusions was warranted, or whether other issues were involved, additional information besides grades would be required.

This book will operate under the principle that a grade should convey, as well as the report card or assignment design will allow, information about student achievement of classroom learning goals—or how well students learned what they were given an opportunity to learn. These classroom goals should be derived from the school's curriculum. The rationale for this philosophy is perhaps best summed up by the cartoon in Figure 1-2. Students and their parents will use grades to draw conclusions about what the student is learning in his or her daily lessons. These conclusions have serious consequences for everyone.

FIGURE 1-2 Report card cartoon

"It may be a report card to you, but in my house it's an environmental impact statement."

Source: Bo Brown. Used by permission of Margaret Brown.

DEFINITIONS OF TERMS

GRADING

Teachers talk about "grading papers," meaning scoring or rating individual assignments, but they also talk about "grades," meaning the marks on report cards. In this book, I will use the language the way you will hear it, but I will try to make each reference clear. "Grades" and "grading" will refer to scoring papers and other assignments, and "report card grades" or "term grades for report cards" will refer to the symbols put on report cards.

Articles about grading written in the early part of the 20th century tended to use the terms "grades" and "grading" in both of these contemporary senses. For a time in the early to mid-20th century, the terms "marks" and "marking" were used instead—but again, "marks" was used in both senses, to refer to the marks for individual assignments and the marks on report cards. It seems that the public use of language emphasizes how important those feelings are that we explored at the beginning of the chapter. Whether they think about grades or marks for a single piece of work or for a collection of work, students experience grades or marks as judgment. Large or small, teachers' appraisals of their work are important to students and are seen as part of the same function.

In this book, we will explore ways that grades on individual assignments and report cards can be *sound* judgment. We will also explore ways that descriptive feedback can accompany the judgments, adding valuable information for understanding current achievement and planning future progress.

ACHIEVEMENT

Grades and other communication about student achievement should be based on solid, high-quality evidence. Teachers should be able to describe that evidence and explain how they arrived at any judgments about the quality of student work.

The term "achievement" will be used to mean student performance of the learning goals on which their classroom lessons were based. This is certainly a narrow, school-based definition of achievement. We all realize that "achievement" in life covers much more territory than school learning goals. But the achievements for which we assign grades *are* defined in the school context. Typically these learning goals are set by the teacher and coordinate with school and district curriculum and state standards. Sometimes, students have a hand in setting their own goals for learning, which can be a very good thing.

Set by the teacher or jointly by teacher and student, school achievements generally are one of four types (Stiggins, 2005): knowledge, reasoning, performance skills, or products (Figure 1-3).

Knowledge of facts and concepts is one type of achievement. Facts and concepts include things like knowing the math times tables, or the chemical properties of various elements, or the causes of the American Revolution, or how plot, setting, and characterization work together in a novel.

FIGURE 1-3 School achievement targets

Note: Target names are from *Student-Involved Assessment FOR Learning,* by R. J. Stiggins, 2005, Upper Saddle River, NJ: Merrill/Prentice Hall.

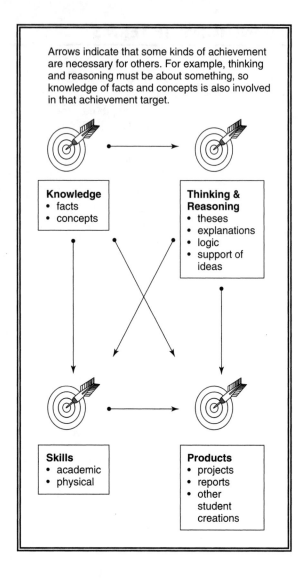

Thinking, sometimes called critical thinking, consists of reasoning with facts and concepts to analyze, compare and contrast, plan, and the like. For example, it is one thing to know what "imagery" is; it is another to be able to explain its use in a particular poem.

Skills include physical abilities, such as using a keyboard or microscope properly, as well as more academic processes like using a library or computer program. Music students are accustomed to demonstrating skills such as the ability to play a particular piece on the violin. Language arts classes often include student speeches where eye contact, clear pronunciation, and vocal expression are important skills.

Products can be fairly concrete or more academic. I still remember the first complete meal I fixed, with group members, in a seventh-grade home economics class. We served hamburgers, green beans, and cookies, and we invited four teachers to come and eat. That meal was a product. But a term paper or report can be a final product, too, subject to judgments of achievement quality.

Stiggins (2005) describes a fifth achievement target, dispositions. A disposition to read for pleasure, for example, is a valued outcome in reading class. It does no good to teach students to read if in the process they learn to hate it and are not disposed to pick up a book if they don't have to. However, we are focusing on grading, and grading dispositions is not recommended. *Assessing* dispositions is good; it's important to know how your students feel about their schoolwork. But *grading* their dispositions is not helpful, and besides—if you ask students about their interests and they know a positive response will get a good grade, of course they will tell you what they think you want to hear. So for grading, we'll stick to considering four kinds of achievement: knowledge of facts and concepts, reasoning, performances of academic or physical skills, and construction of academic products.

VALIDITY

Whether an individual grade for an assignment or a term grade on a report card, grades should convey interpretable, appropriate information about the particular achievement in question. This quality of meaningfulness and appropriateness is called *validity*.

We'll talk more about the validity of information from individual assignments in Chapters 4 and 5, and about the validity of information from report card grades in Chapter 7. For now, think about validity as a general concept: If you want to use information for communicating to students and parents, for making decisions about your instruction, for giving feedback to students to use in their future work, or for any other purpose, you need to make sure that the information is "the right stuff." To use an obvious example, if I want to know whether my students can do three-digit multiplication with carrying, I would not look at their scores on a test comprised of single-digit multiplication problems. I would look at their scores on—you got it!—a test comprised of three-digit multiplication problems with carrying.

For individual classroom assignments, the most important way to approach validity is to ask yourself two questions. First, what do I want to know about student achievement? This question is usually best answered with reference to your instructional goals and objectives. Second, will performance on this assignment give me the information I seek? Sometimes this is obvious, but you have to be careful. You won't get information about whether students understand the themes in *Macbeth,* for example, by asking them to write lines from it that they have memorized. You would have to ask questions that called for interpreting themes.

For a more subtle example, you won't get information about whether students can interpret visual imagery in poetry by asking them to interpret the same poem you discussed in class. All a student needs to do that well is a clear memory of the class discussion, not original interpretive skills. You would need to ask students to interpret the visual imagery in a different poem in order to find out whether they could do that kind of interpretation themselves.

It's important to make sure the assignment matches your classroom instruction, which should also match your goals and objectives. For report card grades, the same validity principle is extended to a set of assignments. Think about this concept of thoughtfully connecting what you assess and grade with what you teach and what you say you want your students to learn. We'll return to this concept in more detail several times throughout the book. It's safe to say this is the single most important principle you will learn in this course.

In the story that began this chapter, Ann's problem was a validity problem, although she didn't use that word for it. She knew that Carla had been a better student in high school than she had, because Carla had stepped up to challenges all four years while she had avoided working too hard senior year. She knew that Carla had learned more, overall, than she had. But when she looked to the grade point average as an indicator, it seemed to convey just the opposite. The meaning encoded in their GPAs and class ranks was that Ann, who ranked first, was a better student than Carla, who ranked fifth. Ann didn't think this was valid information.

RELIABILITY

Whether an individual grade for an assignment or a term grade on a report card, grades should convey accurate information about achievement and not just a chance variation in performance. This quality of accuracy and consistency is called *reliability*. As with validity, we'll return to this principle in more detail later in the book. For now, think of the general principle of reliability like this: The grade students get for an assignment should be the closest possible estimate you can make about their real achievement on whatever the assignment is supposed to measure. It shouldn't be a fluke—a low score underestimating achievement because a student was ill, or a high score overestimating achievement because the student made a lucky guess studying only the one question you happened to pick for a test. It shouldn't be an accident of which teacher grades the paper—a "hard" grader or an "easy" grader. The grade should indicate the level at which students would generally register on any assignment designed to indicate achievement of the same learning goals.

We'll discuss this issue of reliability again, in regard to both individual assignment grades and report card grades. For now, one illustration will suffice. I once worked on a project in a middle school that had two eighth-grade teachers. They were including reviews of student writing, along with several other sources of information, in a major decision about placement for ninth-grade English classes. They used four-point rubrics to score the writing samples. To check how evenhanded they were in their grading, each teacher selected 10 papers from her class. Then both teachers, plus one of the school district administrators, graded the 20 papers. All in all, there were 3 sets of scores for each of the 20 papers.

Of course, not every score was in perfect agreement all across the board. But most of the time, one of the teachers and the administrator agreed on the score (4, 3, 2, or 1) for a given student's paper. The other teacher's scoring matched her colleagues' scoring for the 10 papers written by students in the other class. But she consistently scored her own students' papers higher than her colleagues did. This bias was unintentional: When she looked at tables of the student writing scores and realized what she had done, she was horrified. The look on her face spoke volumes! She hadn't meant to misrepresent her students' writing achievement, and until we did our little experiment she didn't know she had done this.

In talking about this later, she expressed that probably the worst thing was that if her school hadn't been involved in this project about assessment of students for placement in high school, she might never have known she graded her own students more leniently than others. She realized the implications. Students with the same achievement level in writing could end up with different grades—and different consequences at home and in future schooling—based on which teacher they had for English.

ORGANIZATION

This book is divided into three parts. Part 1 gives some background on the grading system. Grading has historical and psychological contexts, traditions, public expectations, and documented effects on students. Grading also has contexts within the cultures of individual schools. Grading practices are inextricably tied to instructional practices and classroom management practices.

Part 2 continues the theme of integrating grading practices with instruction by discussing the use of individual assignments and their grades. We have emphasized that grades should be based on solid, high-quality evidence about student achievement. Grades based on appropriate individual assignments are the most common way to collect this evidence. The assignments are appropriate because they fit with classroom instruction and students' and teachers' learning goals. This all works together, tying classroom instruction and management to assessment and grading and, conversely, ensuring that grading reflects actual instruction and intended learning outcomes. You will learn some helpful ways to "grade" student work, sometimes scoring or lettering, sometimes providing written feedback, and often doing both.

Part 3 discusses how to arrive at the summary statements about student achievement that are required at report card time. Several different methods of putting together individual grades are discussed. You should learn them all so you have different options available to you when you teach, and you should learn how to select the appropriate grading method for the instruction and assignments you have to work with.

SELF-REFLECTION: NOW AND LATER

You may have strong feelings about grades and lots of ideas about how you think grading ought to be done based on your own experiences. It is important for you to identify these feelings and use them to understand your perspectives on the material in this book and on the grading practices you will adopt when you teach. Use the questions in the Exercises to get you started now. Continue to reflect on grading as you read this book, as you work in other teacher education classes and through your professional practice as a teacher.

EXERCISES

1. Do you have a "grading story" to tell from your school experience? Was there a time when you thought grades were used against you, or even for you, in ways that didn't make sense? Briefly tell the story, and then use the key concepts from the chapter to try to analyze what went wrong.
2. Reflect on your own beliefs about learning. What information did you think grades should convey before you started to read this book? How have this chapter's key concepts confirmed or challenged your thoughts?
3. Engage in a short personal goal-setting session. Make a list of the things you would like to learn about grades now, before you read the rest of the chapters. Use the list as your bookmark.

Note: These are intended as "short" exercises at the end of the chapter. See Part 1 Exercises on page 49 for additional exercises.

CHAPTER
2

Grading in Its Contexts

KEY CONCEPTS

- The origins of grading in elementary and high schools in the United States stem from university practices.
- History has seen the rise and fall of various grading practices. The most common have been percentage grading and letter grading.
- Current suggestions for alternatives to grades include mastery grading, pass/fail grading, standards grading, narrative grading, and contract grading. All of these date back in some form to at least the 1930s.
- In schools, grades function variously as evaluations of student work, as a kind of currency ("pay" for "work" students do), as motivators or destroyers, as the vehicle for promotion and retention, and as part of public relations.
- It is important to understand the social psychology of grades—school and community expectations and perceptions—since these tend to preserve the status quo and are major barriers to change.
- Parents tend to perceive grades as a normative, rank order scale—and "translate" alternative reporting scales to this metric.
- Legally, grading is a state issue; however, most (but not all) states do not define "grading" and delegate grading responsibilities to local districts. Many local school boards delegate grading responsibilities to administrators and/or teachers.

W e tend to think of grading in terms of the grading that has been "done to" us. In the first section of this chapter, we step back to get the longer view, the view from a historical perspective. This should help you come to a deeper understanding of current grading issues and methods. The second section of this chapter shows that parents and other community members tend to do the same thing we do: view grades from the perspective of their own experience. Understanding this phenomenon will help you think in terms of grades as communication. The third section of this chapter is a brief introduction to some of the legal issues you'll need to keep in mind as a practicing professional.

THE HISTORICAL CONTEXT OF GRADING

History has seen the rise and fall of various grading practices. Although no attempt is made here to present an exhaustive history of grading, some of the more interesting and significant events remind us of important points. First, much of today's grading literature casts issues that are centuries old as new problems. Most of what you will hear called "alternative grading strategies" are not new! Even more important, perhaps, is that most people's objections to various aspects of grading are not new and seem to have arisen almost immediately upon the adoption of the particular grading practices they complain about. Second, the uses to which grades are put should dictate the methods used to grade. Historically as well as logically, no grading system can serve a variety of conflicting purposes equally well. Table 2-1 presents a summary time line of the history of grading in the United States in K–12 schools. Table 2-2 presents historical background for selected current issues in grading.

GRADING AT UNIVERSITIES, 1640s TO 1800s

Grading practices developed first in higher education. Universities in the United States were founded out of the tradition of European universities. This tradition held that it was the duty of the faculty to evaluate students, and that the merits of students could be estimated rather precisely. Smallwood (1935) concluded that the assumption that faculty should evaluate students was never questioned. The assumption that they could evaluate students accurately was not questioned, at first, either.

TABLE 2-1	Time Period	Major Developments
Summary time line of the history of grading in the United States in K–12 schools	1640s to 1800s	• Grading systems coming into use in colleges become models for grading in K–12 schools • Growth of the common school and the beginning of "report cards" c.1840
	1890–1900	• Percentage grading is the most common form of grading
	1900–1920	• Concern with reliability of percentage grades • Growth of interest in "scientific" measurement, standardized testing, and normal curve theory
	1920–1930	• Letter grading becomes increasingly adopted as a solution to the reliability problem of percentage grading • Growth of concern about normal-curve grading • Beginning of interest in mastery grading
	1930–1960	• Growth of recommendations to grade on absolute standards • More experimentation in elementary than secondary schools because normative grading is seen as useful for college selection procedures • Interest in contribution of grades to increasing student learning
	1960–1980	• The student movement highlights grading issues, especially whether and to what extent student interests are reflected in grades • Increasing pressure on grades and other measures of accountability
	1980–2000	• Concern for teacher competence at grading • Interest in teacher grading practices
	2000–present	• Experimentation with "standards-based grading," more in elementary schools than high schools

Note: Summaries are generalizations of trends reported in the literature. There were, of course, some exceptions in every time period.

Smallwood studied original documents at five institutions to learn about grading systems in early American universities: Harvard (founded 1636), William and Mary (1693), Yale (1701), the University of Michigan (1837), and Mount Holyoke (1837). The earliest evaluations were examinations for awarding a degree, which were sometimes conducted on the day of graduation itself. Scholars would remain in college for varying lengths of time until they were deemed ready to pass a graduation exam. Smallwood (1935, p. 8) quotes from a 1646 document from Harvard College:

Every scholar that on proofe is found able to read ye originall of ye old and new testament into ye Latin toungue, and to Resolve them Logically withall being of honest life and conversation and at any publike act had ye approbation of ye overseers, and Master of Y^e Colledge may bee invested with his first degree.

TABLE 2-2	Grading Issue	Historical Background
Historical background for grading issues in the United States in K–12 schools	Comparability of grades for different levels of courses of study	• Harvard experiments with ability grouping in 1825 and raises this issue • Starting in 1910, the growth of interest in standardized testing brings the growth of ability grouping, and this problem, to the public schools
	Evaluation and grading, especially preparing report cards, as a burden on teachers' time	• Argued in an article by S.G.B. in *The Common School Journal* in 1840 • Still a common grading issue, especially in articles written from teachers' point of view
	Interpretability of grades, especially parents' understanding of what grades communicate about their child's progress in school	• Raised as an issue by S.G.B., 1840 • In the 1940s, the whole child movement rekindles interest in communicating with parents • Studies in the 1990s confirm this issue is still with us • Standards-based report cards in the 2000s attempt to focus on the interpretation of grades
	Reliability of grades	• Starch and Elliott (1912, 1913a, 1913b) and other similar studies raise the issue in some of the first "educational research" ever done • This issue today is often couched in terms of the accuracy of teachers' grading practices
	Achievement and nonachievement factors in grading	• Early research in the 1920s establishes that teachers use both achievement and nonachievement factors in assigning grades • More current research on teachers' grading practices (1980s and 1990s) confirms this problem is still with us and couches it in terms of validity, the meaning and value of grades for multiple purposes
	Role of the student	• In 1762, students at Yale refuse to sit for examinations until the university passes a law requiring it • In the 1940s, the whole child movement prompts a call for student self-evaluation and for more communication with parents (e.g., parent conferences) • In the 1960s, the student movement reinforces the idea that students' points of view should be heard • Currently, the formative assessment movement emphasizes the need for student-centered evaluation in the classroom

Examinations were used in early university life to test student ability, measure the quantity of information (usually facts) that students had learned, and award positions of honor, especially rank at commencement. Students' fear of exams and faculty's opinions about the evils of cramming were recognized from the beginning. There is written documentation of a student "strike," as we would call it now, in the

Yale trustee records from 1762. Students refused to sit for exams until they were required by university law (Smallwood, p. 35). Cramming was noted as a problem in these university-level graduation exams. Partly as a response to this issue, individual professors, and not the universities, were gradually given the responsibility and discretion for giving exams.

If examinations were to be measures of student ability—we would say achievement today—then a scale of measurement is implied. By 1775, various kinds of grading scales had come into use. The first record of a scale for grading is a set of categories (in Latin) at Yale in 1785. Students were classified as *Optimi* (the best ones), *Second Optimi* (second best), *Inferiores* (the lesser ones), and *Pejores* (the worse ones).

The first use of a numerical scale came in 1813, at Yale. Students were graded on a scale of 4, including decimals. The average for each student in the class was recorded. To give an idea of the variation in grades, in 1813 the range was 1.3 to 3.7; in 1814 it was 1.0 to 3.21 (Smallwood, p. 43). Different colleges tried various scales; for example, scales of 20, scales of 100, and rank scales with descriptive adjectives. In the 1850s, the University of Michigan, the only state university in Smallwood's study, experimented with abolishing grades and simply passing or failing students. Gradually it found it had to add categories. The university also tried gradations of failure, as in this description from the 1870s (Smallwood, p. 83).

> At the University of Michigan a student simply "passed," but if he failed there were different degrees of failures, such as "conditioned" and "incomplete." At Harvard the reverse was true, variations were on the side of passing; if he failed, his failure was unmodified. It is quite easy to understand this in terms of the general attitude of the universities. Harvard was always more interested in encouraging and rewarding the good student; Michigan felt that emphasis on the superior attainments and merits of one student over another was neither desirable nor democratic.

Comparability of grades was perceived as a problem once colleges began allowing electives. Comparability also was a problem when, beginning in 1825, Harvard began using ability grouping. These are grading problems that are still with us (see Chapter 8). Colleges tried different weighting schemes for grades to make some subjects more important than others, but eventually adopted the uniform marking system used today. Educators have come to doubt that grades measure "true" ability, but higher education continues to use them because they serve the purposes of awarding credit; recording achievement; advising, retaining, and graduating students; and so on.

GRADING IN THE COMMON SCHOOL, 1800s

In the 1800s, the common school movement saw the establishment of schools for children, and by 1890 as much as 69% of the population aged 5 to 17 was in school (Cuban, 1993, p. 24). It is interesting that one of the earliest articles describing the use of report cards in the common schools also includes the two main complaints still heard today from teachers and parents, respectively: that preparing report cards is time consuming and burdensome and that report card information is difficult to interpret. Writing in 1840, an author who signed himself only as "S.G.B." describes the advent of the report card to the common school: "In some schools, the practice has been adopted of using printed forms, containing blanks, in which, by some system of figures or letters, the advancement and behavior of the pupil are to be expressed by the teacher" (S.G.B., 1840/1992, p. 12).

S.G.B. proposed an original solution, which he tried and deemed successful. "He [the writer] procured a number of cards of different colors;—white, blue, yellow and red. On these, respectively, he had printed the words, 'Entire Approbation,' 'Approbation,' 'Indifferent,' and 'Censure,' with the name of his school, and spaces, for the name of the pupil, and the date and number of the report. By this mode, the color of the card was itself an indication of its meaning" (S.G.B., pp. 12–13). The parents had to sign the colored cards, and students returned them to the school. S.G.B. reported an increase in pupil interest in and response to their reports. Obviously color cards did not catch on in a big way, but they illustrate how longstanding is the concern about student evaluation as a teacher burden and concern about the interpretability of grades for parents.

1890 TO 1920

By the end of the 19th century, percentage grading became common in high schools and colleges (Cureton, 1971). However, colleges gradually began to move to category systems like letter grading. By 1910, basic educators also began to question the reliability of grading and the ability of teachers to estimate achievement with 100 different degrees of precision. In the decade between 1910 and 1920, several studies were done to examine the reliability of grades. Probably the most famous are those of Starch and Elliott.

In 1912 and 1913, Starch and Elliott did a series of studies about the reliability of grading of high school examination papers in English, mathematics, and history. They selected two English exams, one mathematics exam, and one history exam and sent copies of the tests and student answers to about 200 different high schools, requesting that the appropriate subject matter teachers grade them as they would a paper from their own schools. They found that grades on the same English paper covered ranges of 35 or 40 points (using a percent scale of 100). Thus, grades for any individual paper were found to be unreliable. Relative judgments of individual teachers were also found to be unreliable; many teachers rated the poorer paper above the better one. Grades on the math paper (a geometry exam) varied even more than the English papers. Results for the history exam were similar to English and math.

Starch and Elliott (1913b) concluded that four factors contributed to unreliability in grading. Listed in order from the largest contributor to the smallest, they were (Starch & Elliott, p. 681): differences due to teachers' pure inability to distinguish between closely allied degrees of merit; differences in the relative values placed by different teachers upon various elements in a paper, including content and form; differences among the standards of different teachers; and differences among the standards of different schools. Starch (1918) therefore advocated developing standard scales for measuring "academic efficiency." These consisted of a series of graded exercises and rating scales anchored with samples of student work. You will find (see Chapter 5) that the idea of clearly described and anchored rating scales is also emphasized today.

Partly in response to the research about the unreliability of percentage grading, the period from 1920 to 1930 saw the use of more symbols for grades. If you need to group students into only 4 or 5 categories instead of a possible 100, you are more likely to reliably designate the student's performance level.

In the early 1900s, there was growing interest in standardized testing, "scientific" measurement, and normal-curve theory. As psychologists discovered that given enough people, many mental characteristics were distributed in a bell shape, educators began to look toward this scientific discovery and the mathematics behind it to solve the problem of how to assign grades that were fair, equitable, and valid measures of student achievement in school. This led some to argue for norm-referenced grading. Briefly, norm-referenced grading means comparing students' performances to one another and allocating the top grade to the best students and so on, down to assigning the worst grade to the lowest performers (see Chapter 5). Teachers who use norm-referenced grading often use the normal probability curve ("the bell curve") to establish grading cutoff scores. Hall (1906/1992) appealed to these "fundamental, biologic and mathematical laws" (p. 16) and proposed a normal-curve-based grading system based on percentage scores. Meyer (1908/1992) criticized Hall because his system begged the question "percent of what" but proposed another norm-referenced grading system.

The growth of standardized testing also led to greater use of ability grouping in school, which in turn led to marking problems that are still with us today. How do you grade students across classes where expectations vary considerably in amount and difficulty?

1920 TO 1930

Research in the 1920s established the fact that teachers often include nonachievement factors such as effort and attitude in assigning their grades. Herron (1929) reported studies showing that many teachers consciously consider effort, attitude, and other factors in assigning marks, and that some are unconsciously affected by similar factors. Proffitt (1930) concluded that what teachers mean by "achievement" often includes such components as accuracy, mastery, regularity, and ability to apply information" (Smith & Dobbin, 1960, p. 784). What is astonishing about this conclusion is that beginning in the 1980s and continuing to the present, researchers are again interested in the influence of nonachievement factors in grading. Apparently, 50 years have not solved the problem.

Crooks (1933) published an overview of various kinds of marking systems described in literature from the 1920s: ranking, the normal curve, the percentage system, and absolute standards. Ranking and grading on the normal curve both compare students with each other, and Crooks was able to cite scholarly arguments against using these norm-referenced methods for grading even then. The percentage system with its 100 possible grades had already been demonstrated to be unreliable. Crooks advocated achievement of clearly defined absolute standards of performance as the basis for marking, although his article appeared fully 30 years before Glaser's (1963) landmark article that lent the term "criterion-referenced" to this kind of grading.

Mastery grading—grading students only after they have achieved or "mastered" a unit of instruction and demonstrated mastery on some assessment—is one method of grading on absolute standards that received attention from educational writers in the early 20th century. Morrison (1926/1992) was one of the earliest to write about mastery grading.

> When a student has fully acquired a piece of learning, he has mastered it. Half-learning, or learning rather well, or being on the way to learning are none of them mastery. . . . It follows that the course material which we find in the curriculum is valuable in education only as it is analyzed into significant units of learning. . . .It is meaningless to prescribe a course in arithmetic or English or grammar or French, and let it go at that. The issue is not learning any of these but rather the mastery of certain significant units in arithmetic or English or grammar or French. The most learned of scholars would hesitate to say that he had mastered any of these fields. But the child of nine years can indisputably learn to add and to identify situations in which adding is the appropriate process. (pp. 45–46)

Mastery grading is sometimes referred to as "grading time," since the achievement goals remain constant for all students but different students take different amounts of time to reach the goals. This is in large part why mastery grading, which has been around for more than three-quarters of a century, has not become more widely used. It is impossible to administer for large numbers of students over large numbers of learning goals. Also, it works best for knowledge and skills that can be chunked into what Morrison called "units." It works less well in developing skills with a larger scope, such as writing.

1930 TO 1960

In the 1930s, the pendulum continued to swing. The "scientific" multiple-choice tests had been found useful, but not the complete solution to educational measurement problems that some thought they would be. The decade 1930 to 1940 saw concern with the effects of testing and growth of interest in the whole child—including his or her intellectual, social, physical, and emotional development—that had started with Dewey and others in the progressive education movement and increased steadily since the turn of the century. Books with titles like *Adjusting the School to the Child* (Washburne, 1932) appeared.

Concern for the whole child meant concern for home–school relations. Literature in the '30s and '40s discussed the uses and limitations of parent conferences for feedback and reporting of student progress in school and a call for an increased role for student self-evaluation. Studies reporting parents' requests for meaningful, interpretable report cards appeared (DePencier, 1951). Sound familiar? As this text goes to press, educators are in a similar position. Grading is considered a necessary evil, necessary for administrative and communication purposes for mass education. Standardized testing is used, taken seriously, but found to have limitations. Concern for the whole child and for parent and student involvement in assessment is growing. Wow! Déjà vu all over again!

The 1940s and 1950s also saw a trend in public schools toward issuing fewer report cards, from nine down to six or even fewer (DePencier, 1951, p. 520). The same decades found the purposes grading was expected to serve expanded from simply reporting results to parents to include increasing learning for students. In some ways, this was terrific—recognizing the importance of evaluation in ongoing instruction. But in another sense, this made the task of grading more difficult. Any measure is designed to serve some purpose, and the degree to which it does is called validity (see Chapter 1). It is very difficult for one measure to serve different purposes equally well, as discussed earlier. Some of the strains on our grading system are a result of this admirable but perhaps unmanageable goal of having grades serve both to report progress dispassionately to parents and to increase student motivation and achievement at the same time.

Also in the 1940s and 1950s, and related to the concern that grades serve an instructional purpose, concern about achievement of educational objectives and the question of whether to grade on absolute standards or by comparison with other students' work continued to grow. Elementary schools were somewhat successful in implementing standards-based grading. In high schools, norm-referenced (ranking or curving) methods lingered because of the use of high school grades in college admissions. The perception was that sorting students according to their relative accomplishments was useful information for college admissions. High schools persisted in this practice despite the fact that some studies (e.g., Wrinkle, 1947, cited in Smith & Dobbin, 1960, p. 788) confirmed it would be an improvement to establish measurable objectives linked to observable student behavior. The major point about what we would now call criterion-referenced grading is that it moved grading from a function that ranked students after the fact to a function inextricably related to instruction and instructional goals—and therefore curriculum, lesson plans, classroom practices, and all of classroom teaching.

1960 TO 1980

The 1960s and 1970s were decades famous for student unrest and therefore an increased interest in what students thought about grading. Probably the most significant writing on grading from this time period is Kirschenbaum, Napier, and Simon's (1971) book, *Wad-ja-get? The Grading Game in American Education*. These three scholars tried to answer the question, "Is the traditional system of grading—the one most of us experienced throughout many years of schooling—the most educationally useful system of evaluation?" (p. 14). They did a comprehensive literature review but chose to present their findings, and their answer to the question, as a novel. *Wad-ja-get?* is written as a story about fictional Mapleton High School. The authors concluded the novel by designing a two-track grading system, where both students and teachers were allowed to choose whether they would use grades or credit/no credit; where clear statements of objectives were shared with students at the beginning of the course; where student self-evaluations and teacher comments on them were done once a report period; and where student conferences were scheduled if needed.

1980 TO 2000

The 1980s brought increased concern about teachers' "competence" in general, including their grading practices. In 1989, a Buros-Nebraska Symposium on Measurement and Testing addressed the question, "Are our school teachers adequately trained in measurement and assessment skills?" and produced an edited volume of papers on this topic (Wise, 1993). It was against this backdrop of concern for teachers' competence that a round of research on grading practices started. Stiggins, Frisbie, and Griswold (1989, p. 5) asked, "What specific procedures do teachers follow to assign grades to their students at the end of a quarter or semester? How do teachers decide what procedures they will use? How 'good' are the grades that are derived from these procedures?" They surveyed measurement textbooks to find recommendations for grading practices, then analyzed case studies of 15 high school teachers' grading practices in light of the recommendations. This study, and a number of studies afterward, raised several issues—or maybe I should say reminded people of issues. The primary one was teachers' use of nonachievement factors in assigning grades, an issue that had been raised in the 1920s.

In its recent incarnation, concern about the use of nonachievement factors has been cast as an issue of bias specifically as well as validity more generally. Considering factors like effort, attendance, attitude, and other student personal characteristics not only results in grades that mean different things for different individual students, but it also means that certain groups of students are more at risk than others, depending on location and circumstances.

Evidence suggests that teachers' use of achievement and nonachievement factors in grading is related to the multiple-purpose problem we just noted. Achievement criteria are relevant for some of the uses to which grades are put: for example, getting into college. Both achievement and nonachievement factors are relevant for some other uses of grades: for example, parents' responses to their children at report card time. Teachers intuitively understand this, even if they don't always know that the concept they're thinking about is called validity (Brookhart, 1993b).

2000 TO THE PRESENT

The No Child Left Behind Act (NCLB), signed into law in early 2002, is the latest reauthorization of the Elementary and Secondary Education Act. NCLB requires states to establish challenging content standards for students and to report student achievement on these standards. A movement to grade on standards (as opposed to general subject areas) had begun already, but the requirements of the law to report achievement on standards fueled the impetus to also use standards as the basis for report card grading. As I am preparing this edition, NCLB is up for reauthorization; however, it is not likely that standards in some form are going to go away.

Thus the most important change in grading in the early 21st century is the advent of standards-based report cards. These are more prevalent in elementary than in high schools, where grading still tends to be by course name. Standards-based report cards present their own set of challenges, including communication (Guskey, 2004, 2008) and the fact that results do not always align with large-scale assessment results for the same standards (Welsh & D'Agostino, 2008). We will discuss standards-based report cards further in Chapter 7.

CURRENT CONTEXT OF GRADING

Current dilemmas about grading are seen most clearly as a confusion of purposes—and thus a validity problem. As we have seen, dating back at least 50 years, grades have been used to serve three general purposes simultaneously: ranking (for sorting students into higher education, for example); reporting results (accounting to parents the degree to which students learned the lessons prescribed for them); and contributing to learning (providing feedback and motivating students—see Chapter 3). According to current measurement theory, this is a recipe for disaster. One can make the comparisons necessary to construct scales of measurement in three general ways, and each purpose is best served by a different one! Norm referencing (comparing students to each other) is best for ranking purposes, criterion referencing (comparing students to a standard of attainment) is best for reporting results, and self-referencing (comparing students' work to their own prior achievement and to expectations for them) is best for contributing to learning. Which should grades be? The current, unsatisfactory answer is the same now as it has been since the mid-20th century: all three.

Grading is presently enjoying a period of intense scrutiny and interest. Many current books on the market about grading recommend various practices to teachers, and many of these would make excellent further reading. This section describes different current approaches to grading and reminds readers of their historical roots (see Table 2-3). The most common grading systems currently in use employ letters or other symbols and/or percentages. Because the purpose of this book is to prepare you for current teaching practices, most of Parts 2 and 3 will explore how to use these systems effectively. Alternative methods will be described in greater detail in Chapter 10.

TABLE 2-3	Type of Grading	Definition	Historical Background
Types of grading schemes: definitions and historical background	Percentage grading	Using a percentage scale (percent of 100), usually based on percent correct on exams and/or percent of points earned on assignments	• Most common method in use in high schools and colleges c.1890–1910. • Used today as a grading method or as a way of arriving at letter grades.
	Letter grading and variations	Using a series of letters (often A, B, C, D, F) or letters with plusses and minuses as an ordered category scale—can be done in a norm-referenced (standards-based) manner	• Yale used a four-category system in 1813. • In the 1920 letter grading was seen as the solution to the problem of reliability of percentage grading (fewer or criterion-referenced categories) and was increasingly adopted.

TABLE 2-3	Type of Grading	Definition	Historical Background
(continued)	Norm-referenced grading	Comparing students to each other; using class standing as the basis for assigning grades (usually letter grades)	• Was advocated in early 1900s as scientific measurement. • Educational disadvantages were known by the 1930s.
	Mastery grading	Grading students as "masters" or "passers" when their attainment reaches a prespecified level, usually allowing different amounts of time for different students to reach mastery	• Originating in the 1920s (e.g., Morrison, 1926) as a grading strategy, it became associated with the educational strategy of mastery learning (Bloom, Hastings, & Madaus, 1971).
	Pass/Fail	Using a scale with two levels (pass and fail), sometimes in connection with mastery grading	• In 1851, the University of Michigan experimented with pass/fail grading for classes.
	Standards (or Absolute-Standards) grading	Originally, comparing student performance to a preestablished standard (level) of performance; currently, standards grading sometimes means grading with reference to a list of state or district content standards according to preestablished performance levels	• Grading according to standards of performance has been championed since the 1930s as more educationally sound than norm-referenced grading. • Current advocates of standards grading use the same principle but the term "standard" is now used for the criterion itself, not the level of performance. • Since 2002, the scales on some standards-based report cards use the state accountability (proficiency) reporting categories instead of letters.
	Narrative grading	Writing comments about students' achievement, either in addition to or instead of using numbers or letters	• Using a normal instructional practice (describing students' work) in an assessment context.

Percentage grading means assigning grades as percents, usually based on percent correct on exams and/or percent of points earned for other assignments. The percentage method was at first the most common method used in high schools and colleges, and in each case gave way to letter grading or some other symbol system with fewer than 100 categories once it was discovered that it is very difficult to reliably make 100 (101 if you count zero!) different gradations of achievement. You have just read about Starch and Elliott's reliability studies, and those of others concerned with the reliability of percentage grading in high schools in the early 1900s. A history of Harvard written in 1890 sums up how the institution came to a similar conclusion based on its experience from about 1850 to 1890 (Thayer, 1890, cited in Smallwood, 1935, p. 53).

> The marking system . . . has been overhauled and reduced to the least obnoxious condition. Formerly, the maximum mark for any recitation was eight; the students were ranked for the year on a scale of 100, but, though the scale was the same, no two instructors agreed in their use of it. . . . some frankly admitted that it was impossible to get within five or ten per cent of absolute exactness; others were so delicately constituted that they could distinguish between fractions of one per cent. One instructor was popularly supposed to possess a marking "machine"; another sometimes assigned marks *less than zero*. . . . In each of their courses students are now divided into five groups, called A, B, C, D, E. . . . To graduate, a student must have passed in all his courses, and have stood above the group D in at least one-fourth of his college work; and for the various grades of the degree, honors, honorable mention, etc.; similar regulations are made. . . .

Colleges began the switch from percentage grading to letters in the late 1800s. A committee at Mount Holyoke College proposed a method of letter grades equivalent to ranges of percents in 1896. Percentages remained the most common grading method in high schools until the early 1900s. Today, letter grades are often assigned by grading individual assignments with the percentage method, combining those percents, and assigning a report card letter grade based on ranges of percentage points (e.g., 90–100 = A, 80–89 = B, etc.). The ranges vary from school district to school district and are often a matter of district policy.

Letter grading or letter grading with plusses and minuses is currently the most common system of grading in use. Exceptions are most likely to be found at the early elementary grades, especially in kindergarten (see Chapter 8 for a discussion of developmental concerns in grading). Letter grades have the advantage of using a manageable number of categories, typically five (A, B, C, D, E, or F) or sometimes 12 (using plusses and minuses with all grades except F, often without A+).

They also have the advantage of *seeming* to have a shared meaning; "everybody knows" what A, B, C, D, and F mean. It is not unusual for people to use grades as descriptions in common speech. For example, someone who sees what to him seems an excellent movie might say, "I'd give that one an A." The letter-grading scale is sometimes used as a survey response scale, for example in the annual Gallup poll of the public's attitudes toward the public school, because this very quality of shared understanding and experience with the scale makes it a good tool for gathering survey responses. But this quality of apparent shared meaning is also a disadvantage. In the next section you will see how research shows that parents and community members tend to use the letter scale differently from teachers and students. Since the purpose of these letters is to communicate information about student achievement, that's a problem.

Another problem with letter grades is that they can be used for communicating information via several very different methods. The problem is you can't tell by looking at letters on a report card whether they have been arrived at by comparing student performance to a standard (criterion referencing) or to other students' performance (norm referencing). Even when criterion referencing is done and grades do reflect achievement based on standards of performance, the old descriptive labels are still in use in the language and culture of the community. You will still hear people talk about A as "superior," B as "above average," C as "average," and D as "below average." If you think about those descriptions, you will see they imply comparison with other students, even if that is not what was done.

Since letter-grade or percentage systems are the methods most of you will use in your teaching, this book will try to help you use these admittedly imperfect systems in the best way you can. But these systems have plenty of critics, and some schools do use alternative grading methods. Current suggestions for alternatives to grades include mastery grading, pass/fail grading, standards grading, narrative grading, contract grading, and combination methods. These systems are defined briefly here to complete this picture of grades in history.

Mastery grading is a system that allows students to work on an objective until they can pass a test or other assessment at a specified level. As we have seen, this method is not new. It has been around at least since 1926, is used profitably in some important contexts—like most state driving exams!—but for administrative and logistical reasons will probably never become the main grading method for entire districts where thousands of students study dozens of topics or courses simultaneously. Mastery grading became associated with mastery learning (Bloom et al., 1971) because it was the grading method most suited to this approach to instruction. Mastery learning methods generally use frequent assessments during a unit of instruction. These assessments identify students who have mastered the material and those who have not. Students who demonstrate early that they have mastered the concepts or skills are either allowed to move to the next unit of instruction or given enrichment activities while their classmates work on the basic material for the unit. Students who have not mastered the material use the information from the assessments as they continue to study. They move to the next unit only when they have demonstrated mastery of the present material.

Pass/fail grading means using a scale with two levels, "pass" and "fail." Sometimes this method is done in connection with mastery grading, where the levels may be termed "mastery" and "nonmastery." This method is not new, either. In 1851, the University of Michigan experimented with pass/fail grading. This method is still in use in many high schools and colleges, often for noncredit-bearing experiences. Although it has some advantages, research has shown that it can encourage students to do just enough to pass.

Standards grading has historically had several different but related meanings. In the first uses of the term, it meant essentially the same thing as criterion referencing. Growing awareness in the 1920s and 1930s that linking grading to achievement of performance standards based on instructional goals was more educationally sound than linking grading to student standing in the class led to arguments for grading on "absolute standards" (Crooks, 1933). As recently as a decade ago, proponents of the use of rubrics called the levels of performance under each grading criterion the "standards."

So, for example, if the criterion was English grammar and usage, the various standards or levels under it might range from a high standard of performance (very few errors, appropriate use of complex constructions) to a low standard (frequent errors impair meaning).

In the 1990s, states began to promulgate "state standards" for education. State standards are published on state education Web sites. To find the Web site for any state, see the Council of Chief State School Officers (CCSSO) Web site, which has a U.S. map that links to education Web sites for each state (http://www.ccsso.org/chief_state_school_officers/state_education_agencies/index.cfm). This use of the term "standards" differed from previous use and has effectively revised the use of the term. States are legally responsible for public education, so schools must deal with their terminology. If "standards" now means the content of instructional goals themselves, which drive the curriculum, then "standards-based grading" or "standards grading" (Guskey, 2001, 2004, 2008; Marzano, 2000) must mean grading according to student achievement regarding various content standards. Levels of performance are still required but are no longer called the "standards" themselves, since that term has been redefined to mean the areas of study. In current standards-based grading, levels of performance typically are designated "Advanced, Proficient, Basic, and Below Basic," or "Advanced, Proficient, Partially Proficient, and Beginning," or something to that effect.

Narrative grading means preparing written comments about students' achievement, either in addition to or instead of using numbers or letter grades. Sometimes computer report cards have a menu of comments from which teachers can select; sometimes handwritten report cards have sections for teachers' comments; and sometimes teachers, either because of district policy or on their own, send home separate narrative progress reports. Of course teachers' commenting on students' work is not new, either! In this book, you will find information about the use of narratives for grading in Chapter 10. Whether or not you use narrative grading, the use of narrative feedback on individual student assignments is strongly recommended (see Chapter 6).

Contract grading involves specifying on paper what a student must do to earn an A, a B, and so on (or whatever symbols are used). The teacher and student both sign the paper, and then the idea is that the student's grade becomes a matter of his or her choice. In K–12 schools, this method is most often used in the context of special education (see Chapter 8).

Combinations of these methods are often used. Many grading problems or issues are really about trying to use one system for multiple, sometimes conflicting purposes. Any solution to those problems will almost surely involve some sort of combination of methods to meet the different purposes. We have already noted that narrative grading is sometimes used in conjunction with letter or percentage grading. Some districts use a combination of letter grading for achievement and other symbols for effort, conduct, and other nonachievement factors (see Chapter 7). Wiggins (1998) has suggested a combination of grades and scores on report cards to give parents two types of information. "Grades" would communicate, as they often do now, information about how a student performed in current classroom instruction and be based on classroom assessments ("How is my child doing in class?"). "Scores" would communicate student level of achievement relative to external assessments ("How is my child doing in the absolute sense?"). This seems a promising system, since it would provide, and disentangle, the two types of information parents want about their children. It could work only if there existed a fairly detailed and complex set of curriculum-based external assessments, and multiple forms of each at that. Whether this will come to pass is doubtful. Starch (1918) published a whole book of such external scales for measuring students' academic progress almost a century ago, but their use did not catch on.

SOCIAL CONTEXT OF GRADING

In schools, grades function variously as evaluations of student work, as a kind of currency ("pay" for "work" students do), as motivators or destroyers (see Chapter 3), as the vehicle for promotion and retention, and as part of public relations. It is important to understand the social psychology of grades—school and community expectations and perceptions—since these tend to preserve the status quo and are major barriers to change.

One important function of grades is to communicate to parents about their children's achievement in school. Therefore, it is important that grades communicate clearly. Two studies investigated the question of whether parents' and teachers' interpretations of grades are consistent. Waltman and Frisbie (1994) surveyed fourth-grade math teachers and the parents of their students. They selected the teachers from schools representative of the size and achievement level of schools in Iowa. Their conclusions were disturbing, since most of the teachers and parents had a hard time understanding the various meanings grades can have (achievement relative to an absolute standard or achievement relative to other students, progress or status, etc.). The biggest difference between parents' and teachers' perceptions was that parents thought the "average" grade was a C+, whereas the average grade assigned by the teachers was a B; many assigned no D or F grades at all. Thus the parents of a child who was doing C work might think the child was doing satisfactory work when, in fact, the child was receiving one of the lowest grades assigned.

Pilcher-Carlton and Oosterhof (1993) used a case study approach to investigate high school students' and their parents' and teachers' perceptions of grades. They interviewed two average, two above-average, and two below-average high school students, plus a parent of each of the students and their math and language arts teachers. Serious discrepancies were found in these cases between the parents and the teachers and students. Teachers and students both reported knowing that the meaning of grades differed from teacher to teacher. They both realized that achievement as well as effort was involved, with high grades generally meaning both high achievement and good effort and low grades generally meaning a lack of effort and application in class. Teachers and students both reported taking this into account when they used grades; for example, teachers did not use the grades of other teachers to make decisions about their students. But parents, having no other way to interpret grades, assumed they represented achievement of course content.

It is important for you to realize, as you assign grades and send them home to parents, that what you intend to say and what parents or others hear may be two different things. Although this isn't the main argument for grading on achievement—the main reason is consistency with the model of instruction promulgated by most teacher education (see Chapter 4)—nevertheless, it's a point. Parents think that grades indicate achievement.

LEGAL CONTEXT OF GRADING[1]

Education law, and therefore the legal context for grading, differs from state to state. You must check grading policies and education law in your own state and district. Most often, the authority for grading is vested in the school board but delegated to educators in the school district. The delegation is a matter of policy more than law, and the level of delegation (superintendent, principal, teacher, or a mixture) varies.

For a state-by-state survey of legislation that refers to grading, see McElligott and Brookhart (2008). The wide variation from state to state was the main finding from our review of state legislation and case law related to grading. There were, however, a few general conclusions that we present below, with the repeated caution to check your own state when you begin teaching.

CONFIDENTIALITY

Report card grades in official school records qualify as information subject to confidential treatment under the Family Education Rights and Privacy Act (FERPA). Grades recorded in teachers' personal grade books probably do not; cases about this issue have been decided in different ways. Teachers' grading practices are not subject to legal challenge under FERPA. A U.S. Supreme court case involving peer grading was decided in 2002 in *Owasso Ind. Sch. Dist. v. Falvo.* The court held that peer grading does not constitute official educational records. While confidentiality as a legal issue extends only to official educational records, there are times that student perception of fairness (see Chapter 3) is just as important for sound grading practices as the legal basis. Therefore, "public" declaration of grades, like posting scores on charts or calling out scores after peer grading, is not recommended even though it is legal.

GRADE PENALTIES

Students have brought suit to challenge the lowering of their grades for absenteeism or disciplinary reasons. Here are two contradictory cases about students using alcohol on a field trip. In Texas, students who drank alcohol on a field trip received no credit for work assigned while they were away, and their overall grade for that grading period was reduced three percentage points (*New Braunfels Indep. Sch. Dist. v. Armke,* 1983). The court upheld the grade reduction. In Pennsylvania, however, a student who drank

---

[1]The material in this section is based on McElligott and Brookhart (2008).

alcohol on a field trip had her overall quarterly grades in every class reduced by two percentage points for every day of suspension, for a total 10% reduction for 5 days of suspension. The court found the grade reduction to be unfair and illegal (*Katzman v. Cumberland Valley Sch. Dist.*, 1984).

And here are three contradictory cases about lowering grades for absenteeism. In Connecticut, a school board's policies said a student would receive no credit in any year-long class after 24 absences (whether unexcused or excused) and would get a 5% reduction in a course grade for every unexcused absence beyond the first. A student failed one class under the first policy and had his passing grades in three classes reduced to failing grades under the second policy. The court upheld the policies (*Campbell v. Bd. of Educ.*, 1980). In Kentucky (*Dorsey v. Bale*, 1975) and Colorado (*Gutierrez v. Sch. Dist. R-1*, 1978), however, school board policies that reduced students' grades because of absences were found to be invalid because those policies were found to breach state statutes.

Most of the time students and parents have challenged school grades, the courts have upheld the educators and policies in question. Therefore, you should familiarize yourself with district policies about grading and follow them in your grading practices. Some grade reduction and "penalty" policies do not follow sound and recommended educational practice. For example, a grade is intended to convey information about academic achievement, and reducing a grade for reasons of behavior does not fit this purpose. If a policy seems educationally misguided, the best legal advice would be to follow the policy while it is in force, and work within the district to change it.

APPEALS POLICIES AND DUE PROCESS

The two main legal principles under which students and parents have challenged students' grades are both from the 14th Amendment of the U.S. Constitution. These two are the due process provision and the equal protection provision.

The due process clause says that the state (or its actors—in the case of grading, that would be the school board, a superintendent, a principal, or a teacher) cannot deprive anyone of "life, liberty, or property, without due process of law" (U.S. Constitution, Amendment XIV). Due process has two aspects: procedural due process and substantive due process. Procedural due process requires that notice be given to those affected by a decision and that a fair hearing take place; substantive due process requires that the content of the proceedings be fair. In the case of grading, that means grading policies and appeals processes should be in place and clear, and that hearings about grades be conducted fairly.

The equal protection clause says that a person acting for the state cannot deny anyone "the equal protection of the laws" (U.S. Constitution, Amendment XIV). Equal protection cases are all different, but they share the common theme that decision makers cannot treat differently people who are alike in all ways relevant to the decision being made. In the case of grading, that means all students to whom a grading policy applies should be treated in the same way according to that policy.

These cases can be very complicated legally and are generally more about due process or equal protection than about the grades per se. The best advice we can give here is for teachers and school districts to review their grading policies and make sure there are procedures for appeal and due process and that all students are treated equitably.

EDUCATOR RESPONSIBILITIES

Treating students equitably, communicating clearly about grading policies and practices, keeping records confidential, and hearing student appeals are not only "defensive" acts to protect against student litigation. They are positive, proactive teacher responsibilities.

Teachers should find out how grading authority is delegated in their state and district. If a student or parent challenges a grade you assign, does the policy say your principal or school board can change it? In some places the answer would be yes, and in others no. It's not that you would grade differently under the different scenarios. The information in this book should help you establish defensible grading practices and keep good records. However, it's important for you to understand your place in the overall grading policy context in which you work.

The question of whether grades are a protected form of teacher expression, under the 1st Amendment of the U.S. Constitution, has been decided in different ways by different courts. If grading practices are a form of expression (protected or not), then one can also view instructional practices as a form of teacher expression. Both should work together to support and accurately report student learning. Current standards-based language would call this alignment.

In summary, legal issues in grading may have been intensified by the current litigious climate and the increased stakes attached to accountability for student achievement. There is not a lot of specific legislation to give guidance on grading practices. Rather, most grading issues are a matter of policy. Thus at present, thoughtful policies, clearly communicated and uniformly applied, are the key to legally defensible grading practices.

CONCLUSION

This chapter has explored the historical, social, and legal contexts for grading. Few grading issues or methods are really new. The main difficulty driving grading issues both historically and currently is that grades are pressed to serve a variety of conflicting purposes. The next chapter will add educational psychology as another context in which to think about grades. As you learn about the role of grades in learning and motivation, you will realize that students' own uses of grades add to the complexity of the multiple purpose problem in grading. Nevertheless, it is better to understand and to deal with these multiple purposes and contexts than to ignore them. They can inform decisions you make in your own grading practices, as we will see in Parts 2 and 3.

EXERCISES

1. Construct a concept map with "Grading" as the center of the web. Place as many of the issues discussed in this chapter as you can on the map, drawing connections

between issues. Based on the information in this chapter, write a brief (two or three sentences) explanation for each of the connections you drew on your concept map.

2. Select a grading issue or grading method to research in more detail. Look in your library for more information. You might start with the references in this book or a reference work like the *Encyclopedia of Educational Research* to find sources. Write a brief report on the history of that issue or method. In your introductory paragraph, tell why you chose the method as interesting to you. In your concluding paragraph, summarize the importance of what you found and tell why it should be interesting to other educators.

Note: These are intended as "short" exercises at the end of the chapter. See Part 1 Exercises on page 49 for additional exercises.

The Educational Psychology of Grading

KEY CONCEPTS

- Grades play a role in students' learning and motivation—and the particular role they play depends in part upon you and your classroom environment and in part upon the student.
- Therefore, the best thing you can do is make sure your grades convey meaningful, accurate information about student achievement. If grades give sound information to students, then their perceptions, conclusions about themselves as learners, and decisions about future activity will be the best they can be.

The previous chapter described the historical, social, and legal contexts of grading. This chapter describes another important context of grading, its role in student motivation and learning. This is a complex context, in that the same grades may be playing several different roles at once for different students. This chapter will help you understand how, when you grade student assignments or place grades on report cards, your actions play a role in students' learning and motivation—and the particular role grades play depends in part upon you and your classroom environment and in part upon the student.

This chapter is in no way a complete presentation of motivation theory or any other aspect of educational psychology; it merely highlights some of the work in educational psychology that is particularly relevant to grading. The purpose of doing that here is to advance your understanding of how the *same* grades, given by the same teacher for the same assignments, may mean different things to different students and play different roles in their educational experiences. One of the main purposes of this chapter is to raise your awareness that this kind of personal interpretation and use of your grades goes on "inside kids' heads" no matter what your intentions.

Your grading practices can contribute to these motivational states. For example, grades given fairly and based on achievement of known standards for assignments, where students have an opportunity to learn and practice, encourage students to have mastery learning goals but cannot guarantee them. Students bring their own motivational backgrounds and predispositions to the classroom, and you need to understand them. For example, suppose you give several As on a test. One student may use that A as information to conclude: "Nailed it! I knew that extra hour of study would pay off." Another student may, from your point of view, receive that *same* A, for the same score on the same test, but conclude: "I didn't study very hard for this; I guess she just gives easy tests." Yet another student with the same grade might be thinking: "I'm glad I got an A on this test. My sister always gets As, and if I take home anything less my parents might get mad." Some students might even be thinking several of these at the same time, consciously or unconsciously.

Therefore, the best thing you can do is make sure your grades convey meaningful, accurate information about student achievement. If grades give sound information to students, then their perceptions, conclusions about themselves as learners, and decisions about future activity will be based on good information. In this chapter, you will be introduced to some of the research in educational psychology that will help you understand students' perceptions of grades and some theories of the roles grades might play in student motivation and learning. Motivation as it is used in this chapter refers to the energizing of student behavior like studying, paying attention, and so on. Thus motivation is an important part of cognitive psychology, because it has to do with students' attentions, inclinations, and actions that direct their personal learning experiences.

We begin by highlighting the importance of students' perceptions of the grading process. Then we discuss the role of student perceptions in two related areas. Student perceptions play a role in motivation to learn—the wishing, willing, and wanting that results in students putting forth effort (or not!). Students' perceptions of their grades and other feedback about their achievement also give them important information that is directly useful in their cognition: in forming the concepts, developing the skills, and enhancing the knowledge that students and their teachers call learning itself. Finally, we discuss the classroom assessment environment, reminding you that individual psychology is only one part of the picture. In your classroom, there will also be a "social psychology" or "classroom culture" or context effect, and grading and other aspects of assessment are an important part of that.

STUDENT PERCEPTIONS

Students' perceptions of grades are important for two general reasons (Black & Wiliam, 1998; Crooks, 1988; Ross, Rolheiser, & Hogaboam-Gray, 2002). First, grades and other aspects of classroom assessment influence student motivation to learn. Second, grades and other aspects of classroom assessment provide students with information that they use in their learning. These two purposes are related, since the availability of various kinds of information influences students' decisions about how and why to use the information.

Psychologists have recognized that student perceptions are important for a very long time. For example, in the mid-20th century behaviorists conceived of motivation as a drive or emotion. In order to predict behavior from behaviorist theories, one needed to know the strength of the motivational drive, the person's perception of how likely their behavior was to be successful, and the incentive value for them of the reward they would receive. The importance of these kinds of perceptions has endured, even though educational psychology is no longer dominated by behaviorist theories.

Today, cognitive psychologists are interested in motivation (student wishes and intentions) and volition (student actions) as bases for effort in school. What students want and the decisions they make are clearly student perceptions. Some of the same perceptions that once were interpreted in behaviorist terms remain important, reinterpreted according to the theories of cognitive psychology. Since cognitive psychology emphasizes students' thought processes, additional student perceptions have been identified as important; for example, students' perceptions of the *reasons* for their successes or failures. Student perceptions important to the educational psychology of grading include:

- Perceptions of what the task or assignment they are asked to do actually means
- Students' perceptions of what constitutes quality work

- Level of interest in the particular topic or material
- Perceptions of the *difficulty* or *level of challenge* of a particular task or assignment
- Beliefs about whether they can be successful on a task or assignment, called *self-efficacy* (Pajares, 1996)
- Perceptions of the importance of a particular task or assignment for its own sake, sometimes called its *intrinsic value*
- Perceptions of the instrumental importance of a particular task or assignment to something else that is worthwhile (whether it will help with learning in the future, for example), sometimes called *utility value* (Eccles, 1983)
- Beliefs about the reasons for success or failure, sometimes called *attributions*
- Reasons students give for wanting to learn, called *goal orientations* (Ames & Archer, 1988; Elliott & Thrash, 2001)
- Perceptions of the feedback received after doing a task or assignment, especially whether it is *informational* or *controlling* (Deci & Ryan, 1985)
- Their own perceptions of the quality of their work, called *self-monitoring* (Sadler, 1989)
- Perceptions of the distance between their performance as described in the grade or feedback and their conception of quality work

Crooks (1988) reviewed several different bodies of literature and synthesized what we know about the influences of classroom evaluation practices on students. (For an overview list of short-, medium-, and long-term effects, see Crooks, 1988, pp. 443−444. For other excellent reviews of the effects on classroom evaluation practices on students, see Black & Wiliam [1998] and Natriello [1987].) Classroom evaluation practices, of course, include grading, and some of the influences of classroom evaluation in general that are particularly relevant to grading include the following. Grades on individual assignments influence students by

- encouraging (or discouraging) active learning strategies,
- providing knowledge of results and feedback,
- assisting students in self-monitoring,
- influencing the selection of further learning activities to increase mastery, and
- assisting (or discouraging) a sense of accomplishment.

Grades on a whole course or extended learning experience (e.g., report card grades) influence students by

- influencing motivation to study the subject in the future,
- influencing students' perceptions of their abilities in the subject,
- influencing choices of learning strategies and study habits, and
- describing or certifying achievement in the course, thus influencing future course selection.

And finally, long-term consequences of classroom evaluation that are particularly relevant to grading include

- influencing the development of student learning skills and styles,
- influencing ongoing motivation to learn, in the subject and in general, and
- influencing students' perceptions of themselves as learners.

INFLUENCE OF GRADING PRACTICES ON MOTIVATION TO LEARN

Bruner (1966), writing when cognitive psychology was just beginning its surge to the forefront of educational theory, stated, "The will to learn is an intrinsic motive, one that finds both its source and its rewards in its own exercises" (p. 127). Teachers are interested in fostering intrinsic motivation in their students. Many teachers consider developing "the will to learn" itself—more likely today called an interest in lifelong learning—as a learning goal for their students.

Bruner observed that all intrinsic motivation involves one or more of the following categories, the "natural energies that sustain spontaneous learning" (p. 127): curiosity; the drive to achieve competence; the desire to emulate a model; and reciprocity, the need to work together with others to accomplish an objective. I find these categories help me as a teacher to understand the complexity of motivation in classroom processes, which is why this section on learning and motivation begins by discussing Bruner, despite the age of the theory. Bruner's categories were the lens through which I was able to finally understand the complexity of classroom teaching. It made sense to me that the same lessons—and, for our purposes here, the same classroom assessments—were simultaneously functioning in different ways for different students. One student, for example, might want to learn some material because he is genuinely interested in and curious about it. Another student might be paying attention and doing the same tasks because she wants to become competent. A third might be doing the same work, thinking "I want to learn to do that like my teacher does." A fourth student might become motivated to learn when he participates in a group project—he would "get into it," as some students would say. It is also easy to envision combinations of these categories, for example when a student wants to do what the teacher models but also is genuinely curious about a subject.

My point is that Bruner's general theory of intrinsic motivation was my "way in" to realizing how complicated classroom processes were, and how educational psychology needs to drive our educational practices but will never be reduced to a recipe that will guarantee the educational outcomes we desire. As you read the rest of this book, keep in mind this idea of simultaneous processes, of different students perceiving the same things in different ways and doing the same tasks for different reasons. It will keep you from becoming too simplistic in your application of recommendations for grading practices and will allow you to appreciate the myriad effects your grading practices may have on your students.

Several theories about motivation and learning relate the kinds of student perceptions listed above to the development of student motivation. Theories of motivation and learning, of course, are not about grades alone, or even about assessment alone. This section outlines some important developments in understanding motivation that are particularly relevant to grading.

ATTRIBUTION THEORY

Weiner (1979) offered a theory of motivation for some classroom experiences based on attribution theory. Attribution theory assumes that the search for understanding is a basic—if not *the* basic—source of motivation. To understand an event, you need to know what brought it about. The idea was that students identify causes of various class-room events along three dimensions: stability (whether the cause was changeable over time), locus (whether the cause was internal or external to the student), and control (whether or not the student had control over the cause). Thus, for example, if a student receives an F on a test and thinks that happened because he or she is stupid, that causal attribution is stable, internal, and uncontrollable ("I can't help how I was born"). If a student receives an F and thinks it is because he or she didn't study, that's unstable (whether or not I study can change from test to test), internal, and controllable. If a student receives an A and thinks it's because the teacher wrote an easy test, that's unstable, external, and uncontrollable.

Weiner reviewed research that suggested these attributions of cause have psychological consequences. Perceptions of stability are related to the size of changes in expectations following success or failure. If a student attributes success on a project to stable reasons (e.g., "I am good at this"), then he or she can reasonably expect to be able to do even more next time. Perceptions of locus of control (internal or external) are related to self-esteem. Success attributed to ability fosters feelings of competence and confidence, whereas success attributed to luck fosters surprise, but not increased future expectations for success. Failure attributed to lack of ability fosters feelings of incompetence, whereas failure attributed to lack of effort fosters feelings of guilt and shame. Perceived control relates to helping others and emotional responses such as liking others.

Evans and Engelberg (1988) studied student perceptions of school grading. They administered questionnaires to fourth through eleventh graders at four different schools. The questionnaires asked about students' attitudes about being graded, their understanding of grading systems, and their causal attributions about why students get good grades. Their results suggested grading concepts develop gradually. Older students had a better understanding of grading schemes than younger students, although even older students did not comprehend complicated grading schemes. Older students displayed more dissatisfaction and cynicism about grading than younger students, and older students rated grades as more important than younger students.

The causes for grades that students reported to Evans and Engelberg at least partly supported attribution theory. Younger students and low achievers thought that grades were more influenced by external and uncontrollable causes, whereas older students and high achievers thought that grades were more influenced by internal and controllable causes.

This theory gives us two interesting ideas to think about in regard to grades. First, the same grade can be perceived differently by different students, and used by that student as part of a complicated web of perceptions and reasoning to make sense of his or her world. Second, it is possible for a teacher to encourage internal and controllable causal attributions by giving additional feedback in addition to the grade ("I liked the way you wrote this paragraph, Timmy, because I can tell you tried very hard to use lots of descriptive adjectives"). This, of course, will work only if the additional feedback is true and clear, but it underscores the educational importance of helping students to set grades in productive contexts. For a review of the kinds of feedback that research suggests are most powerful, see Hattie and Timperley (2007).

GOAL ORIENTATIONS

Recently, educational psychologists have become interested in the reasons students pursue academic goals, called achievement goal orientations. In the past 20 years, the study of goals has become the predominant focus of researchers and theorists studying achievement motivation (Elliott & Thrash, 2001). As this literature developed, different researchers used different terms for goal orientations: task involved or ego involved, learning oriented or performance oriented, and mastery focused or ability focused (Ames & Archer, 1988).

Currently, most writers use the terms "mastery goals" and "performance goals" to identify these two kinds of achievement goals. Students with *mastery goals* have self-improvement motivations, are interested in the development of competence, and adopt a view of evaluation where they judge their achievement based on how well they did at particular tasks. Students with *performance goals* have self-presentation motives; they want to be seen demonstrating competence. They adopt a view of evaluation where they judge their achievement based on how well they did compared to others.

Motivation theorists who are interested in the differences between approach and avoidance have identified a two-dimensional classification based not only on whether the reasons for learning are self-improvement or self-presentation goals (mastery vs. performance), but also on whether the direction comes from a desirable event or an undesirable one (approach vs. avoidance; Elliott & Covington, 2001). Thus it is possible conceptually to have students wanting to learn more about a topic for its own sake (mastery-approach motivation), wanting not to lose skills they already possess (mastery-avoidance), wanting to be seen as "smart" or competent by others (performance-approach), and wanting not to be seen as "stupid" or incompetent by others (performance-avoidance). Three of these categories have been the topic of recent research. Mastery-avoidance goals are less well studied to date (Elliott & Thrash, 2001).

The implications of theories of achievement goal orientations for classrooms are particularly important because evidence suggests that, in addition to their personal goal orientations, students can perceive classroom goal orientations as well. Ames and Archer (1988) studied students' perceptions of the mastery and performance dimensions of the classroom by asking students to respond to phrases like "The teacher makes sure I understand the work," indicating mastery goal emphases in the classroom, and "Students want to know how others score on assignments," indicating performance goal emphases in the classroom.

In Ames and Archer's study, students who felt the classroom was more mastery oriented reported using more effective learning and study strategies, preferred challenging assignments, had a more positive attitude toward the class, and tended to believe that success was a result of effort. In contrast, students who felt that the classroom was more performance oriented tended to focus on their own ability, in particular, attributing failure to lack of ability.

SELF-WORTH THEORY

Covington (1992, p. 74) based his thinking about motivation on the assumption that "the search for self-acceptance is the highest human priority, and that in schools self-acceptance comes to depend on one's ability to achieve competitively." He reviewed theories of motivation, including attribution theory and theories about achievement goal orientations, and looked for ways to light the way forward. He acknowledged that students were not on equal footing with regard to ability; some students are more able than others. He recommended that schools work to create a condition he named *motivational equity*:

> Obviously, not everyone is equally bright, nor can all children compete on an equal footing intellectually. But at least schools can provide all students with a common heritage in the *reasons* they learn. Everyone can experience feelings of resolve and a commitment to think more, and to dare more; feelings of being caught up in the drama of problem solving, and of being poised to learn and ready to take the next step. Low ability is no barrier to this kind of excellence. (p. 21)

The second recommendation that Covington made was that educators work to foster goal-oriented cognitions. This means providing students practice in the strategies they need in order to learn how to learn and how to think, to set learning goals, and then decide how to achieve them. This involves helping students to see intelligence as a resource that they can use—and even improve—and not an innate, unchangeable limit.

How do we foster motivational equity and encourage students along the road to achieving learning goals they set for themselves? What role does grading play in those efforts? Covington proposed six instructional guidelines (pp. 160–170), broad generalizations for which he provided research evidence (see Figure 3-1). Not surprisingly, grades and grading policies figure in most of them.

First, schools must provide inherently engaging assignments. Intrinsic motivation must have an opportunity to show itself, and everyone is motivated to do *something*. One strategy he suggests is providing assignments that have manageable challenges, arouse curiosity, and stimulate the imagination. This recommendation is supported by more recent work in educational psychology that highlights the role of student interest (Bergin, 1999; Brophy, 1999; Hidi & Harackiewicz, 2000). It also harks back to Bruner's (1966) noting curiosity as a primary driver of intrinsic motivation.

FIGURE 3-1

Guidelines for fostering motivational equity in the classroom

1. COOL STUFF for the CURIOUS—Assignments should be inherently interesting and manageable.
2. GOOD GRADES for GOOD LEARNING–Rewards should be an indicator and result of successful learning (not just participation) and students should have some choice.
3. Set up conditions so EFFORT leads to GOOD OUTCOMES.
4. Set up links between EFFORT and SELF-WORTH.
5. Set up conditions so all students can BELIEVE in their ABILITY.
6. Improve teacher-student relations.

Source: Adapted from *Making the Grade: A Self-Worth Perspective on Motivation and School Reform,* by M. V. Covington, 1992, Cambridge: Cambridge University Press.

Second, teachers must provide sufficient rewards for students who engage in these tasks successfully. Rewards must not be scarce, and they must come in such a way that the act of learning itself becomes a reward. This means that rewards, including grades, should come as a result of learning, not just participation. It also means that grading should be, to as great an extent as possible, under the control of students. Giving students choice in assignments on which they will be graded or having students participate in their own grading (e.g., grading themselves or conferencing with a teacher) are examples of ways grading can become a tool in fostering motivational equity and student development as learners. Research evidence suggests that if you give students the criteria for good performance, students can use them both to accomplish their tasks and also to judge their accomplishments.

Third, Covington recommends working to enhance effort–outcome beliefs. In other words, teachers need to provide opportunities for students to exercise some personal control over their work and have that effort lead to expected and valued learning or achievement. There is some evidence that when students are given choices and have the opportunity to exercise control, they in fact do get better scores. Students who are already mired in a cycle of failure will need special assistance to do this. Teachers will have to help them set realistic goals, so that they can believe they will be able to repeat their successes on future assignments. The grades students get on their work will be their evidence.

Fourth, Covington recommends working to build the connection in students' minds between effort and self-worth. If school tasks are competitive—as, for example, when a limited number of high grades are available—pride in success or shame in failure depend on students' perceptions of their ability. Classroom learning assignments, rewards, and grades should shift so that they emphasize effort, so that pride in success becomes linked to pride at working hard, and so that success is available to anyone who expends effort. This will involve a shift in the types of tasks and the amount of choice involved, so that students who expend effort really will be successful. To be clear, Covington does not recommend giving high grades "just for trying," but rather structuring assignments tailored to students' abilities and interests so that students who do try actually will succeed.

Fifth, teachers should work to promote positive beliefs about ability among their students. An incremental view of intelligence, viewing it as the ability to learn instead of the ability to outscore classmates, will foster motivational equity. Finally, Covington recommends improving relationships between teachers and students. Sharing the power to decide about learning and sharing the responsibility for evaluating that learning will make a big step in this direction.

Covington and Müeller (2001) made the case that approach and avoidance motivations were more important than mastery or performance goal orientations. In particular, any kind of approach-oriented striving, whether for knowledge or for recognition, stood in stark contrast to "avoidance goals driven by the fear of failure." The harm was not whether the goals were internal or external, but whether there was fear:

> These avoidance goals present a worrisome picture. Yet they are unlikely to be caused primarily by the offering of reward such as grades or even by their extrinsic character.

As we see it, the problem is not that grades are essentially foreign—or extrinsic to the act of learning itself—but, quite the opposite: Grades have become inexorably linked to the achievement process. Grades are highly charged with personal meaning. For many students grades carry the burden of defining their worth. The underlying reality is that intrinsic values become imperiled not principally because of the tangible, extrinsic features of the rewards that dominate in school, but because all too often the individuals' sense of worth becomes equated with high marks that are rendered scarce by competitive rules. (pp. 166–167)

Covington and Müeller pointed out that students strive for the highest grade they can achieve for different reasons related to the degree to which knowledge is valued. If students strive for good grades to impress other people or to avoid failure, then learning is valuable only to the extent that it enhances the student's status. If students strive for grades in order to use the feedback to improve their learning, then grades become part of the learning process itself. In this way, Covington and Müeller acknowledge what others have called mastery and performance orientations, but they interpret these as reasons for the primary striving (approaching or avoiding) students exhibit. They described four "kinds" of students that many teachers would recognize. Notice how grades play a role in each.

Failure-avoiding students are not motivated to approach learning, and they are very motivated to avoid failure. They use self-defeating strategies like setting impossibly high goals. When they fail to meet them, they can protect themselves from being thought "failures"; after all, no one could be expected to achieve impossibly high goals. Achievement brings relief, at least temporarily, at not being found out as incompetent. For these students, caring about grades undermines learning not because grades are external rewards, say Covington and Müeller, but because for these students grades have come to mean measures of their self-worth.

Success-oriented students are motivated to approach learning, and are not particularly motivated to avoid failure. They would risk temporary failure in their efforts to learn, and would interpret failure as feedback that a learning goal was not yet mastered. Success-oriented students interpret grades not so much as external rewards, despite the fact that they are usually awarded by teachers, but as information they can use in their own learning.

Overstrivers are motivated to approach learning, but they are also motivated to avoid failure. In effect, succeeding as learners is their strategy for avoiding failure. Getting good grades is the external meter for this group that tells how well they have succeeded. Unfortunately, avoiding failure with a good grade in one assignment carries a natural punishment for this group, since they have that much more to prove next time.

Finally, *failure-accepting students* are motivated neither to approach learning nor to avoid failure. Threats of bad grades will not convince these students to expend extra effort. Offering rewards to these students won't do that, either. Failure-accepting students may drop out of school, or if they stay in school, it is for a reason outside of their success or failure in the classroom. Covington's instructional guidelines for motivational equity (Figure 3-1) are especially important for these students.

FIGURE 3-2	Sometimes, students think grades are
What is a grade?	• "pay" owed for "work" done, • prizes given by a teacher, • a "learn-o-meter" measuring the quality of learning, • proof that they learned something, and • information for future learning. NOT ALL OF THESE VIEWS ARE HELPFUL!

FUNCTION OF FEEDBACK TO STUDENTS

The function of feedback to students is very complicated—and at the same time extremely interesting and useful to teachers—because feedback plays a role in motivation to learn and also a role in learning itself. The previous section reviewed selected developments in motivation theory. We also have discussed how the feedback contained in grades can itself function as an external motivator, such as when students think of grades as "pay" or prizes they earn; how grades function as an external motivator in the sense of a meter on their learning, where the proof that learning has occurred is a badge students want to show to others; or how grades function as an internal motivator, where the information about the quality of performance is rewarding as it furthers the cycle of continued learning (see Figure 3-2).

This section continues the discussion of the role of grades in learning by concentrating on the information contained in grades. Several theorists have examined the meaning and usefulness of information encoded in grades on individual assignments or on report cards. Others have examined the usefulness of the various other information that comes with a grade on an individual assignment; for example, often a "graded" paper includes written comments and other feedback as well as the letter or number grade.

COGNITIVE EVALUATION THEORY

Cognitive evaluation theory describes the effects of students' perceptions of environmental or external factors on intrinsic motivation. The importance of this theory for a discussion on grading is that it offers ways to consider how grades might relate students' motivation to learn to their actual learning. The previous section emphasized the different conclusions individuals might draw from the same grades, based on their individual psychological differences. This section emphasizes that certain kinds of grading and feedback make it easier for students to use the information they contain for learning.

Ryan, Connell, and Deci (1985) offered three propositions. First, anything that encourages students to perceive an internal locus of causality will enhance intrinsic motivation, and anything that encourages students to perceive an external locus of causality will undermine intrinsic motivation. Second, anything that encourages students to perceive themselves as competent will enhance intrinsic motivation, and anything that encourages students to perceive themselves as incompetent will undermine intrinsic motivation. Third, and particularly relevant to grading, events have different *functional significance*. Feedback—or indeed, any event—that students experience as giving them information for improvement is *informational*. Feedback that is principally perceived as pressure to perform a particular way—which, in grading, often includes summary judgments without any information, like "excellent" or "poor"—is *controlling*. Feedback or events that are neither informational nor controlling are *amotivating*.

The important point is that it is not the event, judgment, or grade itself that affects motivation, but its functional significance for the student. In particular, cognitive evaluation theory emphasizes the importance of conveying as much useful information as possible along with grades. The primary opportunities teachers have to convey information are (a) comments and feedback they give along with the grades on individual assignments, and (b) narratives or conferences given to help students and parents interpret the grades on report cards.

Research suggests that it is specific information about the particulars of student work that will be perceived as informational, especially if the information is about both the quality of the work and the process the student used to do it (Hattie & Timperley, 2007). Grades alone, of course, do convey information about the general level of student accomplishment on a particular assignment. But grades alone, or grades and general comments—even if the general comments praise student work—are not associated with improved student achievement or attitudes. Specific comments are associated with improved achievement and attitudes (Butler, 1987; Butler & Nisan, 1986; Elawar & Corno, 1985; Tunstall & Gipps, 1996). This makes sense if you think about the functional significance of the feedback. Students need specific suggestions and comments in order to do better next time. General feedback ("Good job!") does not contain useful information for improvement. For further discussion and practice in the skills involved in providing information to students, see Chapters 5, 6, and 10.

FORMATIVE ASSESSMENT AS FEEDBACK FOR LEARNING

Chapter 5 discusses formative and summative assessment in more detail. For now, think of those terms literally: Formative assessment means information gathered and reported for use in the development of knowledge and skills, and summative assessment means information gathered and reported for use in judging the outcome of that development. As the saying goes, "When the cook tastes the soup, that's formative assessment. When the customer tastes the soup, that's summative assessment."

The motivational theory above suggests that obtaining information students can use to develop their knowledge and skills further contributes to internal motivation. The converse also seems to be true: Students who want to develop their knowledge and skills further will look to all of the information they receive, even grades from final tests, to see what they can learn from it (Brookhart, 2001). Grades themselves—numbers, letters, or other symbols reporting the quality of achievement—are generally considered summative assessment. But the process of grading, especially grading individual assignments, carries with it lots of information that students can use to improve. There is the overall judgment of the level of achievement (the grade). There may be written comments about specific aspects of the work. Information is also available from the questions or other parts of the assignment marked as either correct or incorrect.

Sadler (1989) developed a theory of formative assessment. He suggested that formative assessment "short-circuits" the inefficient process of trial-and-error learning by providing specific information about the difference between the student's current level of performance and the characteristics of satisfactory or excellent performance. He pointed out that three conditions are necessary for learning and improvement. The student himself or herself needs

- a concept of the standard (or goal, or reference level), and a vision of high-quality performance,
- to be able to self-monitor, to accurately compare his or her own work with the standard *while it is happening*, and
- a repertoire of learning strategies that he or she can use to close the gap.

Sadler argued that grading as we usually define it involves the first two elements in a one-shot process, but that true formative assessment (and thus true learning) involves all three steps together in an ongoing process carried out over time. Step 3, where the student actively works to improve, requires effective feedback on the part of the teacher and self-regulation on the part of the student (Butler & Winne, 1995; Hattie & Timperley, 2007).

Students can "learn how to learn" and improve their abilities to use this formative, self-monitoring process. To some extent, students' success with this process of closing the gap between their own performance and a goal is subject- or task-specific. For example, I am much better at learning from my mistakes at cooking than at carpentry, because I know a lot more about food than about wood. The design of classroom assessments can actually contribute to the students' development of a concept of high-quality performance if there are clear directions, rubrics, or other descriptions of criteria, and examples of various levels of work built into the assignments.

THE CLASSROOM ASSESSMENT ENVIRONMENT

Sadler insisted that it was important to give students "direct authentic evaluative experiences" in order to develop their skills at the formative assessment process. Self-monitoring and other learning strategies can be learned. Teachers can foster a classroom climate of achievement and continuous improvement if they construct their classroom environment with certain emphases. Ames and Archer (1988) suggested the following:

- Define "success" as improvement and progress.
- Value learning and hard work.
- Pay attention to how students are learning.
- View errors and mistakes as part of learning.
- Focus your own and students' attention on the process of learning.

- Emphasize learning something new as a good reason for effort.
- Evaluate students' work on the basis of absolute standards or progress toward goals, not student standing in the class.

Teachers create these emphases in their classrooms by both what they say and what they do. The two need to be consistent. For example, teachers who tell students that the process of learning matters, but then do not give students sufficient opportunities to practice new skills before they are tested, are not being consistent.

You have seen that grades influence students' perceptions of what is important to learn and perceptions of themselves as learners. Conversely, how teachers grade influences how they perceive students and their potential and, subsequently, how teachers make decisions about ways to support student learning (Thomas & Oldfather, 1997).

In each particular assignment, and in every other aspect of classroom lessons, students learn what is expected of them, how "good work" is defined, and the meaning and value of effort. The students' overall feelings about these expectations comprise the classroom assessment environment (Stiggins & Conklin, 1992). The classroom assessment environment, as Stiggins and Conklin originally described it, was more about teacher practices than student perceptions. Important to creating a classroom assessment environment were the purposes for which teachers used classroom assessments: the assessment methods used, the criteria for selecting them, and their quality; the teacher's use of feedback; the teacher's preparation and background in assessment; the teacher's perceptions of students; and the assessment policy environment. All of these except the last are under the teacher's control. Thus, a teacher's classes had an assessment "character" or environment that stemmed from the teacher's general approach to assessment. Haydel, Oescher, and Kirby (1999) called teachers' beliefs about testing and assessment practices "the evaluative culture of classrooms," and found that these beliefs were related to teacher efficacy. Teacher efficacy, in turn, is related to student efficacy and achievement.

CONCLUSION

Remember that the information in this chapter was meant to help you understand what is going on "inside kids' heads," not to second-guess or change a grade for any particular student! I once heard a sophomore teacher education student say, about a boy whom she was tutoring in math in her fieldwork placement: "He got most of them wrong, but I told him he did a good job for his self-esteem." Worse than nonsense, this kind of thing can be actively harmful! What the well-intentioned student communicated to the pupil was either incorrect information that he did a good job or, if he knew that he had gotten most of his math work wrong, that for this teacher, getting most of them wrong counts as doing a good job. The student could reasonably draw a number of bad conclusions from this. Perhaps he'll conclude he deserves to be told he's good when he's not—too much of this kind of thinking can lead to laziness in the classroom, belligerence, and a feeling of entitlement. Or perhaps he'll conclude the teacher is stupid—too much of this kind of thinking can cause all sorts of classroom management problems.

In truth, classroom management is one of the most difficult issues related to grading even when grading is done very well. If teachers don't use grades as rewards and punishments (external motivators) to get students to do their work, what then? I have met more than one teacher who insists that students will not do any work unless it "counts," usually defined as graded. It can be hard to share control of grading and let students have any choices or opportunities to self-monitor. Yet the literature suggests that without developing student skills at formative assessment, students will not learn how to learn and remain dependent on their teachers.

The solution seems to be to harness the powerful internal motivation that comes when students receive information and *the power to use it* for their own improvement. Give students as much choice as possible, as much control over the criteria for good work and their visions for their accomplishments as possible, and as much solid information in your grades as you can. In the long run, this will lead to genuine self-monitoring, genuine self-esteem, and genuine learning for most students. Students who are very busy learning will not be so busy at misbehaving.

EXERCISES

1. Define each of the concepts from the chapter in your own words. Then, write a brief story that illustrates the concept. The first example is done for you.
    a. Utility value. Utility value means the importance something has because it's useful to doing or getting something else. Story: Sally paid attention in algebra class, even though she found several of the problems tedious. She wanted to be an engineer like her dad, and she knew that she would need to understand math well in order to learn how to do cool stuff like design bridges.
    b. Goal orientations
    c. Informational feedback
    d. Self-monitoring

2. Describe some grading practices that you as a classroom teacher could use to foster motivational equity in your classroom. Keep this essay, and revise it after you have finished reading the rest of the book.

3. You are a fifth-grade math teacher. You have just given a test at the end of a unit on multiplying fractions and are planning to return the graded tests in class and go over the answers. What specifically would you do (what would your lesson plan be for the day), and what effect do you think your plan would have on success-oriented students, overstrivers, failure-avoiders, and failure-accepters?

Note: These are intended as "short" exercises at the end of the chapter. See Part 1 Exercises on the next page for additional exercises.

Part 1 Exercises

1. Write about how grading functions would be handled in a perfect world (without grades).
2. Make a list of questions you have after reading these introductory chapters and self-reflecting. Interview one or more teachers and report their answers to your questions.
3. Select one of the following books and read it. Prepare a "book report" that is a reflective response to your reading. Identify the three most significant things that you learned, and tell how each of them will affect your thinking about grading.

   Guskey, T. R., (Ed.) (2008). *Practical solutions for serious problems in standards-based grading.* Thousand Oaks, CA: Corwin Press.

   Choose this one if you're interested in reading more about report card grading in the current climate of educational accountability.

   Kirschenbaum, H., Napier, R., & Simon, S. B. (1971). *Wad-ja-get? The grading game in American education.* New York: Hart Publishing.

   Choose this one if you're interested in reading a "novel" about high school students and their teachers and what they decide to do about grading.

   Wiggins, G. (1998). *Educative assessment.* San Francisco: Jossey-Bass.

   Choose this one if you're interested in reading more about grading individual assignments.

Part 2

Integrating Assessment and Instruction

CHAPTER 4

Designing Assessments That Reflect Intentions for Learning

CHAPTER 5

Deciding on the Bases for Grading

CHAPTER 6

Providing Grades and Other Feedback to Students

Designing Assessments That Reflect Intentions for Learning

KEY CONCEPTS

- Assessments and grading criteria must be coordinated with instructional goals.
- The performance task you ask students to do, or the test questions you ask them to answer, must allow students to exhibit understanding or mastery of whatever concepts or skills you are looking for.
- One of the most common errors in classroom test construction occurs when a question seems to tap higher order thinking, but in fact taps recall of predigested information. The way to avoid this is to pose questions that are new to the student.
- One of the most common errors in performance assessment task design is the "close, but no cigar" phenomenon, where a performance task "sort of" taps a learning outcome but also either requires extraneous skills or doesn't require all of the relevant skills.
- Coordinating the test questions or performance task with instructional goals is the first part of matching assessment with instruction. The weights of various parts of the scoring scheme also need to be coordinated with instruction.

A book about grading begs the question, "Grade what?" This chapter treats assessment design in just enough detail to help you think about what you are grading. This textbook is not primarily about assessment design, but it is important to think about assessment as a whole: The task and the scoring, together, form the indicator of student achievement. The task, whether a project or a set of test questions or anything else, must be appropriate to the goals for student learning, and the scoring must accurately place information about student learning onto some meaningful scale.

Figure 4-1 presents one common model for thinking about assessment and instruction together. It's an oversimplification, and has been criticized on those grounds, but it has the advantage of being simple enough to keep in mind as a working principle when you are designing instruction for your classroom. Good teachers will realize there are other things to think about, too; the model doesn't capture everything. For example, student characteristics, the curriculum, and community expectations are all important.

Nevertheless, I encourage you to store this simple triangle in your memory and think of it every time you work in your classroom. It provides a visual organizer for some very important points. Notice that everything is related to what it is you want your students to learn. This can be knowledge of facts and important concepts for recall, thinking and reasoning skills using the particular content, skills like being able to write a certain genre or use a microscope or read a map, or some combination of these things (recall the kinds of achievement targets in Figure 1-3). Figure 4-1 calls this "Goals for Students' Learning." In other classes, you may hear terms like "instructional objectives" or "achievement targets." Whatever you call them, goals for student learning are the destination toward which students and teachers travel. They are the answer to the question "Where am I going?" Think of classroom teaching as creating learning journeys.

Instruction and assessment *both* need to match the goals for learning. If the learning goals are the answer to "Where am I going?" then the instruction shows "How will I get there?" and assessment tells "How will I know when I'm there?" Here's another place where the critics are right that the model is too neat. Assessment happens throughout instruction, sometimes informally and sometimes formally. Students assess themselves, and teachers check how students are doing, all along their learning journey. Think of the two-headed arrow between instructional activities and assessment in Figure 4-1 as an active loop.

Assessment itself has several aspects. Assessment needs to be based on what we want to know—which should be anchored in intentions for learning. Assessment can be

FIGURE 4-1 A common model for the relationship of assessment with instruction

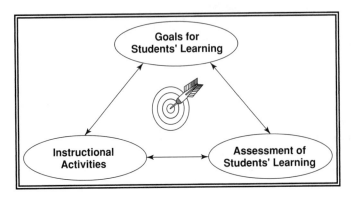

planned to check for prior knowledge, as in a pretest; to check for final level of accomplishment at the end of instruction; or for monitoring learning throughout instruction. In all of these cases, the assessment should be thoughtfully based on the information you need about student achievement of concepts or skills relevant to their learning goals.

Gathering assessment evidence can be done formally or informally. Observing students as they work, asking them questions or answering theirs, provides valuable information about student progress. If you share your insights with students (or they share theirs with you) and they use that information for improvement, you are doing formative assessment. Formal assessments, tests or performance assessments, also can provide information for formative assessment. The evidence you gather to assess achievement that you will use for report card grades will typically be a subset of all of the assessment you do—all results of observations of students' progress should get used, but not everything gets used for report card grading. Airasian and Russell (2008) call the subset of assessment results that are used for report card grades "official assessments."

MATCHING ASSESSMENT AND INSTRUCTION

For several years, I was a seventh-grade English/Language Arts teacher in a middle school in a small city. I often taught large classes of students who were struggling with reading, using a reading textbook the district had selected with stories that were roughly on a fifth-grade reading level but were about subjects that might interest older children. We read about one story a week. For each story, I was interested in students learning their new vocabulary and then reading and understanding the story.

Of course we did some other things too, but typically we would work on a story during the week and then have a short test on Friday. The layout of my tests was the same each time: matching vocabulary words and their definitions and answering comprehension questions about the story. There were usually about 15 vocabulary words a week. The teachers' manual for the reader had five comprehension questions for each story, and I thought they were good ones. They were the sort of short-answer questions you could answer only if you had read and understood the story; for example, "Why was Sam afraid to ask his grandfather about the old days?"

So every Friday, my students had a 20-point test: 15 points for vocabulary and 5 points for comprehension. I did this for 3 years, for hundreds of students! In a college assessment course I took after I no longer had this job, I realized with a sinking feeling the terrible truth—15 out of 20 is 75%. You could have passed all of my story tests without ever having read the story! Why had I never thought of that? Then, of course, I spent several years worrying that hundreds of adults who had been in my class for seventh-grade Reading were stumbling about, warped for life, because I had said some of them could read when they couldn't!

In reality, it is highly unlikely that there were many students who knew all their vocabulary words but didn't read any of the story, so I probably didn't warp anyone for life. Nevertheless, my charge was to give a grade on each test, and then later combine those grades with other measures into a report card grade labeled "Reading."

I hope my story raises your awareness of this issue of matching what your assessment actually *does* with what it is *supposed* to do in order to assess the learning objectives. There are lots of more subtle ways in which the match between the information you need to evaluate whether students learned what you intended them to learn and the actual information you get from an assessment can be askew.

We won't go into great depth about types of assessments. This textbook is about grading, and is intended to supplement other texts on classroom assessment. Instead, we will review the basic types of assessment that are available to classroom teachers. Students are encouraged to read about these assessment types, and how to design them, in more detail (e.g., Nitko & Brookhart, 2007; Stiggins, 2005).

The basic types of assessment include paper-and-pencil tests, performance assessments, oral questioning, and sometimes portfolios (depending on how the portfolio is used, as an assessment itself or as a vehicle for communication of the results of other assessments; Stiggins, 2005). The main point of this chapter is that each individual assessment must be appropriate for providing information or evidence of student learning in the way in which it was intended. In Part 3, we will expand on this point to say that grades from individual assessments must be combined into grades for report cards in such a way that the combination grade provides intended information as well.

PAPER-AND-PENCIL TESTS

You are probably very familiar with paper-and-pencil tests. Students typically take tests individually, by writing or marking the answers to questions on paper. Objectively scored (or "right/wrong") question types include multiple-choice, true/false, matching, and fill-in-the-blank. These questions can be scored by anyone who has the answer key. Subjectively scored question types include essays and show-the-work or partial-credit problems judged with rubrics or other scoring schemes. Paper-and-pencil tests with good questions and thoughtful scoring schemes can do an excellent job of assessing knowledge of facts and concepts and also thinking and reasoning skills.

One of the main advantages of paper-and-pencil tests is that a range of content material can be covered. Because there can be lots of questions on a test, a large number of different concepts can be tapped, typically more than for a project, for example. This is good for validity because a larger portion of the content of the learning goals can be represented. It is also good for scoring reliability, because with lots of answers (one for each test question!), you can estimate the student's level of achievement with more confidence. If you get one terrific answer, you don't know whether it's a fluke or the student's achievement is truly excellent; if you get a whole set of terrific answers, you are on more solid ground when concluding that the student's achievement is terrific.

The major disadvantage of paper-and-pencil tests is that it's easier to write test questions that ask for recall than questions that require reasoning. Another disadvantage may be that if you use prepared tests from textbook publishers or other curriculum materials, they may not match the instructional emphases you used in your classroom. It is worth checking through the questions in published tests before you use them to make sure the questions reflect the mix of content emphases and levels of thinking that you intended for your students to learn. It won't do you much good to get information about how your students achieved on a set of concepts and thinking skills that was different from the set you worked on together in class—which is what may happen if you use a published test without examining it first.

Whether you use a test that you wrote yourself or one that someone else wrote, make sure to check the questions carefully. Each one should clearly ask about some important aspect of intended learning goals. For example, in an English unit where the focus is on reading and interpreting poetry, a test where most of the points are scored by matching poets with the names of the poems they wrote doesn't match.

Or suppose that you are teaching a unit on two-digit multiplication in elementary school math. You have used problems from your textbook, manipulatives, and paper-and-pencil diagrams. You have placed a special emphasis on using estimation first, to guide problem solving and to help students decide whether their solution makes sense. You have emphasized drawing diagrams to help students with estimation. The textbook offers a test and a practice test that are each constructed in two parts: some two-digit multiplication problems and some word problems that require two-digit multiplication to solve. The directions for the test ask students to solve the problems in the first part and solve the problems and label the answers in the second part.

Indirectly, of course, estimation should be helpful, but nothing on this test explicitly asks students to show you that they know how to use estimating appropriately to solve two-digit multiplication problems. If your students take the test as it stands, you'll have direct evidence about only some of your learning goals for the unit. There are a couple of different solutions to this problem of the test matching only some of your learning goals. The key is that you looked at the test first and realized there was a problem! You could add some questions that specifically ask students to estimate. You could modify the word problems on the test to require that students show you their estimation first, then solve the problem and explain how estimation helped. You could give the test as is, and on another day plan a different assessment of students' estimation skills, realizing you would have complete information about the unit only if you looked at the results of both assessments.

NOVEL APPLICATIONS ARE REQUIRED TO TAP HIGHER ORDER THINKING

One of the most common errors in classroom test construction happens when a question seems to tap higher order thinking, but in fact taps recall of predigested information. The way to avoid this is to pose questions that are novel for the student. The questions don't have to be new in the universe—just new to the student. This is something that only the teacher or others who have participated in instruction can judge. Even the most complex reasoning question can become a matter of recall. The question "Analyze the structure and persuasiveness of Jefferson's argument for democracy in the Declaration of Independence" may call for an essay analyzing Jefferson's use of language and rhetoric and the students' understanding of historical and political context, or for an essay recalling the class discussion from last Thursday, if that topic was already addressed in class. The question "Discuss one of the major causes of the Civil War" may call for an essay drawing on historical knowledge and reasoning skills, or for an essay repeating a section of a textbook chapter titled "Causes of the Civil War" and recalling the name of one of its subheadings.

Sometimes teachers do not put anything on a test that they haven't gone over in class to avoid students' complaints of "We never did that!" The way to handle this is to solve novel problems during instruction, too, so that although the student has not done a particular application or analysis before a test, he or she has done others and developed the thinking and reasoning skills that the novel application now tests. Consider this reportedly true story. It happened in a first-year college calculus class, but could just as easily have happened in a high school math class:

> Early one term, [the teacher] and his class were working through some standard motion problems: "A boy drops a water balloon from a window. If it takes 0.8 seconds to strike his erstwhile friend, who is 5 feet tall, how high is the window?" On the exam, the problem took this form: "Someone walking along the edge of a pit accidentally kicks into it a small stone, which falls to the bottom in 2.3 seconds. How deep is the pit?" One student was visibly upset. The question was not fair, she protested. The instructor had promised that there would not be any material on the exam that they had not gone over in class. "But we did a dozen of those problems in class," our colleague said. "Oh, no," shot back the student, "We never did a single pit problem." (McClymer & Knoles, 1992, p. 33)

This strategy of solving new problems for assessment is indeed a good strategy for instruction, too. If students always memorize and recall, they will not develop good critical thinking skills. If students always solve problems of one particular form, they may learn the form but not the concept behind it.

In the article cited above, the authors go on to relate that the students not only had done motion problems that took various forms, but also had been taught to draw or diagram the problem in order to figure out an appropriate solution strategy. So although we may sympathize with the student who could not solve the motion problem, it is a question that yields information from which we can make a valid conclusion: The student could not apply concepts she was supposed to have learned. If the problem had been in a form exactly like a question from class—the solution to which she had memorized—it would not have been a valid indicator of whether she could apply the concepts herself. She might have done it correctly by rote application of a memorized solution strategy.

PERFORMANCE ASSESSMENTS

A performance assessment can be defined as observation and judgment of student performance on a task. We can assess a process (observe an act in which the student engages) or a product (observe something the student makes). The task and its associated scoring scheme together comprise the performance assessment. The band director who audiotapes her students playing scales on their instruments and then grades them according to accuracy of pitch and quality of tone, the physical education instructor who observes his students' broad jumps and then scores them according to distance and form, and the English teacher who assigns her students to write stories about the moon and then grades them with six-trait writing rubrics (Northwest Regional Educational Laboratory [NWREL], 2001) all are observing students and then judging their performances.

Performance tasks vary greatly according to how open-ended the questions are, how much student choice is involved, how many different modes of response are accepted or required (writing, speaking, drawing, diagramming, filming, etc.), how much time may be spent, and how many different concepts and applications are tapped. Performance tasks can be scored with checklists, where qualities are noted as present or absent; with rubrics where quality is judged along a scale; or with scoring schemes that add up points for various qualities observed in the work.

Performance assessments are good for assessing in-depth thinking or study in one area, or for assessing skills or products. The only way to know, for example, how well students can read aloud, or speak French, or sing is to listen to them do it. A test could give you information about whether students understood the story or the French conversation, or whether students knew the words to the song, but those things are not exactly what we had in mind.

One of the most common errors in performance assessment task design is the "close, but no cigar" phenomenon, where a performance task "sort of" taps a learning outcome but also either requires extraneous skills or doesn't require all of the relevant skills. For example, the Chula Vista Elementary School District in California was working on alternative assessment questions for their fifth-grade students to demonstrate knowledge of the water cycle of evaporation and condensation. Their first draft of the assessment task was as follows:

> Imagine you are a falling raindrop. Describe how you became a raindrop and what will happen to you now. Be sure to include pictures with labels to show your adventures. (California Assessment Collaborative, 1993, p. 31)

The teachers intended students' words and pictures to illustrate the water cycle. But with language like "describe how you became a raindrop" and "show your adventures," what they got was—you guessed it—fantasy and fiction style adventure stories. Narrative writing and illustration are good skills to have, but are not the ones the Chula Vista teachers wanted to assess!

After two more drafts, the task read:

> Imagine that you are a falling raindrop. Think about how you became a raindrop and how, after you fall, you will become a raindrop again. Then describe this in writing on page 2. On page 3 make drawings to show each stage in your cycle. Label each stage and as many parts of your drawings as you can. (p. 31)

Another way performance assessments may end up not quite matching the learning goals they are intended to measure happens when the mode of expression is graded, but it is the content of the message that reflects the learning outcome. For example, students may be assigned to give a speech or group presentation or Microsoft® PowerPoint® presentation on a particular topic they are studying. If oral communication or organization of group work or quality of the use of PowerPoint is the focus of observation and grading, then the assessment really taps skill at speaking or presenting, not understanding of the content.

For example, suppose you want to assess understanding of a chapter of a novel your English class is reading by asking groups of students to create and perform an original skit. You would need to be careful that the assignment calls for showing true understanding of the events and characters in the chapter. It would be easy to get sidetracked and focus on grading the dramatic performance, especially if some of your students display a little "ham."

SCORING IS PART OF THE MATCH

Coordinating the performance task or test questions with instructional goals is the first part of matching assessment with instruction. The weights of various parts of the scoring scheme also need to be coordinated with instruction. Remember my reading test!

TESTS

A good way to check the match for test questions is to make a test blueprint. These can be simple lists of content and weight, done as you are planning the test. Think what would have happened if I had only written this before I had written my reading test:

Vocabulary	15
Comprehension	5
	20

I would have seen that vocabulary and comprehension were out of balance. If I had thought vocabulary and comprehension were about equal in emphasis for the particular week, I could have dashed off a change:

Vocabulary	~~15~~	10
Comprehension	~~5~~	10
	20	20

Then I would have selected 10 of the vocabulary words to test. If students had studied all 15, testing their knowledge of 10 would give a reasonable estimate of their knowledge of all 15 words. Of course, this works only if the students do not know ahead of time which 10 words you are going to select.

I could have written five more comprehension questions, to add to the five questions from the teachers' manual. Probably better in this instance would have been to give 2 points for each correct answer to the five comprehension questions from the teachers' manual, since they each required writing a thoughtful sentence—arguably worth more than selecting a definition—and since as a group they covered the story pretty thoroughly.

On the other hand, I could have decided to make vocabulary worth 5 points and comprehension 15, or any other combination I wished. The point is this simple list is a wonderful tool for making sure the score that comes from a test reflects information about instructional goals in relative proportions to their importance and emphasis in your classroom. I recommend the use of this simple blueprint for any test or quiz, no matter how short.

Two-dimensional blueprints can also be used. They take a little longer to create than the simple blueprints, but the advantage is that they allow for planning the proportions of both content and level of thinking. Two-dimensional blueprints are generally best used for larger tests that will weigh heavily in report card grades. The additional planning time will be well worth it in terms of additional confidence that your information is trustworthy and well matched to your learning goals—in other words, that it is valid information for you to use to grade your students.

Since we're already familiar with my awful Reading test—and since it clearly needs all the help it can get!—we'll use it to illustrate what a two-dimensional test blueprint looks like. See Appendix A for more details about how to write test blueprints for longer tests.

Suppose I decided that I wanted vocabulary and comprehension to each count equally in the test score. Suppose further that I wanted to make sure half of the test score reflected knowledge (recall of vocabulary and of events in the story) and half reflected thinking and reasoning. Table 4-1 shows what my test blueprint might have looked like. In order to come up with 20 points distributed in this way, I might have written 5 vocabulary definition questions, 5 questions asking students to use vocabulary words in original sentences, 5 questions asking students to describe events or characters in the story, and 1 five-point question asking students to discuss some aspect of the story. Can you think of other ways I could have constructed questions for these specifications?

TABLE 4-1

Test blueprint
for a simple
story test

Content of Questions	Level of Cognition Required		
	Knowledge	Thinking and Reasoning	Total
Vocabulary	5	5	10 (50%)
Story Comprehension	5	5	10 (50%)
Total	10 (50%)	10 (50%)	20 (100%)

PERFORMANCE ASSESSMENTS

Performance assessments raise the same concern about scoring weights matching instructional goals as do tests. One of the most common weighting problems for performance assessments involves scoring the performance assessment with rubrics that
are heavy on process, delivery, visual effect, and so on, but using the performance assessments as indicators of achievement of content goals like knowledge of facts and
concepts.

For example, I have seen lots of rubrics for grading reports that were organized into
content, mechanics, and organization, each contributing equally to the grade for the
report. Suppose in your eleventh-grade American history class you were studying the
American Revolution. Suppose further that some of your learning goals were for students to (a) develop library research skills, and (b) investigate the role of one of the
country's founders in the First Continental Congress. You set up an assignment requiring students to select a member of the First Continental Congress, read about that person's involvement in the events prior to the American Revolutionary War, and write a
report. Your assignment has format guidelines for the report: create a cover page, include pictures, write at least three pages of text, and use MLA style for references. The
grading scheme awards points equally for the content of the report (accurate facts and
concepts, presented clearly), mechanics (English grammar and usage), and organization (format requirements, bibliography style). This means that one third of the student's grade reflects how well he or she researched and understood the content, and
two thirds reflects how well he or she presented it. What's wrong with this is not that
presentation isn't important—it is. What's wrong is that the learning goals that the
report was supposed to assess were more about content than about presentation, but
the information (grade) that comes from the report reflects more about presentation
than about content. The same thing can easily happen with student speeches, or
posters, or any project that has format or delivery aspects to it.

CONCLUSION

I hope the examples have given you some idea of what it means to match assessments
with the instructional goals for which they are intended to help you evaluate students.

The most valid information for you to use in assigning your report card grades comes from assessment information—whether from tests or performance assessments—that matches intended learning goals in terms of

- content material,
- type of thinking required, and
- mode of response.

Scores for various parts of assessments should combine in ways where the relative weights mean what you intended. If you do this, your assignment grades will be able to make valid contributions to your report card grades. But before we move on to report card grades (Part 3 of this text), we'll take some time to develop your skills at scoring assignments well—and at providing written descriptive feedback, too. Written feedback won't help you calculate your students' report card grades, but it *will* help your students improve along their learning journey before they get to their final grades. That's definitely part of what students and teachers mean when they talk about "grading papers."

EXERCISES

1. Describe in your own words the model for the relationship of assessment and instruction in Figure 4-1. Do you agree that this is an important model to actually "memorize" and keep in mind as you plan your classroom lessons and assessments? Why or why not?
2. Select a learning goal (or a set of goals) from a content area you will teach. Make a list of as many different instructional activities you can think of that you could use in the classroom to help students reach that goal. Make a list of valid assessment methods that could help you decide to what extent students had reached that goal.
3. Suppose that you wanted all 10 of the score points for comprehension in Table 4-1 to reflect thinking and reasoning. Redraw the test blueprint to show what it would look like. Then describe two different ways you might construct test items to match this blueprint.
4. Locate a test published for use with a unit of instruction in a textbook. You could find one in your curriculum library or borrow some materials from a teacher you know. Classify each test question according to content and whether it requires recall alone or higher order thinking. Working "backward," use these classifications to show what the test blueprint would have looked like. What conclusions can you draw about the meaning you will get from students' test scores? Would you give this test? Would you make any changes? Why or why not?
5. Locate a performance assessment (task and scoring rubrics). Again, you could use the curriculum library, borrow from a teacher, or even use the Internet. Make sure that the performance assessment you choose for this exercise has both a task and rubrics or some scoring scheme. You will need both. First, look at the task alone and analyze what knowledge, thinking, and skills students would have to use to accomplish it. Then look at the rubric or scoring scheme and analyze whether these things are all represented in the scoring, and with what relative weights.

Would you use this performance assessment? Would you make any changes? Why or why not?

6. Following are examples of different assessments. What direct information about student learning goals do you think each would give you? What changes, if any, might you suggest so that the assessment gives clearer information about the learning goals you think it is meant to assess?
   a. (test, see this page)
   b. (test, see p. 64)
   c. (performance assessment, see p. 65)
   d. (performance assessment, see p. 66)

7. For each of the assessments in Exercise 6, describe at least one appropriate use for results from the assessment (or for the assessment as you have improved it). Describe at least one inappropriate use for results from the assessment.

Note: These are intended as "short" exercises at the end of the chapter. See Part 2 Exercises on page 111 for additional exercises.

Test for exercise 6a *Source:* Courtesy of the Bethel Park School District, Pittsburgh, Pennsylvania. Used by permission.					
	Name _____				
	Date _____				
	33 −27	14 − 7	47 −39	70 −13	41 −18
	51 −17	40 −15	63 −57	21 −17	62 −43

FIND THE RIGHT VERB

1. If I go to school tomorrow, I _____ my tennis shoes.
   - a. wore
   - b. am wearing
   - c. will wear
   - d. did wear

2. Yesterday the rain _____ my school shoes.
   - a. will ruin
   - b. will have ruined
   - c. did ruin
   - d. ruined

3. I _____ a new pair of shoes soon.
   - a. bought
   - b. will buy
   - c. have bought
   - d. buy

4. The thief _____ my aunt's TV set when he broke in to her apartment.
   - a. will have taken
   - b. will take
   - c. takes
   - d. took

5. My favorite TV show _____ at 7:00 tomorrow night.
   - a. was shown
   - b. shows
   - c. will have been shown
   - d. will be shown

6. A tadpole _____ into a frog, and a caterpillar becomes a butterfly.
   - a. was turned
   - b. would be turned
   - c. turns
   - d. will turn

7. If you want to learn how to fly a kite, you _____.
   - a. should practice
   - b. shall practice
   - c. shall be practiced
   - d. practice

8. I _____ my friend some yellow flowers, but she didn't like them very much.
   - a. give
   - b. will give
   - c. gave
   - d. given

[*Suppose the test had a total of 30 questions like these*]

RECYCLING NEWS

Work with a partner. Select one of these materials:

- plastic
- paper
- aluminum

Find out what happens to the environment after this material is thrown in the trash if it is not recycled. Find out what kinds of things can be done with this material if it is collected for recycling. Find out whether your community recycles this material. Write a story for the Local News section of your town's newspaper describing your findings for local citizens.

Your newspaper story will be graded with this scale:

A – Your story contains correct, detailed information about the material, its effects on the environment, and its possibilities for recycling. You have correctly identified whether your locale recycles the material.

B – Your story contains generally correct information about the material, its effects on the environment, and its possibilities for recycling. You have correctly identified whether your locale recycles the material. Although generally correct, your story does not have much detail or connection among ideas.

C – Your story contains some correct information about the material, its effects on the environment, and its possibilities for recycling. Detail is lacking, and some information is missing or incorrect.

D – Your story is about the material, but it doesn't help the reader understand its effects on the environment or its possibilities for recycling.

F – Your story wasn't about recycling, or you didn't write a story.

"BEFORE YOU WERE BORN"

Select an event in recent U.S. history that happened before you were born. Examples might be the resignation of President Nixon, or the first moon landing. Try to pick something that interests you. If you are not sure about your selection, talk with me.

Write a report on this event. Collect your information from at least two of the following kinds of sources:

- newspaper or news magazine accounts from the time of the event
- interviews of friends or relatives who lived through the event
- books
- encyclopedia articles

Your report should include (total at least 5 pages): an introduction, body, conclusion. It should also include at least two pictures (a graph or table may be substituted for one of the pictures), a title page, and a bibliography page. Use good writing skills (paragraph and sentence structure, punctuation, spelling).

You will be graded with the following points:

Content—up to 10 points each except for correct information

- Information is correct (up to 20 points)
- Event's place in U.S. history is explained
- Introduction sets the focus of the report
- Report is organized
- Resources are used (at least two kinds of sources)
- Direct quotes are appropriate and cited
- Details support thesis statement

Mechanics—up to 5 points each

- Grammar
- Spelling
- Punctuation
- References in MLA style

Deciding on the Bases for Grading

KEY CONCEPTS

- All student assignments should receive some sort of feedback. Some assignments should receive grades or scores.
- Feedback is usually classified as one of two types: formative or summative. *Formative* feedback is intended as information for improvement, whereas *summative* feedback is intended as judgment of an outcome. In classroom practice, these waters get a little muddied. Good students learn how to make all feedback formative, and good teachers learn how to make even summative assessments "episodes of genuine learning."
- There are three possible bases for grading or scoring. Each method involves making a comparison. Grading on the basis of comparing a student's work to a standard is called *criterion referencing*. Grading on the basis of comparing a student's work to his or her own past performance is called *self-referencing*. Grading on the basis of comparing a student's work to the work of other students is called *norm referencing*.
- Teachers should be able to describe how their basis for judgments about the quality of student work matched intended learning targets. The most appropriate basis for grading individual assignments that will count toward a report card grade is criterion referencing. The most useful kind of feedback to give on practice work is self-referenced. Norm referencing is not recommended for classroom use.
- For work that is to be graded or scored, several types of scales can be used. Points or percents and rubrics are the two most common ones.
- Rubrics may be *analytic,* where each criterion is evaluated separately, or *holistic,* where all criteria are evaluated at the same time. Rubrics may be *general,* applicable to several different assignments, or *task specific,* applicable to only one assignment.
- Factors other than achievement should be assessed, but not graded. For these other factors—ability, effort, attendance, and attitude—the best feedback is verbal and self-referenced.

This chapter appears in Part 2—Integrating Assessment and Instruction—because decisions about the bases for grading are properly considered as issues about intentions for instruction and feedback. By the end of the report period, when it is time to combine individual grades into a report card grade, the main opportunities for feedback are already past. But decisions you make about the kind of scoring and feedback you will use for each assignment will affect what happens at the end of the report period. The kind of scores or individual grades you collect should affect the procedures you'll use to combine them in a meaningful way.

All student assignments should receive some sort of feedback. It doesn't always have to be teacher feedback. For example, a review of student rough drafts during the writing process may be done in peer editing pairs. If an assignment is worth doing at all, it should be worth some consideration. Some student assignments should receive grades or scores that are recorded. These are the "official" assessments (Airasian & Russell, 2008), the ones that will count toward the report period grade.

FORMATIVE AND SUMMATIVE ASSESSMENT

Assessment feedback is usually classified as one of two types: formative or summative. *Formative* feedback is intended as information for improvement, whereas *summative* feedback is intended as judgment of an outcome. In educational research circles, especially in writings by European authors, you may hear the term "formative assessment" as a synonym for all classroom assessment. In U.S. practice, assigning a report card grade is certainly a summative function (remember the cartoon in Figure 1-2!), even though the grade comes from classroom assessments. In this book, we will use the terms "formative" and "summative" as we have just defined them.

If students are to improve they must have a concept of their learning goal, the ability to compare actual with desired performance (for which assessment information is helpful), and the ability to act in such a way as to close the gap (Sadler, 1989). Teachers are responsible for providing the feedback students need to do this; providing the feedback itself is sometimes called "formative assessment." Considering assessment to be formative only when the information it provides is used for improving performance places the student—the learner—in the central role. Yet, perhaps because it is teachers who plan and administer classroom assessments, much of what has been written about assessment has focused on the role of the teacher, not the student. Indeed, Sadler distinguished between "feedback," information about performance supplied to students by the teacher, and "self-monitoring," information about performance from students' own appraisal of their work.

The key is having a concept of the goal or learning target, which originally is the teacher's but which ideally the student will internalize, eventually setting his or her own goals and monitoring progress toward them. Students' conceptions of what constitutes high-quality performance develop over time. As students refine their own performances, their knowledge about desired performance also improves. Teaching students to monitor their own performance is the ultimate goal of providing feedback. We have seen in Chapter 3 how the effects of feedback on student performance have been examined in the educational psychology literature. Informational feedback, that is, information students can use to improve their performances, is intrinsically motivating. But feedback, however detailed, will not lead to improvement until a student understands both the feedback itself and how it applies to his or her work. This appraisal process itself is part of the learning.

One of the best ways for students to develop self-monitoring skills is to work with rubrics. If students are familiar with the characteristics of good work, they can write their own rubrics and then apply them to their own work and the work of others. If students are not familiar with the characteristics of good work, as for instance in areas where they are just starting to learn, student practice at interpreting and applying rubrics that the teacher provides will help students develop an understanding of the achievement targets toward which they are aiming.

Summative assessment is an "overview of previous learning" (Black, 1998, p. 28), either by accumulating evidence over time or by testing at end-phase or other transition times. Using classroom assessment for summative purposes can create tension in the relationship between teacher and student. Yet, for grading and other times of accountability, teachers do indeed collect and use summative assessment information. Any assignment that receives a score or grade that "counts" toward the report card grade is part of summative assessment. In classroom practice, some assessments serve both formative and summative functions. Good students learn how to make all feedback formative (Brookhart, 2001), and good teachers learn how to make even summative assessments "episodes of genuine learning" (Wolf, 1993).

Gipps (1994), building on the work of others, considered two different summative processes. "Summing-up" means creating a picture of achievement based on accumulating evidence from assessments that were originally formative. "Checking-up" means assigning tests or tasks at the end of learning specifically to collect information for summative judgments. Most K–12 grading practices in the United States would be classified as using a summing-up model. It would generally not be appropriate to give grades based solely on a series of unit tests and final examinations, not counting any other work. In part, this is because a fuller and more reliable picture of student achievement can be developed using more examples of student work. Also, most teachers use a summing-up model because they work on different learning goals in turn and combine them for the report card grade. This summing-up model is also used partially because of the instructional and management principles that would argue against pressuring students with one "monster test" instead of taking several smaller measurements of their achievement.

Several authors have questioned the relationships between formative and summative assessments, arguing whether it is even possible to have a summing-up process that uses information originally intended as formative assessment for a summative purpose. It can be argued that students will pay less attention to feedback and more to the grade or score that "counts" in the final grade and thus learn less from the feedback than they might otherwise. As a counterargument to this point of view, Biggs stated that "sensible educational models make effective use of both FA [formative assessment] and SA [summative assessment]" (1998, p. 105). Biggs concluded that formative and summative assessment need not be mutually exclusive if one's model of assessment is inclusive:

> Instead of seeing FA and SA up close as two different trees, I would zoom to a wider angle conceptually. Then, in the broad picture of the whole teaching context—incorporating curriculum, teaching itself. . . and summative assessment—instead of two tree-trunks, the backside of an elephant appears. [See Figure 5-1.] Summative assessment is often assumed to have entirely negative consequences, but if it matches instructional goals and clearly offers information about what students have been expected to learn, then classroom summative assessment, such as a test at the end of a teaching episode or unit, can have positive effects. (p. 108)

FIGURE 5-1 Formative and summative assessment

Source: Illustration of a metaphor in "Assessment and Classroom Learning: A Role for Summative Assessment?," by J. Biggs, 1998, *Assessment in Education*, p. 108.

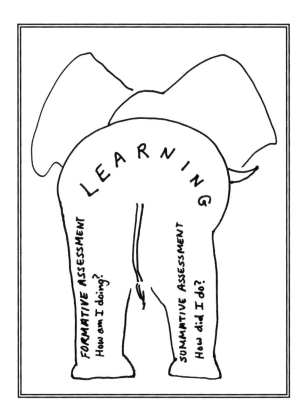

There are three possible bases for grading or scoring. Each method involves making a comparison. Grading on the basis of comparing a student's work to a standard is called *criterion referencing*. Grading on the basis of comparing a student's work to his or her own past performance is called *self-referencing*. Grading on the basis of comparing a student's work to the work of other students is called *norm referencing*. Table 5-1 summarizes these three types of comparisons.

Criterion-referenced scores are most appropriately used for grading decisions. The standard of performance you use for comparison should be, of course, the standard that comprises your instructional goals or achievement targets. You can see from the example in Table 5-1 that most grading decisions are not based on true criterion referencing, which would allow statements of what a student can do ("John can spell these 18 words").

More typically, grading decisions are based on a kind of pseudocriterion referencing. John, for example, might be given a score of 18 out of 20 words, or 90%. That would still be criterion referencing if you could logically conclude that John achieved 90% of his learning goals in spelling, but for most classroom tests and performance assessments, this logic doesn't work. One test might be much harder than another test of the same material, so the percent method of grading compares student performance to a "floating" standard based on the difficulty of the assessments. A score of 80% on a difficult assignment, for example, might reflect the same level of achievement as 90% on an easier assignment.

This textbook argues that this kind of criterion referencing is still better for grading than self-referencing or norm referencing, for the reasons outlined below. It works best and makes the most sense if the assessments are pitched at a difficulty level that matches the teacher's instructional goals. Then at least the standard against which students' performances are judged fits with the curriculum on which the school is obliged to report.

Self-referenced scores compare students with their own past performance, or with expectations for their ability level. This is the most powerful kind of formative feedback

TABLE 5-1	Type of Comparison	Basis for Comparison	Example	Use of Information
Bases for comparing student performance	**Criterion referenced**	A standard of performance	John can spell these 18 words.	Grading
	Self-referenced	One's own prior performance or expectations	John spelled 5 more words correctly on the posttest than he did on the pretest.	Instruction
	Norm referenced	Other students' work	John is the best speller in the class.	Competition

to give to students for their further development. If I know, for example, that the paragraph I wrote today is better than the one I wrote yesterday, I have reason to continue to work. Even better for learning than self-referenced scoring is specific self-referenced narrative feedback. If I know, for example, that the paragraph I wrote today demonstrated much improved use of descriptive adjectives, but the details are still not organized very logically, then I know what to continue to do and what to work on in the paragraph I will write tomorrow.

Self-referencing does not work very well for grading purposes. Imagine a student with a poorly written paragraph who sits next to a student whose paragraph was well written. The poor paragraph has a B on it because it is much better than that student's previous work, and the good paragraph has a C on it because it isn't as good as the paragraph that student wrote before. Absent a long discussion with the teacher, what are these students to conclude about the qualities of a good paragraph? When they take home their papers, what are their parents supposed to conclude? The same C might mean, variously, that the paragraph is good but not what was expected for the child, or that the paragraph is of mediocre quality, or that the paragraph is poor but represents some improvement over previous work. A grade or score that is not interpretable is worse than useless, because incorrect conclusions might lead to inappropriate consequences for the student.

Norm-referenced scores compare students to each other and communicate student standing in the class. This is good only for the students who have a chance at coming out on top, which by definition can't be very many. There are very few legitimate uses for norm-referenced assessments in school, and all of them are situations where students are competing for limited resources. For example, band and orchestra directors need norm-referenced information to decide who will play first chair, second chair, and so on, in a section. But even when norm-referenced information is used for seating, the student's grade in the class is usually based on criterion-referenced information. You may play first-chair violin, but if you didn't learn to play the assigned music, you don't get an A.

A true norm-referenced grading scheme would give top grades to the top few students, whatever their absolute level of performance, and bottom grades to the bottom few students. Most of the students would have middle grades. Clearly, that doesn't match with the model of instruction in Figure 4-1. If all the students learned what they were supposed to learn, why would some of them have to fail? By the same token, if none of the students learned what they were supposed to learn, why would you give some of them top grades anyway?

KINDS OF GRADING SCHEMES

Knowing that we need criterion-referenced scores for our grades—scores that will give students information about how well they hit the achievement target represented by a particular assessment—how do we get them? For work that is to be graded or scored, several types of scales can be used. Points or percents and rubrics are the two most common ones.

POINTS OR PERCENTS

Points or percents divide an assessment into parts and give students credit for the quality of their performance on those parts. If you are going to use percents to figure a grade, make sure there are enough points available. There is no hard-and-fast rule, but if there aren't at least 25 points to an assignment, you should think about using some other scoring mechanism besides percents. Thirty is even better. The reason for this is just a little arithmetic and a little logic. If an assessment has 25 points, then possible grades are 100% (25 points), 96% (24), 92% (23), and so on. Depending on the scale you use, fewer than 25 points may result in some letter grades being represented by only 1- or 2-point values. If that's the case, there's a rubric scale in your mind trying to break free, and you are forcing this rubric scale into a percent scheme.

Point schemes work well for tests, both those with objective scoring (right/wrong) and objective-essay combination tests, where some of the points come from essay questions scored with a scoring scheme. Point schemes also work for projects that have several parts to be evaluated. Figure 5-2 shows an example of a seventh-grade lab report point grading scheme. Notice the instructional choices that are coded into the point scheme. This was a group report, and about 20% of the grade (35 out of 170 points) is based on the individual's contributions to the group lab. About 56% (95 out of 170 points) is based on the content of the lab report and data charts, and about 24% (40 out of 170 points) is based on neatness, sentence structure, and punctuation. The distribution matched the teacher's instructional intent, since part of what she was trying to teach was how to write the lab report, not just how to do the lab. Communicating this point scheme could benefit the students; for example, the teacher could explain (as part of the instruction) how the points for each section, especially the larger ones, would be allocated. The number of points is large enough (170) that a grade based on percent of 170 would be reasonable.

RUBRICS

Oftentimes the term "rubric" is used to mean any scoring scheme. This textbook uses "rubric" to refer more specifically to rules for judging the quality of student work that are based on relatively short, descriptive scales. The quality the rubric is judging is referred to as the *criterion,* and the descriptions of various levels of performance relative to that criterion are called *performance levels.* The term "standards" was formerly used for this purpose, until states began creating state standards for learning that used the term differently. Some people get around this terminology problem by calling the descriptions of performance levels "performance standards." At any rate, think of the criterion as the title of the rubric and the performance levels as the numbers and their descriptions.

Suppose, for example, that you were working with your sixth-grade students on solving the kind of word problems in math class that have one right answer but may have several ways of arriving at it (e.g., using pictures or a diagram, using an algorithm). Suppose further that you have decided you want to focus on four aspects of problem solving. First, when students read the problems, you want them to be able to identify the information they will need to solve the problem. Second, you want them

FIGURE 5-2

Example of a
point scheme
for a seventh-
grade lab
report

Source:
Courtesy of
the
Washington
School
District,
Washington,
Pennsylvania.
Used by
Permission.

GROUP MEMBERS _____   MISS XXXXXX
_____   SCIENCE PER. _____
_____

PENDULUM LAB REPORT

__75__   POINTS POSSIBLE   POINTS RECEIVED   _____

               Pendulum Lab Report in Scientific Method Format

__5__   * Purpose (Given in class)   _____
__5__   * Hypothesis   _____
__20__   * Experiment (in detail)   _____
__10__   * Analysis   _____
__5__   * Conclusion   _____
__10__   * Neatness   _____
__10__   * Sentence Structure
             (Complete sentences)   _____
__10__   * Punctuation   _____

__60__   Data Charts on Graph Paper   _____
__5__   * Proper Format (Given in class)   _____
__45__   * Accuracy
             (Complete data info, labeled, etc.)   _____
__10__   * Neatness   _____

__35__   Cooperative Group Evaluation   _____
__20__   * Collaborative effort
             (collecting data, writing report)   _____
__5__   * Accurate Information
            on all Data Sheets   _____
__5__   * Complete Folders   _____
__5__   * Organization   _____

TOTAL POINTS POSSIBLE   TOTAL POINTS EARNED

__170__ _____   _____

             PERCENTAGE & GRADE _____

COMMENTS:

to be able to see a way to use that information to solve the problem, maybe by drawing a diagram or by setting up an equation or other algorithm. Third, you want them to be able to explain why their solution strategy is appropriate and thereby demonstrate understanding of the mathematical concepts involved. Fourth, you want them to arrive at the correct answer and report it with proper labels. These will become the

Problem Solving

Identify Relevant Information
4 — Identifies all relevant information
3 — Identifies most relevant information
2 — Identifies some relevant information
1 — Does not identify relevant information

Choose Solution Strategy
4 — Uses the most efficient, appropriate solution strategy
3 — Uses an appropriate solution strategy
2 — Uses an inappropriate solution strategy
1 — Does not use a solution strategy

Demonstrate Understanding
4 — Explanation, diagram, or algorithm shows clear understanding of mathematical concepts
3 — Explanation, diagram, or algorithm may not be clear
2 — Explanation, diagram, or algorithm shows lack of understanding of mathematical concepts
1 — No explanation or complete lack of understanding

Report Solution
4 — Reports correct solution, clearly labeled
3 — Reports correct or nearly correct solution; minor computational errors may be present
2 — Reports incorrect solution; major computational errors may be present
1 — Reports no solution or guesses

criteria from which you will build rubrics. For each criterion, you can envision a range of work quality, from very low to very high. Describing these levels will result in the performance levels (or performance standards) for your rubrics.

Rubrics may be *analytic,* where each criterion is evaluated separately, or *holistic,* where all criteria are evaluated at the same time. Rubrics may be *general,* applicable to several different assignments, or *task-specific,* applicable to only one assignment. Figure 5-3 gives an example of an analytic rubric, and Figure 5-4 gives an example of a holistic rubric for problem solving, using the criteria and standards identified. They are both built around the same four criteria. Analytic rubrics rate one criterion at a time and are good for diagnostic feedback to a student. For example, if a student scored 4 on the first two criteria and 2 on the last two, the student would know he got started with the right information and strategy but didn't understand it clearly enough to explain it or follow it through to a correct answer.

Holistic rubrics consider all the criteria simultaneously. To assign a holistic score, you need to ask yourself which group of descriptions best fits the work you are grading. The fit won't always be perfect. Holistic rubrics have the advantage of being easier

FIGURE 5-4

Example of a
general
holistic rubric
for math
problem
solving

Problem Solving

4   Identifies all relevant information
     Uses the most efficient, appropriate solution strategy
     Explanation, diagram, or algorithm shows clear understanding of mathematical
       concepts
     Reports correct solution, clearly labeled

3   Identifies most relevant information
     Uses an appropriate solution strategy
     Explanation, diagram, or algorithm may not be clear
     Reports correct or nearly correct solution; minor computational errors may be
       present

2   Identifies some relevant information
     Uses an inappropriate solution strategy
     Explanation, diagram, or algorithm shows lack of understanding of mathematical
       concepts
     Reports incorrect solution; major computational errors may be present

1   Does not identify relevant information
     Does not use a solution strategy
     No explanation or complete lack of understanding of mathematical concepts
     Reports no solution or guesses

and quicker to use, but they don't give specific enough information for students to use for further learning. They are best used on end-of-unit assignments where all that is required is a grade.

These rubrics are general. They could—and should—be shared with the students during instruction. They could be used for student self-evaluation and peer evaluation, during instructional time in the classroom. Practice applying these criteria and standards to their own and others' work would help students learn more clearly the concepts represented in these criteria. Since learning these concepts is the instructional goal for problem solving, we have not only a nice match for valid grading but also good consequences for instruction and learning.

I recommend that you use general rubrics like those in Figures 5-3 and 5-4 whenever possible, for three reasons. First and most important, general rubrics include a statement of the instructional goal or achievement target, usually in the description of "top" performance. This leads to the second reason, which is almost as important, namely that you can and should share general rubrics with students as part of their instruction. As students use the rubrics, they will come to internalize the concepts (learn!) and also come to appreciate the assessment of high-quality work as something *they* can do and for which *they* are responsible, which is important for motivation. A third reason to recommend using general rubrics is that task-specific rubrics, such as those in Figure 5-5, have to be rewritten for each problem and cannot be

FIGURE 5-5

Example of a
task-specific,
holistic rubric
for solving
a math
problem

Lizards and Turtles

Tina keeps lizards and turtles for pets. She has 13 pets in all. She feeds them insects. Each lizard eats 5 insects a day, and each turtle eats 4 insects a day. One day she fed her pets 58 ants. How many lizards and how many turtles does Tina have? Show and explain all your work.

Scoring Rubric for "Lizards and Turtles"

4   Correctly reports and labels 6 lizards and 7 turtles
       EITHER sets up and solves simultaneous equations
           $5 \cdot (lizards) + 4 \cdot (turtles) = 58$
           $(lizards) + (turtles) = 13$
       OR draws 13 pets with 4 ants in each, then adds a 5th ant to 6 of them
       OR multiplies 13 pets $\times$ 4 ants = 52 ants eaten, and then subtracts
           $58 - 52 = 6$ more ants to eat means 6 lizards to eat one more ant each
           then subtracts 13 pets − 6 lizards = 7 turtles
       OR uses some equivalent strategy
       AND explains the selection of strategy using mathematical concepts

3   Correctly reports 6 and 7, may label one or both of these (lizards and turtles)
       Identifies the numbers of insects and pets needed to solve the problem
       Uses one of the strategies above, but may not explain clearly

2   Identifies some of the numbers needed to solve the problem, but does not apply
           an appropriate solution strategy
       Does not arrive at 6 lizards and 7 turtles for the answer

1   Does not identify the numbers needed to solve the problem
       Does not apply a solution strategy
       Gives no answer or incorrect answer

shared with the students. This means they are good only for grading, not for learning, and thus are a less efficient use of teacher time and forfeit a good learning opportunity for students.

You don't always have to write your own rubrics. Lots of rubrics are available in textbooks and curriculum materials and on the Internet. If you choose a rubric someone else has written, make sure that it matches the criteria you want to measure, based on the achievement goals you had set for your students. No matter how clever or elegant a rubric is, it is the wrong thing to use if it doesn't match with what you want your students to demonstrate.

In general, plan a rubric or scoring scheme each time you plan an assignment. The scoring scheme and the task together form the assessment; one is not complete without the other. Develop a repertoire of generalized rubrics that your students will see over and over again in important domains in the subject you teach: writing, problem solving, critical thinking and analysis, and so on. Reusing these rubrics will support student learning in those domains, specifically developing whatever skills the rubric specifies. This is a case of "be careful what you wish for," because you will get what you ask for if you tie students' grades to particular rubrics. So choose them carefully, focusing on worthwhile concepts and skills.

ASSESSMENT VERSUS GRADING

Factors other than achievement should be assessed, but not graded. For these other factors—interest, effort, attitude, even attendance—the best feedback is verbal and self-referenced. Speak or write to students and tell them how they are improving or need to improve. Listen to their responses.

There are a number of methods for assessing dispositions: interest, attitude, and the like. Journal writing and other self-reflection methods are important ways of helping students see the relationship between their interests and their schoolwork. Oral questions and discussions with students, individually or in groups, will give you a sense of students' thoughts and feelings. Conferences with students should foster two-way communication between students and teacher; however, these assessments should not be scored or graded, nor should they "count" in the report card grade. Since this is a book about grading, we will not focus on nongraded assessments. To learn more about assessing nonachievement factors that should not be included in grades, see Anderson and Bourke (2000) or Stiggins (especially Chapter 8; 2005).

The general assessment principles we've been using apply to disposition assessment as well. Disposition assessments need to be valid and reliable; they need to provide meaningful, useful information about whatever you intended to measure, in a manner that is accurate, and should be followed by nonjudgmental, descriptive feedback. It's safe to say that assessment of dispositions should always be formative, intended to give students information they can use to reflect on their own attitudes and interests.

CONCLUSION

We began this chapter with a definition of two kinds of feedback, formative and summative. All student work should receive some kind of feedback, and we will discuss this further in Chapter 6.

When student work is to be scored or graded, use a criterion-referenced scoring scheme that refers to the qualities of good work you tried to teach students. These qualities should match your instructional goals or objectives. Several different kinds of scoring schemes were described: points and percents and various kinds of rubrics. Rubrics can be analytic or holistic, and they can be general or task-specific. It's important to realize that these are two separate characteristics: Rubrics can be analytic and general, or analytic and task-specific, or any other combination of the two characteristics.

EXERCISES

1. For each of the situations below, decide whether the assessment information is intended to be formative (information students will use to help them improve) or summative (information that will be used to make a final decision of some sort).
   a. Your English class writes an essay over the course of a week. The first day, students brainstorm ideas. The second day, they write individual first drafts. The third day, they work in pairs to peer edit each other's work. The fourth day, they revise. The fifth day, they prepare a final version, which they turn in to you. What is the function of the peer feedback on the third day?
   b. What is the function of the teacher's feedback on the essay turned in on the fifth day?
   c. Your math class does homework, which you go over the next day in class, as they work on a unit about fractions and mixed numbers.
   d. Your math class does homework, which you collect at the start of class the next day, in the same unit on fractions and mixed numbers.
   e. Your math class takes a test at the end of the unit on fractions and mixed numbers.

2. Describe each of the following judgments about students as criterion referenced, self-referenced, or norm referenced. Identify the basis of comparison for each.
   a. Richard took a test at the end of a unit on the planets in his fourth-grade class. His score was 83% correct.
   b. Richard's class also made models of the solar system. The teacher selected the best five to be displayed in the hallway display case.
   c. Pearl, a student in the same class, did better on the test than her teacher expected her to. The teacher called Pearl's parents to tell them how pleased she was with Pearl's improvement.
   d. In Bettina's keyboarding class, her teacher required students to practice until they could key 40 words per minute (wpm) with 5 or fewer errors. One day, Bettina keyed 35 wpm with 6 errors. She was assigned to do practice exercises again the next day.
   e. Students in a high school social studies course made class presentations about local political figures of their choice. The teacher graded the presentations with an analytical rubric. There were two criteria: content, which counted double, and delivery. Each criterion had four performance standards. The description of a "4" for content was "Detailed, relevant and correct information." The description of a "4" for delivery was "Clear, articulate, logical presentation of information."

3. Review the performance assessments in the end-of-chapter exercises in Chapter 4. Two were provided, and you may have located additional performance assessments for Exercise 5. Describe the scoring (rubrics or a point scoring scheme? analytic or holistic? general or task-specific?). See if you can write different scoring schemes for the assessments, keeping the relative weight of each of the criteria the same.

Note: These are intended as "short" exercises at the end of the chapter. See Part 2 Exercises on page 111 for additional exercises.

Chapter

6

Providing Grades and Other Feedback to Students

KEY CONCEPTS

- The kind of feedback a teacher uses helps create the classroom's climate for learning. The best kind of feedback, whether accompanied by a grade or not, gives students information they can use to improve their work.
- Matching criteria to student work is a skill that must be learned. Grading reliability is enhanced by the use of clear criteria and clear descriptions of each level of performance, and by the use of exemplars. Exemplars are examples of student work that cover the range of performance levels.
- Student involvement in assessment presents a powerful opportunity for learning. Students can be involved in creating grading criteria, applying criteria to their own work, giving feedback to peers, and going over test results. Each of these assessment situations can generate further learning.
- Anyone who is careful can grade objectively scored tests with an answer key. Applying rubrics with good judgment, however, is a skill that must be mastered.

$\mathbf{T}$his chapter is intended to give you an understanding of the basic concepts underlying the practical skill of grading. It describes the procedures for grading assignments and giving feedback and gives you opportunities to practice them.

PROVIDING INFORMATIVE FEEDBACK

The kind of feedback a teacher uses helps create the classroom's climate for learning. The best kind of feedback, whether accompanied by a grade or not, gives students information they can use to improve their work. Tunstall and Gipps (1996) did an extensive analysis of teacher feedback in the primary years; however, the resulting typology is useful for considering feedback to students of other ages, as well. They analyzed both oral and written feedback, thus their typology included feedback for socialization purposes as well as feedback on student achievement. Table 6-1 presents the academic portion of their typology for feedback on student work. They classified feedback as either evaluative or descriptive, corresponding to what in Chapter 3 we called providing judgment or information (Ryan, Connell, & Deci, 1985). As previously discussed, feedback that students can use to improve—descriptive or informational feedback—helps learning in two ways. First, it stimulates intrinsic motivation, specifically, the desire to become more competent. Second, it provides needed information. If a student does not know what to do in order to improve, he or she can hardly be expected to do it!

From their observation of teachers interacting with students and comments written on students' papers, Tunstall and Gipps determined that in addition to the evaluative/descriptive dimension, feedback could also be classified as either positive or negative and achievement-related or improvement-related. Notice in Table 6-1 that the closer you move toward the descriptive category, the more the feedback becomes constructive. If you are careful, you can point out what needs to be improved without using a cutting, critical tone. If you are constructive, and couch criticism in the context of pointing out what is already good about the work and what more could be done to make it even better, then even pointing out flaws becomes "constructing the way forward."

All of the kinds of feedback in Table 6-1 are useful in at least some situations. In general, however, the more descriptive you can be, the better. The legitimate uses of Tunstall and Gipps's categories A2 and B2, Punishing and Disapproving, are mostly

TABLE 6-1

Typology of teacher feed-back

Source: Adapted from "Teacher Feedback to Young Children in Formative Assessment: A Typology," by P. Tunstall and C. Gipps, 1996, *British Educational Research Journal, 22,* p. 394. Used by permission of the publisher, Taylor & Francis Ltd: http://www.tandf.co.uk/journals

	Evaluative Feedback		Descriptive Feedback	
	Type A	Type B	Type C	Type D
1–Positive Feedback	**A1–Rewarding** • giving rewards • giving stickers, smileys • giving treats • clapping	**B1–Approving** • positive personal expression • general praise • positive non-verbal feedback	**C1–Specifying Attainment** • specific knowledge of attainment • use of criteria or models in relation to work • specific praise	**D1–Constructing Achievement** • mutual articulation of achievement • additional use of emerging criteria, student role in presentation	1–Achievement Feedback
2–Negative Feedback	**A2–Punishing** • giving punishments • removal from social contact • deprivation of something the student enjoys	**B2–Disapproving** • negative personal expression • reprimands • negative non-verbal feedback	**C2–Specifying Improvement** • correction of errors • more practice given • training in self-checking	**D2–Constructing the Way Forward** • mutual critical appraisal • provision of strategies	2–Improvement Feedback

limited to very short-term classroom management situations. I advise you not to use punishment or disapproval for the purposes of grading student work. In written feedback, aim for statements of positive evaluation and descriptive, constructive specifications of achievement and recommendations for improvement.

STUDENT INVOLVEMENT IN ASSESSMENT

Student involvement in assessment presents a powerful opportunity for learning. Students can be involved in creating grading criteria, applying criteria to their own work, giving feedback to peers, and going over test results. Each of these assessment situations can generate further learning.

CREATING GRADING CRITERIA

If students know the qualities of good work, they can participate in writing the rubrics by which they will be graded. Of course this wouldn't work with totally new content, but think of how much students actually do know about the qualities teachers look for in their schoolwork. Brainstorming the criteria for good work, by itself, is a good way to focus students on the achievement target they are being asked to hit. Taking the next step and organizing those criteria into rubrics you and the students will actually use to grade them makes a statement to students. It affirms that they do indeed know the criteria, that you know they know, and that you accept their definition.

APPLYING CRITERIA TO THEIR OWN AND PEERS' WORK

Whether or not the students have written the rubrics, they will benefit from practice applying them. It is one thing for a student to say "my description should have complete details" and another thing to recognize complete details when he or she sees them. Using a class period for students to review one another's work and make suggestions would be a worthwhile learning experience and a worthwhile formative assessment.

GOING OVER TEST RESULTS

A teacher-made test may seem the ultimate in lack of student involvement in assessment, but it doesn't have to be so. Many teachers already go over the answers when they pass back graded tests, and good students know a lot of valuable information may be gained from paying attention and noting where they made their mistakes. The problem is that often there is nothing "in it" for the students except their own satisfaction. If a test is reviewed after the grade has been recorded, especially if students will not be working with that material again in the near future, many students will simply see what they "got" for a score and bide their time during the review.

One strategy to increase the amount of productive student involvement in going over objective test results is to turn it into an additional assessment. After you grade tests, group the students heterogeneously according to their scores on the test, into groups of about three. This works especially well when most students did not do as well as they would have liked on the test.

Return individual graded tests to the students, then give each group of three a worksheet you have prepared, similar to Figure 6-1. List each test item and its correct answer (a, b, c, d, or T/F, etc.). Make one column for the number of students in the group who got the item wrong. If that number is zero, they write it and move on

Group member names_____

NAME OF TEST

Look at each question on your test, and then look at the correct answers below. If no one in your group got the question wrong, note a 0 (zero) in answer to that question and move to the next item. If one or more of your group members got a question wrong, note how many and then write an explanation of why the correct answer was correct. You may use your book or other materials.

Test Item	Correct Answer	Number in Your Group Who Got This Wrong	Why was the correct answer correct?
1.	A		
2.	D		
3.	C		
4.	B		
5.	B		
6.	D		
7.	C		
8.	A		
9.	A		
10.	D		
11.	B		
12.	C		
(etc.)			

to the next test item. If one or more of the group members got the item wrong, the group must write an explanation of why the correct answer is correct—which can be anything from citing a forgotten fact from a textbook to a sequence of logical reasoning, depending on the question. The grade for these explanations may be counted as an additional grade toward the report card grade. The real power of the exercise is that it says to the students that learning the content behind the items is the main point, and it gives them a second chance to do that. The fact that the content was "on the test," especially if the student got it wrong the first time, by definition registers it as "important."

GRADING IS A SKILL

Matching criteria to student work is a skill that must be learned. It is one thing to understand the different types of rubrics and scoring schemes described in Chapter 5; it is another thing to apply them consistently and accurately to student work. It is one thing to know that in addition to the grade, you should provide constructive, informative feedback so the students know their work has been valued and they have information they can use to continue to improve; it is another thing to actually provide that feedback skillfully. Oddly, we don't get much practice at articulating the qualities of good work in specific detail, and so many teachers provide "feedback" that is cheerful but not particularly helpful. "Good job!" is a nice affirmation, but it doesn't help the student do any better next time. The student may not even be sure what it was you liked about his or her work.

Grading reliability is enhanced by the use of clear criteria and clear descriptions of each level of performance, and by the use of exemplars. Exemplars are examples of student work that cover the range of performance levels. You will also hear the term "anchor papers," which means more or less the same thing as exemplars but usually refers to examples used by teachers or other graders, not students. The term "anchor papers" is most likely to be used in a large-scale assessment context, to refer to examples of work used in rater training. The term "exemplars" is used more broadly. Examples of good work, or exemplars of work across the range from poor to excellent, can be used in classroom instruction and assessment. Bennett and Collins (1994) pointed out that even tasks that arise during instruction can be graded if the grading is based on solid criteria, anchored at each level with student work and rationales, and checked for reliability.

Let's try some samples of student work. The school district that shared these with me is located in Pennsylvania. One of the fifth-grade-level state standards for Reading, Writing, Speaking, and Listening (Writing standard 1.5.5.B) reads:

Write using well-developed content appropriate for the topic.

- Gather, organize, and select the most effective information appropriate for the topic, task, and audience.
- Write paragraphs that have a topic sentence and supporting details.

Recently, a middle school in this district experienced a bomb threat, fortunately without a real bomb. The school used emergency procedures that it had put in place, gathered the students in the gymnasium, and eventually released students if parents or guardians came to get them. The next day, they followed up with school-wide activities. Some of the fifth-grade classes tied this to written expression. Students were asked to describe how they felt during the bomb threat and any other information they would like a judge to know. As you will see, this double prompt led most students to write paragraphs that were mostly about their feelings and actions during the bomb threat, with one sentence at the end about punishing the criminal.

Nevertheless, these papers allow us to see how well, in a spontaneous situation, students can select details of content and organize them into paragraphs. This is a state learning target that was mirrored in the district's and school's curriculum. We will use them to help you practice three skills:

- Reading papers for content and not primarily grammar or usage
- Applying a rubric to real student work
- Writing descriptive, as opposed to evaluative, feedback for students

These papers will also be good illustrations of some general principles about grading:

- It is easier to apply criteria if you have examples of various performance levels.
- It is much easier to write evaluative feedback ("Good job!" or marking something wrong) than to write helpful descriptive feedback.

As a brief exercise, first read the papers in Figures 6-2 through 6-13 for content. Then see if you can sort them into three categories based on their selection and use of detail. Selection and use of detail is part of the state standard, and was also reflected in their work in class over the year. Suggested categories include the following:

3 – A variety of relevant details are organized to support the topic sentence.
2 – Some details are present; they are related to the topic sentence.
1 – Minimal details are present, or unrelated details do not support the topic sentence.

What did you learn from this exercise? The three categories seem fairly clear until you try to apply them. Perhaps you had questions like how many details, or how much variety, is enough? What about when the student writes the same idea twice? What were your thoughts while you were rating these papers?

Once you have rated each paper, the next step is to compare your findings with a partner. On how many of the 12 papers did you agree on the rating category? Discuss any discrepancies. Why did each of you categorize each paper the way you did? After discussion, you may come to a consensus about the quality level of each paper. In a real teaching situation, two teachers who check their ratings against one another are checking reliability, and this coming to a consensus is called "group moderation" (Gipps, 1994). But in that situation, teachers would have discussed the criteria and probably looked at some student work ahead of time. Another method for arriving at a grade when two raters are in dispute takes less time but also provides fewer professional benefits: you can simply average the two scores.

FIGURE 6-2 Bomb Threat student paper

> "Bomb-Threat"
>
> I was scared and nervous I didn't know what was going to happen. We didn't know what was going on. They told use that we had to go to the gymnasium. Then my cousin came to pick my cousins and I. I think he shoul to jail for life or until he knows better. I hope this will never happen agian. and I didn't come back the next day. That was the most scariest day of my life and I hope it never happens agian.

FIGURE 6-3 Bomb Threat student paper

> "Bomb A Threat"
>
> I felt alittle nervous about the bomb threat. At first I didn't know what was going on but soon after I found out I got scared. I thinks that the person that did this should pay for his action's in jail for atleast one year or two. I just feel that if a person that has done something like this young or old they should pay for their actions depending on what they did wrong and when one person threatens another person's life they should pay the penalty for what they've done wrong.

FIGURE 6-4 Bomb Threat student paper

> ## Bomb Threat
>
> The day of the bomb threat I felt very scared. When my class went to the gymnasium I didn't know why untill I asked the teacher. I felt really scared and I wanted to go home. But I wasn't aloud. I thought the kids should be taken to the buses to go home. I think that the person should be put in jail for a couple of years. If he doesn't what if he does this to another school and really does have a bomb in that school. I was so scared to go to school the next day. This was a waste of time. Whoever did this scared eyeryone in this school and a wasted a day. I hope this person gets punish for what he/she did and he/she doesn't do it again.

FIGURE 6-5 Bomb Threat student paper

> ## the Bomb threat
>
> I think that the Bomb war the scards time in school I wauld help him to lernu to never do that anging I think that he sauld be pull in steel for the seat for the russt of his lift. the jrust shald pret him away and lurt him in farm and mach him warbs for the rest of his lift.

FIGURE 6-6 Bomb Threat student paper

"Bomb Threat"

After I heard from the Teacher's
I was veary, veary scared. I was
treeing to not cry and I was really
shacking I whanted to go home /
but I couldn' t because we were
not alead to call are parents. It was
veary, veary scarey. I whanted to know
were my brother was and if he was
ok because, he my brother and I whanted
to know if he was ok. I think
the person that did the bomb threat
should get 20 eyears in jail
and get some help. And stay away
from other Kids.

FIGURE 6-7 Bomb Threat student paper

Bomb Threat

After the bomb threat I felt
very nervous about going back to school.
I thought that the older teachers might
get scared and even some might
have a heartattact, I think school
teachers and parents should go
talk to him/her after hes behind
lars. I think they should tell
him/her how much fear they put
the children in every district.
I think he should be put in
jail forever,

FIGURE 6-8 Bomb Threat student paper

> Bomb Threat
>
> During the bomb threat I feel scare that the scool might get blowing up and everybody will die. After that I told my mom about it and me and my brother was not going to come back to this school at all but we ask or mom could come back to the school on Friday. The person who did it should get killed. And he should be in Jail for his life and never let him go.

FIGURE 6-9 Bomb Threat student paper

> "Bomb Threat"
>
> During the bomb threat I was confused, scared, and mad. I was confused because parents were yelling and trying to get their kids out of the building which made me scared. It made me mad because no one would tell me anything about why we were in the big gym.
>
> The next day my mom said that I wasn't going to school for the rest of the week. My mom felt guilty for herself. She was crying because she felt so bad.
>
> I hope the person is punished. If he or she wanted something that they couldn't have or wanted revenge, they shouldn't put other people in danger.

FIGURE 6-10 Bomb Threat student paper

Bomb Threat

When we had went back to the class room I didn't know what was going on. My aunt came to pick me up and she told me there was a bomb threat. Then I relised my friends; family, and myself could of been dead. I think the person who did it should be sentenced for a very long time. They also need to get the person alot of mental help. Why would they want to over a thousand people? Exspecialy their friends.

FIGURE 6-11 Bomb Threat student paper

Bomb Threat

Obut the Bomb Threat I got scary becouse
aver fride sady thery is a bomb in school
My Mom got me out of school
Then we hard on the newos They sady home
from School That man I hod put hom in
jall from I afl of has lofl plucs faid Home
He shod Not put a bomb in school.

FIGURE 6-12 Bomb Threat student paper

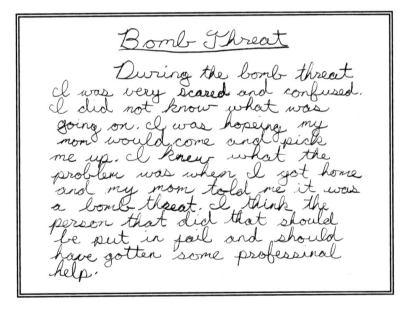

Bomb Threat

During the bomb I felt really scared because I didn't know what was happing. We had to go to the big Gym until after lunch. There wasn't really a bomb, but there could have been. Someone could have been killed. I think he should go to jail because he shouldn't scare kids like that. I was really scared that day.

FIGURE 6-13 Bomb Threat student paper

Bomb Threat

During the bomb threat I was very scared and confused. I did not know what was going on. I was hopeing my mom would come and pick me up. I knew what the problem was when I got home and my mom told me it was a bomb threat. I think the person that did that should be put in jail and should have gotten some professinal help.

Although we have used this partner discussion as a learning experience, as a teacher it is worthwhile to discuss ratings with another professional from time to time to double-check reliability. Perhaps your uncertainty when you first looked at these bomb threat essays will convince you that is important! Don't worry if this "grading practice" seemed difficult. The more student work you see, the more you will become used to what it looks like, and the more confident you will feel judging it. For now, just begin to appreciate the task. You can check your ratings against the ratings of the author and some of her students in Appendix D.

Besides, we haven't done the hard part yet! All we have so far is a score or grade for the paper. Since this assignment was a response to an actual bomb threat, it is not likely you would count these papers toward report card grades. But you might provide scores or comments as formative feedback. What would you say to each of these 12 students?

Try writing some descriptive feedback about the use of supporting details. Don't mark or correct each spelling, grammar, or usage error. Instead, try to identify something the student did well or bravely attempted to do, or something that he or she said that caught your attention, and respond to that. Then make a suggestion or two, using statements or questions, on how the use of detail and content might be improved. Make sure you respond to the substance of even the worst paper, and provide a suggestion for even the best paper.

When you have done this, share your feedback with a partner. Use Tunstall and Gipps's categories to make sure you have both written descriptive feedback. Note that for some purposes, evaluative feedback is appropriate—although, I recommend you always be as descriptive as possible in your feedback.

EXEMPLARS

Recall your first try at scoring Figures 6-2 through 6-13 on the 3-point rubric. Now let's try that task again, only this time assume you are given additional information. Each level on the rubric will be illustrated with an example. Suppose you were told to consider Figure 6-9 an example of a "3" level performance (a variety of relevant, organized details), Figure 6-10 an example of a "2" level performance (relevant details), and Figure 6-8 an example of a "1" level performance (minimal or unrelated details). Now try to rescore the other nine papers by comparing them to these exemplars, sometimes called anchor papers. Easier, isn't it? You will also find that teachers are more likely to agree on the ratings for each paper, that is, that reliability will be enhanced, when they use exemplars. For some assignments, students can be given exemplars along with the rubric. You can even have a productive lesson by asking students to work together to describe why and how the various examples fit the descriptions for each performance level. As they do that, students will internalize the criteria for good work and be more likely to produce quality work in the future.

MORE PRACTICE

Let's practice two types of scoring of student essays: using rubrics and using points. The focus of your work should be to develop skills at both assigning the score (rubric or points) and providing feedback to the student. For each example, one elementary-level and one secondary-level, you will follow the same procedure.

1. Identify the learning goal(s).
2. Familiarize yourself with the assignment and scoring scheme.

3. Think about how well the assignment and scoring scheme reflected the learning goal(s).
4. Read the student work.
5. Reread the student work, this time deciding on a score or grade.
6. Write comments for the student, concentrating on descriptive feedback (see Table 6-1).

FOURTH-GRADE "DOGS AND CATS" ESSAYS

Fourth graders in one school were asked to write a personal essay. The main learning goal was for the students to take a position on an issue meaningful to them and to describe the reasons for their position, using their developing sentence and paragraph writing skills. They had been taught to include topic sentences, supporting details, and concluding sentences in their paragraphs. The specific assignment asked them to write a paragraph, telling whether they thought dogs or cats were better and explaining why.

First, think about how you would have written this paragraph if you were in this fourth-grade class. Think about cats and dogs. Think about topic sentences, supporting details, and concluding sentences. Then (and only then!) read the selections in Figures 6-14 to 6-19.

After you have read the six selections, read the rubrics in Figure 6-20. Then find, among the selections, three examples that you think represent levels 4, 3, and 2. Set them aside as your exemplars. Group the rest of the selections into categories according

FIGURE 6-14 Dogs and Cats student paragraph

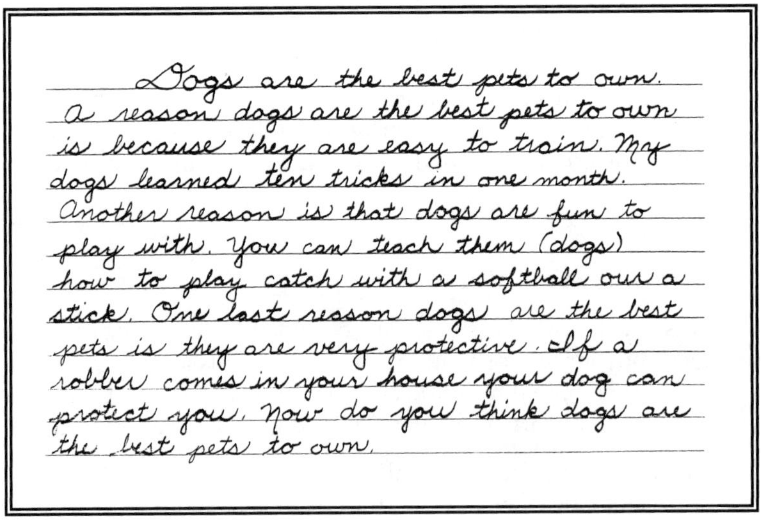

> Dogs are the best pets to own. A reason dogs are the best pets to own is because they are easy to train. My dogs learned ten tricks in one month. Another reason is that dogs are fun to play with. You can teach them (dogs) how to play catch with a softball our a stick. One last reason dogs are the best pets is they are very protective. If a robber comes in your house your dog can protect you. Now do you think dogs are the best pets to own.

FIGURE 6-15 Dogs and Cats student paragraph

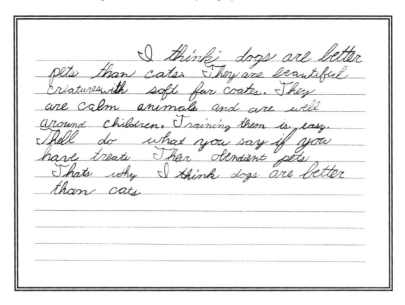

I think dogs are better pets than cats. They are beautiful creatures with soft fur coates. They are calm animals and are well around children. Training them is easy. They'll do what you say if you have treats. Thier obedient pets. Thats why I think dogs are better than cats.

FIGURE 6-16 Dogs and Cats student paragraph

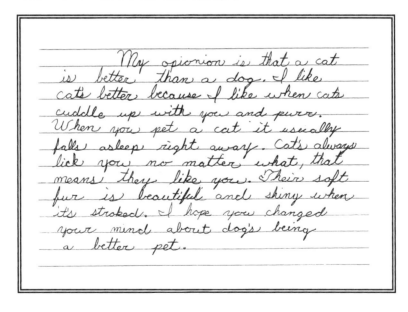

My opionion is that a cat is better than a dog. I like cats better because I like when cats cuddle up with you and purr. When you pet a cat it usually falls asleep right away. Cat's always lick you no matter what, that means they like you. Their soft fur is beautiful and shiny when it's stroked. I hope you changed your mind about dog's being a better pet.

FIGURE 6-17 Dogs and Cats student paragraph

> This is why it is good to have a dog instead of a cat. I think that a dog can chase away a robber what will a cat do meow? Plus you do not have to buy all that stuff. With a dog you buy a bowl and food and your set to go. Plus when you go somewhere you put the dog on the leash. But with a cat you have to take it. I like cats in all but they shed to much they shed every day. Plus you can wash a dog with a hose but can you do that with a cat? No!!! That is why you should get a dog.

FIGURE 6-18 Dogs and Cats student paragraph

> My opinion is that dogs are better than cats. One reason dogs are better are that they have good smelling to find out a case on a robery and they are strong and brave. Another reason is they are men best friend and can make you happy when you are sick or unhappy. If you like to hunt dogs are good for receiving small animals that you kill. They can help blind people and cats cant do that The dogs will not let any of their owners down. Thats why a dog is a good pet to have.

FIGURE 6-19 Dogs and Cats student paragraph

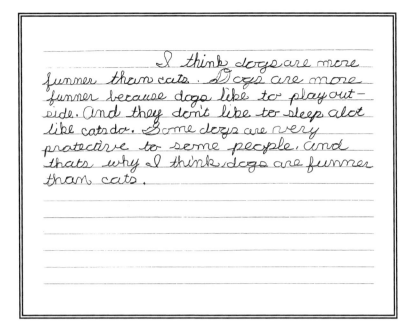

FIGURE 6-20

Rubric for personal opinion essays

4 Personal opinion is stated in a topic sentence and is clear
Support for opinions is detailed and organized
Concluding sentence summarizes paragraph
Word choice, style, and tone are appropriate for topic
Few grammar and usage errors; errors do not interfere with meaning

3 Personal opinion is stated in a topic sentence and is clear
Support for opinions is organized, may not be detailed
Concluding sentence summarizes paragraph
Word choice, style, and tone are appropriate for topic
Grammar and usage errors do not interfere with meaning

2 Personal opinion is stated in a topic sentence, but may not be clear
Support for opinions is not organized or detailed
May have a concluding sentence
Word choice, style, and tone are somewhat appropriate for topic
Grammar and usage errors begin to interfere with meaning

1 Personal opinion is not clear
Support for opinions is lacking
Word choice, style, and tone inappropriate for topic
Grammar and usage errors make reading difficult

to the rubric by placing them with the exemplar they most closely resemble. Provide a rationale for why you think each paper exemplifies the performance level you chose.

Compare your scores and rationales with a partner's. Discuss any discrepancies, paying special attention to why you disagreed. What written feedback would you give for each paper?

HIGH SCHOOL ENGLISH ESSAYS

Figure 6-21 shows an eleventh-grade English essay assignment, and Figure 6-22 presents the grading sheet the teacher used with this project. Using a grading "cover" sheet like this is a good idea for larger assignments. For all of the standard objectives listed, the teacher needs to note only how many points the student earned for each. Then the teacher can make individual notes on the cover sheet next to a point entry, or at an appropriate location in the student's work.

FIGURE 6-21

A Raisin in the Sun Act One essay assignment

English 11
***A Raisin in the Sun* by Lorraine Hansberry**
Act One Essay

Head a new sheet of loose-leaf. Title it with the above title. Follow the instructions below.

Instructions:

Respond to the following prompt in essay form. Be sure to create an introductory paragraph that includes the title of the play (and act) and its author. It should also fully restate the prompt, identify the conflict, and tell why you relate to that conflict. Create body paragraphs that contain plenty of details from the play and explanation. Include a quotation for support if you can. End with a concluding paragraph that restates (not repeats) the ideas in the thesis statement.

Double-space this response. You may write on the backs of paper.

You will have two thirty-minute sessions to plan, write, revise, and edit your response.

Prompt:

In Act One of the play *A Raisin in the Sun*, Lorraine Hansberry portrays many conflicts between members of the Younger family. Identify the conflict that you relate to the most. Recount several incidents that portray this conflict and explain why you relate to this conflict more than to the others.

FIGURE 6-22

A Raisin in the Sun Act One essay grade sheet

Name _____

Date _____   Class _____

Essay Evaluation

	Possible points	Points achieved
Entire essay addresses the given topic	10	_____
Entire essay maintains unity	10	_____

Introductory paragraph   20   _____
- Engages reader   _____
- Includes title and author of selection   _____
- Strong two-part thesis statement   _____
- Thesis that reflects prompt   _____

Body   50   _____
- Paragraphs' topic sentences are focused   _____
- Adequate development   _____
- Coherent development   _____
- Unity maintained   _____

Concluding paragraph   10   _____
- Ties back into piece   _____
- Brings piece to a close   _____
- Does not repeat   _____

Points deducted for errors in conventions   _____

Total points: 100   _____

Grade: _____

This grading sheet can be shared with students when they receive the assignment, so that they can refer to it as they prepare their papers. Take a moment to think about the assignment and the grading sheet. One learning goal was for the students to be able to use essay form. Another learning goal was for students to express personal responses to literature. Given the way points were allocated, can you tell which was the primary goal assessed?

As you did for "Dogs and Cats," take a few minutes to consider how you would respond to this prompt. If you have not read *A Raisin in the Sun,* at least think about family relationships that are important to you and about essay format. Then read the three selections in Figures 6-23 to 6-25. Use the grading sheet to score each paper, and write constructive comments for feedback. Comment on the substance of the writing, not just grammar and usage.

FIGURE 6-23 *A Raisin in the Sun* student essay

In Act One of the play *A Raisin in the Sun*, Lorraine Hansberry portrays many conflicts between the Younger family. The conflict I can relate to the most is the conflict between Walter and Beneatha.

Walter and Beneatha fought about what to do with the money mama is going to receive in the mail. Walter wants Mama to give the money to him so he can invest it in a liquor store, but Beneatha says that the money is Mama's and they should let her decide how she wants to use it. Then Walter says that Mama will probably put some of it away for Beneatha so she can go to medical school. He thinks that she wants everything to be handed down to her.

I can relate to that because my brother and I always fight about money. He thinks that just because I am the youngest of the family that I have everything given to me.

want to go to college too and to become a music teacher, but my brother thinks I want my parents to pay for everything.

So many siblings want the same thing. Not everybody can have everything that they want and parents can't give their children the same thing. This the one conflict I can relate to.

FIGURE 6-24 *A Raisin in the Sun* student essay

A Raisin in the Sun
Act One

In Act One of the play *A Raisin in the Sun*, Lorraine Hansberry portrays many conflicts between members of the Younger family. One of the conflicts in this Act was between Mama and Walter Lee. This conflict is over money and how it should be spent or where it should be put.

This is Mama's side of the conflict. Mama said she wants the money to go into the bank. Mama doesn't want to use the money to help provide people with alcohol. She doesn't want to be the cause of people who drink dieing in alcohol related accidents.

On the other side Walter Lee says he really needs the money so he can get his family off the ground.

Walter doesn't want Mama to waste the money. He wants her to invest it.

In this conflict I think Mama is right. She should do whatever she wants with the money; its hers. So in conclusion to this conflict I feel that Walter doesn't need to be part owner. The way I relate to this conflict is; well, I'm a middle class person. I'm not poor nor am I rich, but when my dad gets some cash in his pocket I automatically want something big, but I don't get it because its his money. I feel that me and Walter are the same.

FIGURE 6-25 *A Raisin in the Sun* student essay

<u>Essay</u>

The play *A Raisin in the sun* by Lorraine Hansberry had a specific Conflict I recanized right away. The conflict was between mama and her kids Beneatha and Walter. Mama tried to grow up her kids in the right way, but her kids were fighting to go in anathor direction. Her kids began to change as they grew older.

One time mama got stern with Beneatha for using god's name in vain, and also for Beneatha saying " I'm tired of hearing about god what has god ever done for me?" Walter on the other hand is a disgrace to his father according to mama. One time he refused to talk to his wife about an obortion; he just got up and walked out. To mama Walter also seems selfish. He wanted to start a liqour business but that's not what Mama had in mind. That opened Mama's eyes to see Walter's selfishness. I relate to this conflict very much.

This shows the conflict that me and mom have with each other. We go through the same thing. Me and my mom argue know and then about stuff. Sometimes she thinks I'm selfish and think only of my self, but she only says that when she is mad. So as you can see it's perfectly normal to see mothers and there children get into conflicts.

Objectively scored tests can be scored by anyone who has an answer key. It is common, however, for tests to include some constructed response questions that are "worth more points." Some tests are entirely made up of multiple-point questions. Whether the test is partly or entirely made up of "partial credit" questions that require judgment for scoring, make sure that the weights of the various parts are in proportion to the emphasis you intend for your measure of achievement.

Figure 6-26 presents a grading example of a high school math test. The entire test is worth 71 points. A percentage grade can be calculated by dividing the number of points

FIGURE 6-26 High school math test grading example

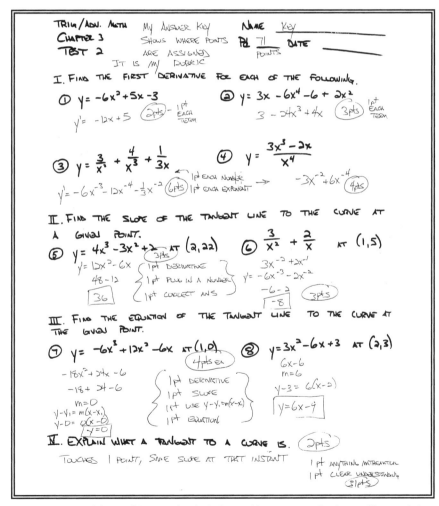

Source: Courtesy of the Washington School District, Washington, Pennsylvania. Used by permission

(continues)

FIGURE 6-26 *(continued)*

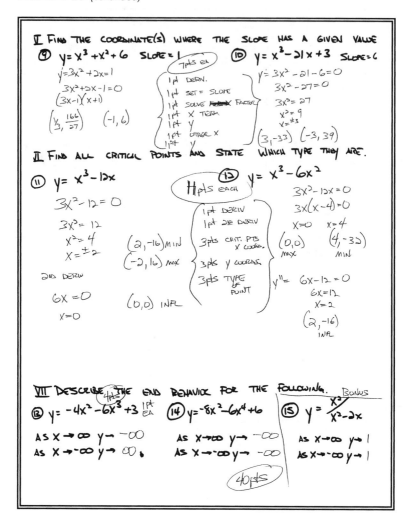

V. FIND THE COORDINATE(S) WHERE THE SLOPE HAS A GIVEN VALUE

⑨ $y = x^3 + x^2 + 6$ SLOPE = 1

$y' = 3x^2 + 2x = 1$

$3x^2 + 2x - 1 = 0$

$(3x - 1)(x + 1)$

$\left(\frac{1}{3}, \frac{166}{27}\right)$ $(-1, 6)$

7pts ea
- 1pt   DERIV.
- 1pt   SET = SLOPE
- 1pt   SOLVE ~~FACTOR~~ FACTOR
- 1pt   X TERM
- 1pt   Y
- 1pt   OTHER X
- 1pt   Y

⑩ $y = x^3 - 21x + 3$ SLOPE = 6

$y' = 3x^2 - 21 - 6 = 0$

$3x^2 - 27 = 0$

$3x^3 = 27$

$x^2 = 9$

$x = \pm 3$

$(3, -33)$ $(-3, 39)$

VI. FIND ALL CRITICAL POINTS AND STATE WHICH TYPE THEY ARE.

⑪ $y = x^3 - 12x$

$3x^2 - 12 = 0$

$3x^2 = 12$

$x^2 = 4$

$x = \pm 2$

$(2, -16)$ MIN

$(-2, 16)$ MAX

2ND DERIV

$6x = 0$

$x = 0$

$(0, 0)$ INFL

⑫ $y = x^3 - 6x^2$

11pts EACH
- 1pt   DERIV
- 1pt   2ND DERIV
- 3pts CRIT. PTS X COORDS.
- 3pts Y COORDS.
- 3pts TYPE OF POINT

$3x^2 - 12x = 0$

$3x(x - 4) = 0$

$x = 0$ $x = 4$

$(0, 0)$ $(4, -32)$
 MAX   MIN

$y'' = 6x - 12 = 0$

$6x = 12$

$x = 2$

$(2, -16)$
 INFL

VII. DESCRIBE THE END BEHAVIOR FOR THE FOLLOWING.   *4pts*   BONUS

⑬ $y = -4x^2 - 6x^3 + 3$ *1pt EA*

AS $X \to \infty$ $y \to -\infty$

AS $X \to -\infty$ $y \to \infty$

⑭ $y = -8x^2 - 6x^4 + 6$

AS $X \to \infty$ $y \to -\infty$

AS $X \to -\infty$ $y \to -\infty$

⑮ $y = \frac{x^2}{x^2 - 2x}$

AS $X \to \infty$ $y \to 1$

AS $X \to -\infty$ $y \to 1$

40pts

a student receives by 71. As you can see, the teacher who shared this with me called this key "my rubric," by which he meant his rules for scoring. Students who took this test and got some, but not all, of a problem correct received points for what they did understand.

GRADING TERM PAPERS, WRITTEN REPORTS, AND PROJECTS

It would take too much space in this book to print a set of student term papers for you to practice grading. But it is worth noting that the skills you used to develop rubrics or scoring schemes for essays and partial credit problems are the same skills you would use to grade term papers, written reports, and projects. Typically, you will use some kind of analytic scoring scheme for a term paper, since there are usually several different criteria involved. In fact, one of the main reasons for assigning a term paper is to assess how students combine content-area knowledge with academic process skills such as locating and organizing relevant information, and how they use academic presentation skills such as effective use of term paper format, illustrations, bibliographies, and so on.

In an earlier article (Brookhart, 1993a), I described some characteristics of term paper assignments that contribute to their being valid assessments of this combination of content, process, and presentation skills. The term paper or report assignment should

- be a meaningful task, both for the student and the content area,
- require that the student frame his or her own question or write his or her own thesis statement,
- require that the student locate and analyze information and draw conclusions from it (not just repackage it),
- require that the student communicate his or her results clearly in writing, and
- if possible, require that students work together for part of the assignment, as "real" reporters do.

In order for your grading scheme to support reliable ratings of the qualities you want to measure, the criteria you use to judge the final paper should do the following:

- Focus on important aspects of the subject matter content and of student strategies for dealing with the content
- Match the particular kinds of achievement you want the students to show with their work on the term paper or report
- Be complete, covering all aspects of the students' performance that you need to assess
- Have clear, interpretable labels or descriptions
- Have clearly described levels of performance, with descriptions of each level phrased in positive language

To illustrate, consider an example of an eighth-grade American history teacher who assigns a term paper. This teacher has two main learning goals. One is cognitive: Students will understand the importance of social structure on people's lives and political events in Colonial America. A second is affective: Students will dvelop a sense of their own participation in history.

The students' assignment reads: Describe one aspect of life in colonial America, then compare and contrast it with your experience of life today. Figure 6-27 outlines how the assignment incorporates the above criteria. Figure 6-28 shows how a set of criteria and performance levels could be written to the quality specifications for grading schemes just discussed. The final grade for the paper could be arrived at in several different, defensible ways, depending on how you will use the final grade—especially how you will combine it with other assignments for the report period grade. One way to assign a grade would be by adding the total points and dividing by 29. Another way would be to use a decision rule where mostly 5s (or 3s for the 3-point rubrics) is an A, mostly 4s a B, mostly 3s a C, and so on.

FIGURE 6-27

Exercise for
eighth-grade
social stud-
ies example

LIFE IN COLONIAL AMERICA

Describe one aspect of life in Colonial America, then compare and contrast it with your experience of life today.

Start with a question of the type, "How did Colonial Americans _____? How is my experience similar (or different)?" For example, "How did Colonial Americans dress? Is our clothing similar or different today?"

Possible topics include: The family unit
Roles of men, women, and children
Education
Religious beliefs
Work in urban and rural settings
Slavery

You should have at least three sources, which can include library books, magazines, films, museum exhibits, or the Internet. If you use the Internet, use at least one other kind of source, too.

Your report should have the following format:

• Introduction—state your question and tell why it's important
• Section with historical details
• Section with contemporary information
• Comparison and contrast section—include both text and a visual organizer like a table or chart
• References

[*Teacher provides class time for group brainstorming of topics and question framing, discussing comparisons, designing charts, and peer editing.*]

CONCLUSION

Practice with examples is important. I encourage you to look at as much real student work as you can. In fieldwork placements, for example, ask your cooperating teacher if you can review a set of papers. Even better, observe students in the process of doing some work, and then observe the work itself after students hand it in. Student work is a gold mine of information about student learning, and the whole point of grading and feedback is to mine that information in the most accurate and useful ways possible.

EXERCISES

1. Write a brief self-reflection about what you learned from the bomb threat essay exercise. What did you learn from reading them? scoring them? comparing your scores with others? writing feedback to the student authors? What did you learn about grading? about yourself as a reader and a grader?

Scoring Rubrics for "Life in Colonial America" Paper

Does the paper describe an aspect of life in Colonial America that is important?
5–Intro asks a clear question and tells why important
4–Question clear, explanation of importance not clear
3–Question clear, topic not important
2–Topic trivial
1–Topic unrelated to assignments

Is there evidence of student understanding of the historical importance?
3–Student explains historical material clearly
2–Student presents material clearly but without reasons
1–Student does not present any historical context

Is the presentation of historical facts accurate and complete?
5–Description accurate, complete, clear
4–Most facts accurate, but some information is missing
3–Most facts accurate, much information is missing
2–Inaccurate information is presented
1–Cannot tell from writing what information is presented

Is the description of the current experience accurate?
5–Description accurate, complete, clear
4–Most facts accurate, but some information is missing
3–Most facts accurate, much information is missing
2–Inaccurate information is presented
1–Cannot tell from writing what information is presented

Are comparisons and contrasts with present-day life made logically and clearly?
5–Clear, logical comparisons at all appropriate points
4–Clear comparisons, some lapses of logic
3–Most comparisons make sense
2–Many potential comparisons overlooked
1–No comparisons made

Is prescribed format (text sections, references) followed?
3–Format model followed
2–Model followed for the most part, some errors or omissions
1–Format not followed

Is the visual organizer (chart or table) complete, logical, readable?
3–Chart is complete, presents information discussed in text
2–Chart is readable but does not coordinate with discussion
1–Chart is missing or does not make sense

2. Write a reflection about what you learned grading the "Dogs and Cats" essays.
3. Write a reflection about what you learned grading the essays on *A Raisin in the Sun*.
4. If you have kept any of your projects or term papers from previous classes, select one and design a rubric for grading it. Be able to explain how the rubric matches the assignment and the learning goals as you understood them, and why you allocated the values as you did.

Note: These are intended as "short" exercises at the end of the chapter. See Part 2 Exercises on page 111 for additional exercises.

Part 2 Exercises

INTEGRATING ASSESSMENT AND INSTRUCTION EXERCISES

1. If you have a field placement in your education program, ask your cooperating teacher to share student work from a performance assessment such as an essay test or a project—something that did not have objective scoring that anyone could grade with an answer key. Use photocopies of the work without student names, so you can "practice" grading. The teacher will want to do his or her own grading and return the students' papers to them. You will need to look at the assessment itself (including the scoring criteria); it would also be helpful for you to talk with the teacher about what the assignment's objective was. Work with a partner to do this, if you can.
    a. Determine what the students were supposed to learn, and how their learning can be assessed. Think about what high-quality work would look like, emphasizing the criteria. Talk about this with your partner.
    b. Grade the student work independently. Also write feedback to the student.
    c. Compare your grading with your partner's. On what percentage of the papers did you agree? Where you disagreed, can you find any patterns for your disagreements (that is, were your disagreements systematic or just chance differences)? If you did have systematic differences, can you explain why?
    d. Review your partner's written feedback to see how descriptive and constructive it was. Then give feedback to your partner on the feedback!
    e. Write a reflection on what you learned from grading this set of papers and providing student feedback.
    f. If possible, meet with your cooperating teacher and discuss what you've learned from grading the assessments. Ask for the teacher's observations and comments about your work.
2. Collect some of your own previously graded work. Reflect on the kinds of feedback you received and your responses to it.
3. Interview an elementary or secondary school student—a friend or relative, perhaps—about grading. Ask how he or she has been graded in his or her school career, what kinds of feedback he or she usually receives, and what he or she usually does with the information. What kinds of feedback are most helpful? least helpful? Does the subject matter make a difference?

Part 3

Combining Grades into Marks for Report Cards

CHAPTER 7

Grading Policies and Formats

KEY CONCEPTS

- Report card grading should be based on achievement of learning goals for the report period.
- Important nonachievement factors such as effort and attitude should be assessed, but should not be included directly in grades. Of course, they will have indirect effects on student achievement. Communication about effort and attitude is best done verbally. Some report cards also include "effort" grades.
- There are many kinds of report cards. Elementary report cards vary more than middle school and secondary school report cards.
- Whatever reporting system a teacher is required to use—even if it's not ideal, and even if the school or district is working to improve it—a teacher should make the best use of it, given its limitations, for the sake of the students. "Best use" means that the report conveys the most accurate and clearest information possible about students' achievement.
- Grade point averages are not particularly reliable or valid measures of achievement. They are, however, reasonably good predictors of future grades and are therefore a measure of "studenting" in some sense.
- Schools and districts benefit from self-reflection about grading. Uncovering assumptions and making them explicit helps students, parents, teachers, and administrators to communicate more clearly.

This chapter lays the foundation for "doing" grading. How teachers assign grades depends in part on the report cards and grading policies they are required to use. Grade assignment also depends on how teachers understand the nature and purpose of the summative enterprise—what, exactly, should be reflected in a report card mark?

GRADES SHOULD REFLECT ACHIEVEMENT

Brainstorm for a minute all the different factors that have counted toward a report card grade, in your experience. Many measures of achievement come to mind; tests and exams, quizzes, book reports, lab reports, term papers, and projects have all probably counted in various report card grades you received. Most teachers would agree that grades should be based on achievement; however, not all would agree that grades should be based on achievement *alone* (Stiggins et al., 1989) as recommended in this textbook.

Have other characteristics ever "counted" toward the report card grade you or your classmates received? For example, has any teacher ever "let you slide" because you made an effort, maybe giving a B to a report that might otherwise have been worth a C? Would you even be aware of it? One of the problems with "cutting students a break" is that typically teachers don't tell students that they're doing it, and the students think the grade is bona fide (Lantos, 1992). Students get the wrong idea about how well they're doing. But many teachers do consider effort when assigning grades (see Brookhart, 1994, for a review). If you "take off points" or lower grades for work that is turned in late, for example, are you grading the work itself or the student's work habits and effort?

Ability is another factor teachers sometimes consider in grading: "He did a really nice job, considering what he was capable of." Or improvement: "She did so much better on this test than on the last one." Educators argue about whether and how to consider these factors in final grades. This textbook recommends a different solution to the problem of ability. Start with the learning objectives, and modify those to reflect student ability. If a student cannot achieve an objective, why would you have that objective in mind for him or her? See Chapter 8 for a fuller discussion of this issue.

There is a whole class of personal factors that, it is generally agreed, shouldn't be counted in a grade (Stiggins et al., 1989): personality, attitude, class, gender, ethnicity, and so on. Sometimes these are counted anyway, however. In one of my college classes, only tall women with blonde hair got As (a sad but true story, happily from long ago). Sometimes these practices are much more subtle. The more subtle personal biases are in grading, the more difficult they are to identify and overcome.

Some teachers base grades on a combination of achievement, effort, ability, attitude, and behavior. There are several problems with this. First, research shows that teachers who count effort as well as achievement assess students of varying ability levels differently. For example, it's much more common for a teacher to consider effort in the case of a low-achieving student than for a high-achieving student (Brookhart, 1993b). Second, the models of instruction and assessment on which the teaching profession is based (see Chapter 4) all are anchored in goals for student learning. To fit our model of instruction—the model of instruction used to learn to write lesson, unit, and year-long plans, and to select learning activities and methods—grades *must* be based on those goals for student learning. Third, "effort" is very difficult to measure. Students can easily pretend to look interested when they are not, or look "out-to-lunch" when in fact they are thinking about their work. Indicators of effort in a classroom are hard to separate from decorum and good behavior, which are important for classroom management but clearly not the same thing as intellectual effort.

One reason teachers may resist the "achievement-only" rule for grading is that they are acutely aware of the importance of some of the nonachievement factors for developing the learning skills and dispositions that will serve students well. A disposition to be a lifelong learner is one of the most important overarching goals for schooling, and teachers are quite right to be concerned about it. The diagram in Figure 7-1 may help clarify this point. A recommendation for grading on achievement alone does not mean that effort and ability are unimportant, or that they fail to facilitate learning. It is important to realize that effort and ability *do* affect achievement. It's also important to assess these factors and to communicate with students and parents about them (Winger, 2005)—but not with a grade! It is usually more effective to talk with a student about his or her effort than to mix effort and achievement ratings into one report card grade. Conversations with students and parents can, and should, include discussions about the relationship between effort and achievement. You can tell a student, "I think if you'd spent another couple hours in the library, you would have found more references for that paper," and the like. Or, often better, ask a student how he or she thinks the work could have been done differently, and suggest that the student try that next time. This kind of coaching clearly requires both assessing and communicating about effort—but not for a grade.

Most of the uses of grades are as achievement measures. School districts use grades to monitor students' progress through a curriculum of study. Studies of parent perceptions of grades indicate they interpret grades as measures of achievement (Pilcher-Carlton & Oosterhof, 1993; Waltman & Frisbie, 1994). Teachers have been found to object to basing grades on achievement only, preferring instead to take effort into account (for a review, see Brookhart, 1994). But when teachers use grades to make

FIGURE 7-1 What information should go into a grade?

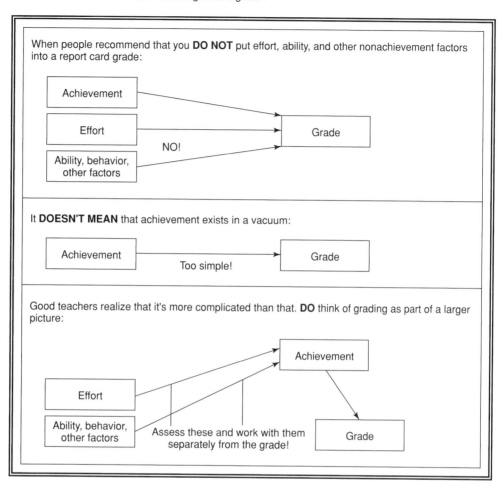

When people recommend that you **DO NOT** put effort, ability, and other nonachievement factors into a report card grade:

Achievement

Effort

NO!

Ability, behavior, other factors

Grade

It **DOESN'T MEAN** that achievement exists in a vacuum:

Achievement

Too simple!

Grade

Good teachers realize that it's more complicated than that. **DO** think of grading as part of a larger picture:

Achievement

Effort

Ability, behavior, other factors

Assess these and work with them separately from the grade!

Grade

decisions, they are most often decisions about instruction (for example, "How well did they do on this unit? Should I take more time with this concept? Should I teach it the same way next time?") or decisions about communication (such as "What should I tell this student or parent about the student's progress?"). Such decisions should be based, logically, on information about achievement of the concepts and skills that the student was expected to learn.

It is not recommended that you include every assignment from the report period in a final grade. Following the suggestion in Figure 7-1, you can find other ways to provide feedback for practice work and to emphasize its importance. If everything counts in a final grade, students will do relatively little risk-taking, preferring instead to stick to tried-and-true—and already successful—methods. You won't be able to assign challenging new work, because everything students do they will need to do at a mastery level. Base the final grade on major tests, quizzes, papers, projects, and so on: work for which students are sufficiently prepared to demonstrate whether or not they have reached acceptable, "gradable" levels of work that should be reported to parents and recorded as official marks of achievement. These official assessments are summative assessments, and good students also use them for formative (learning) purposes. If students can clearly see how their graded work reflects how well they have achieved clear learning goals, they can also use this information formatively, to inform their own future studying, writing, reading, and other learning activities.

REPORT CARD FORMATS

Report cards are like meatloaf: everyone has a different recipe. Even if this book were the size of an encyclopedia, it wouldn't be able to include all the different examples that exist. What this book will do, then, is to identify the various characteristics of report cards. One of your first responsibilities as a teacher should be to understand the particular report card format you will be using for your students. Figures 7-2, 7-3, and 7-4 present some concrete examples, showing a kindergarten, third-grade, and high school report card, respectively. Note that these reports are from three different districts. Researchers who have collected and reviewed report cards (Friedman & Frisbie, 1995; Schuster, Lynch, Polson-Lorczak, & Nadeau, 1996) note great variation among reporting formats.

Report card formats are usually adopted by a district, and their use is a matter of policy. Thus, for example, you probably will not have any choice about what sort of grade (letter or percent, for example) you will report or how often you will report. Whatever reporting system a teacher is required to use—even if it's not ideal, and even if the school or district is working to improve it—a teacher should make the best use of it, given its limitations, for the sake of the students. "Best use" means that the report conveys the most accurate and clearest information possible about students' achievement.

PHYSICAL CHARACTERISTICS

Report cards include spaces for the name of the student and often the teacher, and are usually printed with the name of the school and district and the date. Physical characteristics vary and can include

- size of paper and format (e.g., 8.5 × 11-inch single-page format),
- method of recording information (e.g., handwritten, computer generated), and
- carbon copies (for parents to file and/or return) or no carbon copies.

The examples shown in Figures 7-2 through 7-4 illustrate some of these physical differences. The kindergarten report card in Figure 7-2 is printed on card

FIGURE 7-2 Example of a kindergarten report card

TEACHER COMMENTS (1ST SEMESTER)

TRINITY AREA SCHOOL DISTRICT
KINDERGARTEN PROGRESS REPORT

Student's Name _____

Teacher's Name _____

School _____

School Year _____ - _____

PARENT'S SIGNATURE _____
(Please return report card in one (1) week)

TEACHER COMMENTS (2ND SEMESTER)

RECORD OF ATTENDANCE:

	1ST Semester	2nd Semester
Days Absent		
Days Tardy		

5/00 K

ASSIGNMENT FOR NEXT YEAR:

PROMOTED TO FIRST GRADE	
PLACED IN FIRST GRADE	
RETAINED IN KINDERGARTEN	

(Continued)

119

FIGURE 7-2 (Continued)

READING and LANGUAGE ARTS

	1ST Semester	2ND Semester
READING READINESS		
*follows pattern of working from left to right and top to bottom		
*recognizes and names capital and lower case letters of the alphabet		
*identifies the sounds that each letter represents		
*matches beginning sounds		
*matches capital with lower case letters		
COMPREHENSION		
*follows oral directions		
*demonstrates an understanding of text by drawing and/or writing		
*can orally retell a story in sequence		
PHONEMIC AWARENESS		
Sound Matching - identifies words beginning with the sound		
Sound Isolation - identifies the beginning sound		
Sound Blending - blends sounds to make a word		
Sound Segmenting - separates the sounds in words		
Rhyming - matches rhyming pictures		
Rhyming - oral rhyming		
WRITING READINESS		
*draws to convey meaning		
*demonstrates knowledge of letters and sounds		
*creates words using temporary and/or conventional spelling		
*uses groups of words to express a complete thought		

MATH

	1ST Semester	2ND Semester
NUMBER OPERATION		
*counts 1-10		
*counts 1-30		
*writes numerals 1-10		
*writes numerals 1-20		
*identifies numerals 1-10		

MATH (continued)

*identifies numerals 1-20		
*matches sets 1-10		
*matches sets 1-20		
*uses appropriate vocabulary		
PROBLEM SOLVING		
*solves problems using basic math concepts		
DATA ANALYSIS		
*analyzes data using concepts of largest, smallest, more or less		
*interprets graphs		
*uses appropriate vocabulary		
GEOMETRY/MEASUREMENT		
*identifies basic geometric shapes		
*understands basic concepts of measurement		
*uses appropriate vocabulary		
PATTERNS		
*recognizes, describes, extends and creates a pattern		
WORK HABITS		
*works independently and completes tasks		
*raises hand and waits turn to speak		
*listens attentively		
*works cooperatively in a group		
*follows classroom rules		
*works in an organized manner		
*exercises self-control		

EXPLANATION OF PERFORMANCE CODES:

* * commendable achievement in kindergarten
* \+ acceptable achievement in kindergarten
* ✓ making progress toward acceptable achievement
* \- area of concern

5/00 K

Source: Courtesy of the Trinity Area School District, Washington, Pennsylvania. Used by permission.

FIGURE 7-3 Example of a third-grade report card

South Fayette Township School District
SOUTH FAYETTE ELEMENTARY SCHOOL
Student Progress Report
Third Grade
2000-2001

Name: _____   Teacher: _____

Superintendent – Dr. Linda B. Hippert   Principal – Denise Beverina Moore, M.A., NCSP

CURRICULUM AREAS	NINE WEEKS				
	1	2	3	4	Final
Reading/Language Arts					
Consistently uses decoding strategies					
Reads with understanding					
Grammar (English)					
Writing Rubric Grade*					
Spelling					
Mathematics					
Knows basic math facts					
Applies basic facts for problem solving					
Communicates mathematics orally and in writing					
Social Studies					
Science					
Health					
Art					
Physical Education					
Music					
Library					
Foreign Language: German					

Days	1	2	3	4	Total
Absent					
Tardies					

EXPLANATION OF MARKING SYSTEM
A	100% - 93%	T - Taught but not graded
B	92% - 85%	S - Satisfactory
C	84% - 75%	N - Needs Improvement
D	74% - 65%	M - Mastered
F	64% or below	P - Partially Proficient
		NM - Not Mastered

Writing Rubric Grade*
4 - Exemplary
3 - Competent
2 - Developing
1 - Emerging

YOUR CHILD IN SCHOOL
Completes classwork assigned				
Completes homework assigned				
Uses agenda properly				
Is organized				
Exhibits self-control				
Is attentive to instruction				
Applies handwriting skills				
Follows directions				
Interacts appropriately with peers				
Uses time effectively				

PROMOTED TO GRADE: _____   TEACHER: _____

TEACHER'S COMMENTS

Please sign the report card envelope and return the envelope to your child's teacher.
If you are interested in having a conference, please call _____ at (412) 221-4542, Ext. ____, or send e-mail to _____

Source: Courtesy of the South Fayette Township School District, McDonald, Pennsylvania. Used by permission.

FIGURE 7-4 Example of a high school report card

WASHINGTON HIGH SCHOOL

NAME		GRADE LEVEL		SCHOOL YEAR		STUDENT NO.

		1ST			2ND			3RD			4TH			FNL EX GRD	FINAL GRADE
COURSE	TEACHER	GR	COMM	CL ABS	GR	COMM	CL ABS	GR	COMM	CL ABS	GR	COMM	CL ABS		

	CREDITS ATTEMPTED	CREDITS EARNED	QUALITY POINTS	QUALITY POINT AVG.		1ST	2ND	3RD	4TH	CUM
CURRENT MARKING PERIOD					DAYS ABSENT					
CUMULATIVE TO DATE					TIMES TARDY					

SEE REVERSE SIDE FOR KEY TO GRADES AND COMMENTS

GRADING KEY

A - SUPERIOR ACHIEVEMENT

B - ABOVE AVERAGE ACHIEVEMENT

C - AVERAGE ACHIEVEMENT

D - BELOW AVERAGE ACHIEVEMENT
    MINIMUM ACCEPTABLE ACHIEVEMENT

F   UNSATISFACTORY WORK
    NO CREDIT ALLOWED
    (CONFERENCE WITH TEACHER RECOMMENDED)

I - WORK INCOMPLETE, NO CREDIT ALLOWED
    (CONFERENCE WITH TEACHER
    RECOMMENDED TO DETERMINE IF WORK
    CAN BE COMPLETED AND GRADE REMOVED)

P - PASSED

W - WITHDREW

TEACHER COMMENTS

1. PUTS FORTH BEST EFFORT

2. COMMENDABLE EFFORT, GOOD ATTITUDE. COOPERATES IN CLASS.

3. AVERAGE PREPARATION AND PARTICIPATION IN CLASS ROUTINE

4. CARELESS PREPARATION OF ASSIGNMENTS AND WRITTEN WORK.

5. POOR PREPARATION, UNCOOPERATIVE AND INDIFFERENT TO CLASS ROUTINE

6. EXCESSIVE ABSENCE OR TARDINESS

7. BEHAVIOR PROBLEMS LIMIT LEARNING PROGRESS

8. DEFICIENCY REPORT SENT

9. INTERVIEW WITH PARENTS REQUESTED

SCHOOL PHONES

WASHINGTON HIGH SCHOOL OFFICE
223-5080

GUIDANCE OFFICE
223-5079

Source: Courtesy of the Washington School District, Washington, Pennsylvania. Used by permission.

stock, folded into a booklet format, and designed to be filled in by hand. The other elementary report cards in this district are also booklets designed for handwritten entries.

The third-grade report card shown in Figure 7-3 is constructed as a word-processing file and is printed on standard 8.5 × 11-inch paper. Teachers fill in symbols or comments by selecting the template in their word-processing programs and entering the information. They save each student's records in a file after they have typed them. All of the teachers in this district have computers on their desks.

The high school report card shown in Figure 7-4 is a computer form with printer carriage strips and is the size of a half-sheet of paper. There are two copies, a white copy labeled "Student Copy" and a yellow copy labeled "Office Copy." The forms are made from No Carbon Required paper, so both copies are printed at the same time by the district's administrative computer.

ADMINISTRATIVE POLICY

The design of a report card incorporates administrative policy, although this may not be obvious. For example, the number of times a report card is issued (twice a year, every 9 weeks, every 6 weeks) is reflected by the number of columns or lines or other recording features of the card. Many other administrative policies are built into report card design that varies between districts and often among grade levels within districts. Report cards also differ in whether and how they include

- attendance and/or tardiness records,
- selection and detail of subject areas or other areas of study,
- space for effort, behavior, citizenship, and/or attitude ratings,
- kind of symbols used (A, B, C, D, F; percents; other letters, numbers, or symbols),
- grade point averages and/or number of credits,
- final examinations,
- space for teacher comments (sometimes from a list of standard comment selections),
- space for parent comments,
- space for parent signature,
- a school or district mission statement,
- district grading philosophy or policy statements,
- space for indicating assignment for next year (e.g., "promoted to first grade, placed in first grade, retained in kindergarten"), and
- space for indicating any special services the child receives (e.g., speech, hearing, learning support).

The examples shown in Figures 7-2 through 7-4 illustrate various administrative policies. For example, the kindergarten report card (Figure 7-2) is designed for use once a semester. The third-grade and high school report cards (Figures 7-3 and 7-4) each assume a report is issued once every 9 weeks. As another example, the kindergarten report card uses a symbol system. The third-grade report card uses a criterion-referenced letter-grade system, where each letter is defined as a percentage. As noted in Chapter 5, this is not true criterion referencing: The comparison is to an external standard but the standard "floats." The high school report card uses a similar list of letters (A, B, C, D, F), but the descriptions are written as "average," "above average," and so on.

INSTRUCTIONAL TARGETS

There are several approaches to listing the substantive areas for students' achievement targets on report cards. One way is to list subjects by name (e.g., "Spelling," "Mathematics," "Social Studies," as in Figure 7-3). Sometimes these have subheadings. Thus, for example, the heading "Mathematics" may have subheadings like "Knows basic math facts," "Applies basic facts for problem solving," and so forth (see Figure 7-3). Computer forms usually have a space for "Course" (as in Figure 7-4) or "Subject" that is printed only with those subjects the student is taking, and often will also have a space for the teacher and/or section number of the class.

Another method of identifying instructional targets for grading is to list more specific instructional goals (e.g., "Matches beginning sounds," as in Figure 7-2). Elementary report cards vary more than middle school and secondary school report cards; they are more likely to list instructional goals instead of subject areas. Kindergarten report cards rarely use letter grades, whereas some first-grade report cards do use letter grades. By third grade, many report cards use letter grades; however, there is still a great amount of variation in this practice. Even in high school, where letter grading is quite common, not all high schools follow this practice.

Increasingly since the signing of the No Child Left Behind legislation in 2002, districts are experimenting with *standards-based report cards*. These are report cards that, instead of categories based on subject names or district learning targets, use state learning standards as the categories to which grades are assigned. The example in Figure 7-5 is from a school district in the state of Washington. The grading categories in bold on this report card are from the Washington Essential Academic Learning Requirements. Note the grading rubric, as well. The rubric levels refer to progress toward the particular standard being graded. This is consistent with the state-level accountability reporting for NCLB. In Washington, schools report "percent meeting standard" in Reading, Math, Writing, and Science for their "school report cards," as the school-level NCLB reporting is called.

To date, districts have revised more elementary school report cards than high school report cards to be standards-based. High school courses do not lend themselves to subdividing into standards as easily as elementary school subjects do. In fact, some state standards are grouped by subject for elementary school and change to course style standards in secondary school. For example, California (http://www.cde.ca.gov/be/st/ss/) has content standards for Mathematics for each grade K through 7, and for course subjects (e.g., Algebra I) for grades 8–12.

Another issue is that standards-based report cards highlight the difference between teachers' grades and state standardized tests. Because the state tests and standards-based report cards purport to measure the same state content standards, an obvious expectation is that the information in these two sources would be related. In fact, that is not always the case. Welsh and D'Agostino (2008) found that student grades on

FIGURE 7-5

Example of a
standards-
based fourth
grade report
card

Source:
Courtesy of
the Everett
Public School,
Everett,
Washington.
Used by per-
mission.

Everett, WA

Report to Parents - Grade 4

Dear Parent: The teachers and staff of the Everett Public Schools are committed to helping all children develop the knowledge and skills they need to be successful. Regular communication with parents about their child's progress is critically important. Although a report card cannot capture all that a child learns, it will give you regular information about your child's progress and current achievement level. Our desire is to help each child become a lifelong learner.

Carol Whitehead, Ed.D.
Superintendent

Student:
Teacher:
School:
Grade: 4
Year:
Principal:

Everett School District Attendance	1st	2nd	3rd
Present			
Absent			
Tardy			

EVALUATION KEY
4 **Exceeds Standard (area of excellence)** - The student demonstrates superior performance and skills appropriate to content and grade level. The student consistently goes beyond requirements in subject areas
3+ **Meets Standard (area of competence)** - Student is working beyond level 3 but does not yet consistently perform at level 4.
3 **Meets Standard (area of competence)** - The student demonstrates solid performance appropriate to content and grade level. The student applies skills in a variety of situations.
2+ **Progressing Toward Standard (area of development)** - Student is working beyond level 2 but does not yet consistently perform at level 3.
2 **Progressing Toward Standard (area of development)** - The student shows partial accomplishment of the knowledge and skills in specific situations or with support. The student is showing progress over time.
1 **Not Progressing Toward Standard (area of concern)** - The student demonstrates little or no progress or achievement.
NE **Not Evaluated** during this evaluation period.

(Continued)

FIGURE 7-5

(Continued)

Reading	1st	2nd	3rd
Understands and uses different skills and strategies. Identifies setting, character, plot and theme. Recognizes the characteristics of different genres.			
Understands the meaning of what is read. Analyzes, interprets, and summarizes what is read. Thinks critically about author's language, style, purpose and perspective.			
Reads different materials for a variety of purposes. Reads to learn new information, to perform a task and for literary experience.			

Communications	1st	2nd	3rd
Speaking. Prepares, organizes, and presents for a variety of purposes.			
Listening. Comprehends and listens attentively.			

Writing	1st	2nd	3rd
Writes clearly and effectively. Develops concepts and design and uses appropriate style.			
Applies writing conventions (writes in complete sentences and paragraphs, and uses correct spelling, punctuation and capitalization).			
Writes legibly using correct cursive letter formation.			
Writes in a variety of forms for different audiences and purposes, Writes to entertain (self-expression, short stories, folk tales, poetry) and writes to inform (biographies, reports, instructions).			
Accepts and gives feedback on own writing and offers feedback on writing to others.			
Analyzes and evaluates the effectiveness of written work. Uses criteria to evaluate and improve own and others' writing.			

Literacy Comments:

(First Grading Period: by)

Science	1st	2nd	3rd
Understands and uses scientific concepts and principles.			
Participates in and understands grade level content, skills and processes.			
Connects content and study of concepts to real life.			

Science Comments:

(First Grading Period: by)

FIGURE 7-5

(Continued)

Mathematics	1st	2nd	3rd
Understands and applies math concepts.			
Knows and uses math facts.			
Selects and uses a variety of strategies to mathematically solve problems. Identifies different ways to solve problems, shows work, and explains the solution.			
Communication. Gathers, organizes and shares information.			
Uses mathematical reasoning. Justifies reasonableness of solution.			
Mathematics Comments:			
(First Grading Period: by)			

Social Studies	1st	2nd	3rd
Understands major ideas, themes and developments in history.			
Uses maps and other geographic tools.			
Understands and compares the interaction between people, the environment and culture.			
Understands the rights and responsibilities of citizenship and the purpose of government.			
Understands basic economic concepts and how they impact the past and present, e.g., scarcity, supply and demand.			
Social Studies Comments:			
(First Grading Period: by)			

Health and Fitness	1st	2nd	3rd
Health: Demonstrates knowledge and skills necessary to maintain a healthy lifestyle (nutrition and safety).			
Demonstrates the knowledge and skills necessary to maintain personal safety in a variety of situations.			
Physical Education: Physical skills			
Follows rules and demonstrates safety procedures and good sportsmanship.			
Effort			

Art	1st	2nd	3rd
Demonstrates and applies art skills and knowledge.			
Uses the creative process to develop his/her ideas.			
Uses art skills to communicate ideas and feelings.			

(Continued)

FIGURE 7-5

(Continued)

Music	1st	2nd	3rd
Demonstrates knowledge of music skills and concepts.			
Contributes positively to group activities.			

Cooperative Worker	1st	2nd	3rd
Cooperates and interacts positively with others			
Participates actively and appropriately			
Respects property of school and others			
Respects rights, feelings and ideas of others			
Solves problems with peers independently			
Follows school and room rules			

Quality Worker	1st	2nd	3rd
Shows willingness to try			
Shows persistence			
Keeps workspace and materials organized			
Completed work is done neatly			

Self Directed Worker	1st	2nd	3rd
Works independently			
Follows directions			
Evaluates own progress			
Completes classwork on time			
Returns home assignments on time			
Makes productive use of class time			
Is prepared with materials and ready to work			
Attends and arrives on time			

General Comments:

(First Grading Period: by)

standards-based report cards in one large district were only moderately related to performance on standards on the state test, and that this relationship varied considerably among teachers.

Why look so closely at the format of report cards? Because the form of a report influences the information that it conveys. The selection and description of subject areas, or behavior or effort categories, and the marks that are used to rate them have implications for what the report cards seem to be intended to communicate. As a teacher, you need to know what your report card looks like and what kind of information it is capable of conveying, so you can do two things. First, you need to match the collection and evaluation of evidence with the kind of rating you need to give, so that within the limits of the report card you can do the best job possible of communicating with students and parents. Second, you need to identify what additional information you would like to give students and parents that cannot be communicated through the report card, and determine the best way to provide that information (see Chapter 10).

GRADING POLICIES

If it's possible, grading policies are even more variable than report card formats! Grading policies may include statements about any—or none—of the following areas (Austin & McCann, 1992):

- Purposes for grades (reporting progress, achievement, providing information for decision making, etc.)
- Intended audience for grades (parents, students, school district personnel)
- Criteria for grading (what kinds of information may be taken into account in assigning grades)
- Number of marking periods
- Grading system (letters, numbers, and their meaning)
- Weight of final exam
- Definition of "passing"
- Calculation of grade point average and class rank
- Guidance for teachers in calculating grades

Grading policies are typically adopted by school boards, and the amount of use and reference they receive differs from district to district. Some are quite detailed, whereas others contain only general statements. Some districts do not have written grading policies, and some districts' grading policies are subsections in larger policy documents. Figure 7-6 presents one district's grading policy. It is an example of a grading policy that is part of a larger document about academic standards in the district. The larger document includes information about graduation requirements, progress toward graduation, and a district assessment plan. Note that this policy is included only as an example, and not necessarily as a "typical" policy. Because policies vary so much from district to district, there is no typical example.

FIGURE 7-6

Example of a
district grad-
ing policy

Source:
Courtesy of
the Washington
School District,
Washington,
Pennsylvania.
Used by per-
mission.

*The following is an excerpt from a unified document that contains three sections: (a)
Organization Overview for Washington School District, (b) Core Purpose (including
Mission and Vision statements), and (c) Academic Standards. The "Grading System"
subsection reprinted here is from the Academic Standards section.*

Grading System

Washington Park Elementary School Grading Scale for Grades K–5

A = 90–100%
B = 80–89%
C = 70–79%
D = 60–69%
F = 59% and below

**Washington High School (Grades 9–12) and Washington Park Middle School
(Grades 6–8) Grading Scales**

Letter Grade	Equivalent % Score	Quality Point Value (QPV)	Weighted Quality Point Value (x 1.25)
A+	97–100	4.0	5.0
A	93–96	3.8	4.8
A−	90–92	3.6	4.6
B+	87–89	3.3	4.1
B	83–86	3.0	3.75
B−	80–82	2.7	3.4
C+	77–79	2.3	2.9
C	73–76	2.0	2.5
C−	70–72	1.7	2.1
D+	67–69	1.3	1.6
D	63–66	1.0	1.25
D−	60–62	0.7	0.9
F	<60	0	0

Letter Grade

How yearly QPA is calculated:

Add the Quality Point Value based on the final grade and divide that number by the
credits attempted for the school year. Using the example below, the total QPV is 22.3
and the credits attempted is 8. 22.3 ÷ 8 = 2.7875, QPA for year = 2.7875.

GRADE POINT AVERAGES

For students in high school, especially in their junior and senior years, class standing or "class rank" can be an important consideration. Remember Ann's story from Chapter 1. Students and their parents can get very emotionally involved in a number that is not terribly meaningful in its own right. The power of the grade point average lies in its uses. Many high schools designate the top student in the class as "valedictorian" and invite him or her to make a speech at graduation. Some schools designate the student ranked second as salutatorian, and this person also sometimes speaks at graduation. Some colleges take class rank into consideration for admission and/or scholarship decisions.

The calculation of grade point averages will be a matter of district policy over which teachers will not have direct control. However, teachers will live with the consequences of that policy and will be the first point of contact for many students and parents with questions. Teachers should understand their district's grade point policy and its implications. They should be able to describe it clearly to students and parents. Teachers may choose to argue for changes in policies they think are harmful to students.

Any system where there are "winners" and "losers" risks undermining the developmental intentions of education, not to mention risking political firestorms. But the various solutions people have offered have not been very helpful, either. One year, one district decided to designate all students above a certain high grade point average as "valedictorians," and all 17 of them were seated on the graduation platform! This appeared a bit silly to the community.

In some school systems, class rank is computed by considering the scale A = 4.00, B = 3.00, C = 2.00, D = 1.00, F = 0.00, weighting each by the number of course credits each grade reflects (typically 1.0 for a high school academic course and sometimes 0.5 for electives that do not meet every day). But there are many variations on this theme. Sometimes the grade point average is updated for each report period; sometimes it is updated at the end of the year.

In other districts, honors or other advanced courses are given extra "weight." "Weighted grading" is something of a misnomer, since every time you put together numbers they have weights, even if they're all equal. So "unweighted grading," mathematically speaking, is weighted grading where all the weights are ones. Nevertheless, in common parlance weighted grading usually means using some algorithm that allows advanced courses to pull up the grade point average. In some cases that means using a scale of A = 5.00, B = 4.00, C = 3.00, D = 2.00, and F = 0.00. In other cases it entails some kind of calculation system, as illustrated in the grading policy in Figure 7-6, where the 0–4 scale is multiplied by 1.25 for weighted grades. Talley and Mohr (1993) surveyed high schools and found that in 1990, 55.4% of the respondents in their national sample used some kind of weighted grading.

Several times I have been asked what I think of weighted grading. For me that's a loaded question, since it assumes that grade point averages are a good idea in the first place. Grade point averages are not particularly reliable or valid measures of achievement constructs. Each student's grade point average is made up of a slightly different selection of courses, some of which are harder than others. In fact, some of those courses would be harder for some students than others. A student who finds math and physics easy may have a difficult time with even an introductory-level foreign language course. A student who revels in advanced literature courses may have a difficult time even with Algebra I. The average of all of this is not really a valid measure of any clearly definable construct.

On the other hand, grade point averages can do a reasonably good job of predicting future grades (Young, 1993). Grade point averages are therefore a measure of "student-ing" in some sense. At a broad level, college admissions decisions can be made using grade point averages as one measure. College admissions personnel prefer weighted grading, giving advanced courses more weight in grade point averages, over unweighted calculations of grade point averages (Talley, 1989; Talley & Mohr, 1991, 1993).

You will hear all sorts of anecdotes illustrating the fuss about weighted grading in the cases of individual students. For example, a high school principal told the story of a talented trombone player who wanted to take music as an elective course in his senior year. But he didn't. He needed to use the spot in his schedule for a course with weighted grades, so that his grade point average would be higher and he could qualify for a more elite college. That story seems to argue for all course grade weights being equal. But then there is the fear that gifted students will not take challenging courses, preferring instead the "guaranteed" As, and high class rank, that would come with taking regular courses. That scenario argues in favor of weighted grading.

What to do? A wise school superintendent summed it up very well. "Any system you invent," she said, "students will find a way to play it." In a perfect world, there would be no grades. The best advice I can give for getting along in this imperfect world is to have grades reflect achievement of learning goals, to combine them in a way that has meaning for your district, and then be able to clearly communicate *what that meaning is.* If grades reflect learning goals, and if the curriculum enacted in teachers' classes and lessons is aligned with the district's curriculum, then the grades will at least be indicators of learning as defined by the district—which is arguably what districts should be obligated to provide (as opposed to character references or indicators of psychological traits). If the districts articulate what meaning is conveyed in their method of grade point averaging, at least teachers and administrators will be clear about how those grade point averages should be used. Thus, if you want a system where the valedictorian each year is likely to be an advanced-placement student, use weighted grading. If you want a system where the valedictorian is likely to be any student who achieved the learning goals set for him or her, use unweighted grading.

SELF-REFLECTION IS CRITICAL

Self-reflection is an important component of any professional practice. Teachers who take the time to reflect on their teaching give themselves the opportunity to improve—and to take charge of their self-improvement. This principle works for all aspects of teaching: instruction, classroom management, relations with parents and colleagues, and so on. It is especially critical in grading precisely because so little self-reflection is done. Teachers do, usually, think about their instruction and classroom management, reflecting on what went well and wondering about what they could do to improve things if they weren't satisfied (Cochran-Smith & Lytle, 1999).

Grading, however, sometimes happens as an afterthought, as numbers "done" or calculated at the end of a report period when it's too late to do much besides meet the deadline for turning in reports. As you have seen, grading plans should be made at the same time as instructional plans, and they should be based on instructional goals. Reflection about instruction and assessment can and should go together.

Another reason to reflect on grades and grading practices is the documented fact that grades mean different things to different constituencies—students, parents, teachers, school administrators, and the public. Communication about grades is impossible without a shared understanding of what grades mean. Where there are discrepancies between the information you *intend* to convey with a grade and the information the student or parent *think* is being conveyed, there is room for trouble! At best, you won't make yourself clear, and at worst, some inappropriate consequence (like no TV for a week!) might ensue for the student. Remember the cartoon in Figure 1-2.

Table 7-1 presents a survey-style reflection tool that you might find helpful as you are called upon to assign grades. The items listed are based on research about grading practices, and include both recommended and nonrecommended practices. There are several ways you might use this survey for self-reflection, both as a student and as a teacher.

- **As a "consciousness-raising" for yourself:** Answer the questions the way you are personally inclined right now. Then look over your answers and ask yourself why you answered the way you did, what the implications are for the kind of communication your grading would afford, and whether or not you might want to modify any of the beliefs you have identified.
- **As a study tool:** Answer the questions according to the recommendations made thus far in this book, and then ask yourself what grading practices would follow. Note that there will not be "one right answer" even if you use the survey this way, but there will be some "wrong" ones!
- **As a discussion starter with colleagues:** Once you are assigned a teaching position, form a study group with other teachers. Use the survey to find out their perception of how grading is done, and how it ought to be done. See how far you are from consensus, and whether you can generate more agreement by discussion—or at least identify areas of disagreement and determine whether the reasons for them relate to subject area, teaching philosophy, tradition, and so on.
- **As a planning tool** if your district decides to work on grading issues as a school target. Many districts have chosen to make grading a topic of school- or district-wide study and improvement recently, or are planning to do so soon.

CONCLUSION

The above exercise in self-assessment is intended to be formative. What did you learn? Did what you learn support your understanding of the key concepts of this chapter?

TABLE 7-1

Survey or discussion-starter on grading practices

What grade(s) do you teach? What subject(s) do you teach? *[If you do not have your own class yet, reflect upon how you would assign grades in a subject/grade you plan to teach.]*

What method do you use to calculate or assign report card grades? If you teach several classes and use more than one method, select the method you use most often.

☐ Quality judgment, using A, B, C, D, and E as a holistic scale
☐ Averaging, using a 4, 3, 2, 1, 0 scale
☐ Averaging, using a 0–100 scale (percents)
☐ Using the median grade the student received that period
☐ Using the most frequent grade the student received that period

What meaning do you try to encode into your grades?

☐ Student achievement of classroom and curriculum learning goals for the period
☐ Student standing relative to others in the class on the subject matter taught during the period
☐ Student improvement or achievement relative to a student's own potential
☐ Student progress on individual learning goals for the period

What do you do when a student's grade is just *below* the borderline or cutoff for a letter grade?

☐ I just give the grade as is.
☐ I review additional information about the student, to decide whether to raise the grade or not.
☐ I offer the student extra-credit work.
☐ I just give the grade as is, unless the missed cutoff was between a D and an F.

What do you do when a student's grade is just *above* the borderline or cutoff for a letter grade?

☐ I just give the grade as is.
☐ I review additional information about the student, to decide whether to lower the grade or not.

For the following list of items, please make two judgments. For each, check the selection that most closely matches your practice. **If you teach more than one class, select one to report.** You can answer the questions separately for each class if you wish to reflect on all of them.

First, tell whether and, if so, how you assess these things in the course of your teaching. Indicate everything you assess, formally or informally, and

TABLE 7-1

(Continued)

whether or not the assessment becomes part of the official report card grade. Your choices will include the following:

NOT CONSIDERED—factors that you do not consider at all in your teaching
INFORMALLY ASSESSED—factors for which you make a mental note about students, but do not write or record anywhere
NARRATIVE—factors for which you make a written record in words
GRADE OR RUBRIC—factors for which you assign an A, B, C, etc., or a category from a rubric
PERCENT—factors for which you assign a percent-correct score

Second, tell whether and, if so, with what weight that item contributes to the grade you assign students on their report card. Your choices will include the following:

NOT INCLUDED—factors that do not "count" into the report card grade, whether or not you have assessed them in class to help you with your teaching
SMALL PORTION—factors that count 10% or less of the report card grade
MODERATE PORTION—factors that count 11 to 40% of the report card grade
LARGE PORTION—factors that count 41 to 100% of the report card grade

Factor	How Assessed	How It Contributes to a Report Card Grade
Classroom tests	☐ Not considered ☐ Informally assessed ☐ Narrative ☐ Grade or rubric ☐ Percent	☐ Not included ☐ Small portion ☐ Moderate portion ☐ Large portion
Standardized tests	☐ Not considered ☐ Informally assessed ☐ Narrative ☐ Grade or rubric ☐ Percent	☐ Not included ☐ Small portion ☐ Moderate portion ☐ Large portion
Announced quizzes	☐ Not considered ☐ Informally assessed ☐ Narrative ☐ Grade or rubric ☐ Percent	☐ Not included ☐ Small portion ☐ Moderate portion ☐ Large portion
Unannounced quizzes	☐ Not considered ☐ Informally assessed ☐ Narrative ☐ Grade or rubric ☐ Percent	☐ Not included ☐ Small portion ☐ Moderate portion ☐ Large portion

(Continued)

TABLE 7-1

(Continued)

Factor	How Assessed	How It Contributes to a Report Card Grade
Projects done (mostly) in class	☐ Not considered ☐ Informally assessed ☐ Narrative ☐ Grade or rubric ☐ Percent	☐ Not included ☐ Small portion ☐ Moderate portion ☐ Large portion
Projects done (mostly) outside of class	☐ Not considered ☐ Informally assessed ☐ Narrative ☐ Grade or rubric ☐ Percent	☐ Not included ☐ Small portion ☐ Moderate portion ☐ Large portion
Term papers or written reports on a topic	☐ Not considered ☐ Informally assessed ☐ Narrative ☐ Grade or rubric ☐ Percent	☐ Not included ☐ Small portion ☐ Moderate portion ☐ Large portion
Book reports	☐ Not considered ☐ Informally assessed ☐ Narrative ☐ Grade or rubric ☐ Percent	☐ Not included ☐ Small portion ☐ Moderate portion ☐ Large portion
Lab reports	☐ Not considered ☐ Informally assessed ☐ Narrative ☐ Grade or rubric ☐ Percent	☐ Not included ☐ Small portion ☐ Moderate portion ☐ Large portion
Homework	☐ Not considered ☐ Informally assessed ☐ Narrative ☐ Grade or rubric ☐ Percent	☐ Not included ☐ Small portion ☐ Moderate portion ☐ Large portion
In-class written exercises	☐ Not considered ☐ Informally assessed ☐ Narrative ☐ Grade or rubric ☐ Percent	☐ Not included ☐ Small portion ☐ Moderate portion ☐ Large portion
Group projects	☐ Not considered ☐ Informally assessed ☐ Narrative	☐ Not included ☐ Small portion ☐ Moderate portion

(Continued)

TABLE 7-1

(Continued)

	☐ Grade or rubric ☐ Percent	☐ Large portion
Class participation	☐ Not considered ☐ Informally assessed ☐ Narrative ☐ Grade or rubric ☐ Percent	☐ Not included ☐ Small portion ☐ Moderate portion ☐ Large portion
Spelling/grammar on papers or tests (of other material)	☐ Not considered ☐ Informally assessed ☐ Narrative ☐ Grade or rubric ☐ Percent	☐ Not included ☐ Small portion ☐ Moderate portion ☐ Large portion
Neatness of assignments	☐ Not considered ☐ Informally assessed ☐ Narrative ☐ Grade or rubric ☐ Percent	☐ Not included ☐ Small portion ☐ Moderate portion ☐ Large portion
Completing work on time	☐ Not considered ☐ Informally assessed ☐ Narrative ☐ Grade or rubric ☐ Percent	☐ Not included ☐ Small portion ☐ Moderate portion ☐ Large portion
Ability level of student	☐ Not considered ☐ Informally assessed ☐ Narrative ☐ Grade or rubric ☐ Percent	☐ Not included ☐ Small portion ☐ Moderate portion ☐ Large portion
Effort level of student	☐ Not considered ☐ Informally assessed ☐ Narrative ☐ Grade or rubric ☐ Percent	☐ Not included ☐ Small portion ☐ Moderate portion ☐ Large portion
Improvement during grading period	☐ Not considered ☐ Informally assessed ☐ Narrative ☐ Grade or rubric ☐ Percent	☐ Not included ☐ Small portion ☐ Moderate portion ☐ Large portion
Improvement since previous grading period	☐ Not considered ☐ Informally assessed ☐ Narrative	☐ Not included ☐ Small portion ☐ Moderate portion

(Continued)

TABLE 7-1

(Continued)

Factor	How Assessed	How It Contributes to a Report Card Grade
	☐ Grade or rubric ☐ Percent	☐ Large portion
Inappropriate classroom behavior	☐ Not considered ☐ Informally assessed ☐ Narrative ☐ Grade or rubric ☐ Percent	☐ Not included ☐ Small portion ☐ Moderate portion ☐ Large portion
Paying attention in class	☐ Not considered ☐ Informally assessed ☐ Narrative ☐ Grade or rubric ☐ Percent	☐ Not included ☐ Small portion ☐ Moderate portion ☐ Large portion
Attendance	☐ Not considered ☐ Informally assessed ☐ Narrative ☐ Grade or rubric ☐ Percent	☐ Not included ☐ Small portion ☐ Moderate portion ☐ Large portion
Cooperation with other students	☐ Not considered ☐ Informally assessed ☐ Narrative ☐ Grade or rubric ☐ Percent	☐ Not included ☐ Small portion ☐ Moderate portion ☐ Large portion

We have seen that both report cards and grading policies vary from district to district. Your challenge as a teacher will be to incorporate sound grading practices into whatever format and policy you must follow, and to identify grading formats and policies that you and your colleagues might try to change.

EXERCISES

1. For each of the scenarios below, tell whether the grade is based primarily on achievement, effort, ability, attitude, or behavior. For all of the scenarios where achievement is not the primary attribute that the grade indicates, rewrite the scenario so that the grade does indicate achievement in a manner that is reasonable, fair, and "do-able" in a classroom.

a. Mr. A gave his third-grade class a unit test at the end of a science unit on butterflies. There were 15 multiple-choice "fact" questions about butterflies and a 15-point question asking for pictures and labels that would illustrate the life cycle of a butterfly. The test was graded on a percent-correct scale.

b. Ms. B assigned students in her kindergarten class to draw themselves and the members of their family and pets. She observed how the students held the crayons and asked students to explain each figure included in their pictures.

c. Mr. C asked his eleventh-grade social studies students to select a favorite character from American history, research his or her life, and present it to the class. He graded on the enthusiasm and pizzazz of the presentation.

d. Ms. D assigned a project to her fifth graders. They were to read a chapter book, select their favorite chapter, and create a shoebox diorama. She allowed class time for students to work on the project, during which Byron was more interested in throwing art supplies than working. When she graded the dioramas, she gave Byron an F because he didn't respect the work.

e. Mr. E taught an advanced placement English class to high school seniors. During the course of the year, he taught students various aspects of the writing process. Their "big test" during the third report period was a public version of the AP English exam (an AP exam question that had been used in former years and was released for school use). He graded the papers according to the AP scoring scheme.

f. Ms. F assigned a term paper to her eighth-grade social studies class. It was the first "real" term paper they had done, so she wanted to be very rigorous in her grading. Claire turned in her paper three days after the due date, so Ms. F deducted a letter grade from Claire's paper.

g. Mr. G gave the same spelling test to all of his fourth graders. They had 20 words to memorize, and 5 dictated sentences for which they were expected to spell the words correctly. Most of the students were graded with a percent-correct scale that translated on the scale he used at 90%—A, 80%—B, etc. Larissa was a poor speller, so when she scored 70% he thought that was terrific for her and recorded an A.

2. For each of the situations below, indicate whether the assessment is intended to be primarily formative or summative, and whether or not you would count it in the final term grade.

a. A middle school teacher assigns students to do a report on the use of electric power in the United States, using newspapers, magazines, and books from the library.

b. A second-grade teacher gives a timed test on the 2×, 3×, and 4× multiplication tables, and records how many problems the students could do correctly in 1 minute.

c. A second-grade teacher asks students to write their spelling words five times each, then corrects the papers to see what students should emphasize when they study for the spelling test.

d. A high school math teacher assigns homework problems from the textbook each time a new concept is introduced.

  e. Students pair up in the back of the third-grade classroom and test each other with math flash cards.

  f. A social studies teacher gives a unit test at the end of a unit on Ancient Egypt.

3. Imagine you are a parent in a school district that has conventional A, B, C, D, F grading in the high school and currently calculates grade point average in the unweighted manner (A = 4.0, B = 3.0, C = 2.0, D = 1.0, F = 0.0). All courses count equally. The district is trying to decide whether to institute a weighted grading policy—and if so, what method of weighting to use. Prepare to attend a parents' meeting supporting one of two positions: keeping the system as it is, or changing to a weighted grading policy. Make sure that there are some "parents" on either side of the issue. After you have prepared your arguments, stage this meeting in class. If you wish, you can assign roles (e.g., superintendent, board member, principal, teacher, parent of a gifted musician, parent of a student with learning disabilities, parent who was a good student in school herself, parent who can't read, parent of a student who takes honors courses, etc.). Make sure that the exercise reflects different reasoned points of view. Your mock meeting should be a meeting of the minds as well as the emotions.

4. Report your findings from the self-reflection exercises you did earlier to summarize this chapter.

Note: These are intended as "short" exercises at the end of the chapter. See Part 3 Exercises on page 189 for additional exercises.

Developmental Concerns in Grading

KEY CONCEPTS

- Grading adaptations for special education students can be made in two ways: by changing the nature of grades for individual assignments, or by changing the methods of arriving at and reporting report card grades.
- Two practices are recommended for grading special education students in regular classes, to the extent possible within the district's grading policy: (a) Use multiple grades to report on both process (effort, promptness, etc.) and product (achievement of learning goals), and (b) base achievement measures on IEP learning goals, preferably by modifying individual assignments to reflect these before combining them for report card grades.
- Early childhood educators recommend that number or letter grades, if used, be accompanied by feedback, written comments, and formative evaluation against learning goals.

Developmental concerns in grading are very important and can be complicated and difficult issues. Which students are "ready" for letter or percentage grades, the most common grading? What should we do for students who are not developmentally ready for letter or percentage grading? What is "fair," and how do we manage differential treatment appropriately and without bias? These developmental issues in grading make many teachers long for that perfect world where there are no grades!

GRADING IN SPECIAL EDUCATION

Consider the following parable (Gallagher, n.d.):

> Statureland is an island nation with one major industry—purple fruit. Since purple fruit picking is essential to the welfare of the whole society, the Statureland schools' basic curriculum is intended to train effective purple fruit pickers. Because purple fruit grows only at the top of eight foot trees, the most important and critical course within the curriculum has been Growing. All children are required to take Growing and are expected to complete six feet of growth, which is the minimum criterion for graduation as purple fruit pickers and is the average height of Staturelandians, based upon standardized growing tests. The course content of Growing includes stretching, reaching, jumping, tip-toeing, and thinking tall.
>
> Each year, each child's skill and abilities in Growing have been assessed and each child assigned a grade. Those children who achieved average scores on the standardized Growing tests were assigned C grades. Students who through their commitment to Growing exceeded expected levels received As. Slow Growing students received Fs and were regularly and publicly admonished for their lack of effort and inattention to task. These latter children often developed poor self-images and anti-social behavior which disrupted the school program and interfered with children who really wanted to grow. "This will never do," said the people. "We must call a wise man to consider our problem and tell us how to help the children grow better and faster and become happy purple fruit pickers."
>
> So a wise man was sent for and he studied the problem. At last he suggested two solutions: (1) plant pink fruit trees that grow only five feet so that even four foot students may be successful pickers; and (2) provide ladders so that all students who wish to pick purple fruit can reach the tops of the trees.

"No, no," said the people. "This will never work. How can we then give grades if eight foot trees are goals for some students and five foot trees are goals for other students? How can it be fair to the naturally tall students if children on ladders can also stand six feet tall and reach the purple fruit? However shall we give grades?"

"Ah," said the wise man. "You can't. You must decide whether you want to grade children or have fruit picked."

A consistent question of educators with diverse classrooms is "How do I grade?" How does one assign a comparison physical education grade to a student in a wheelchair, a public-speaking grade to a deaf child, a handwriting grade to a child who has Cerebral Palsy, a reading grade to a child with cognitive challenges? If children with learning challenges need individual rather than class goals, how can one assign comparative grades fairly?

The author of this parable takes the position that comparative grades are inherently unfair to students with special needs. How, then, should we assign grades to special education students? For special education students in separate classrooms, the typical answer to that question is to go with those individual goals, that is, to grade students according to progress on their Individualized Education Plans (IEPs).

The discussion in this book will focus on how to assign grades to special education students for their work in regular education classes. Sometimes the regular education teacher has responsibility for assigning grades to all the students in her class, both regular and special needs. Other times, the regular education teacher and a special education teacher work together to assign those grades. In both cases, there are several important issues: what to "count" and how to count it, how to ensure that the grades are interpretable, and how to treat all students fairly. Bursuck and colleagues discuss the importance of grading decisions for special education students in regular classrooms (Bursuck et al., 1996, p. 301): "Classroom grades earned by students with disabilities provide a direct measure of the successful performance of the students and an indirect measure of the success of integration efforts in general."

Various authors have noted that simply grading special education students in the same manner as their regular education classmates does not work very well. When this is the policy, most of the special education students pass their classes but end up with very low grade point averages (Donahoe & Zigmond, 1990). They go to school, they do their work, and they end up "D" students. This very quickly frustrates both the students and their teachers, and it does not communicate clearly to parents about how the students are doing in school.

Grading policies may or may not be helpful for special education students. In a survey of school superintendents, Polloway and colleagues (Polloway et al., 1994) found that 65% of districts had a formal grading policy, although compliance with the policy was required for only 78% of those districts. For the rest, the grading policy was only recommended. Sixty percent of those districts with grading policies had a policy on modifications for students with disabilities. Using the IEP was the most frequently noted of these.

But if the classroom grading system is to be adapted for special education students, what specifically should a teacher do? Grading adaptations for these students can be made in two ways: by changing the nature of grades for individual assignments or by changing the methods of arriving at and reporting report card grades. Table 8-1 presents

TABLE 8-1	Grading Adaptation	What Teachers Think	What Students Think
Use and fairness of report card grading adaptations for students with special needs *Source:* The middle column of this table is adapted from "Report Card Grading and Adaptations: A National Survey of Classroom Practices," by W. Bursuck et al., 1996, *Exceptional Children, 62,* 301–318. The right-hand column is adapted from "The Fairness of Report Card Grading Adaptations," by W. Bursuck et al., 1999, *Remedial and Special Education, 20,* 82–94, 105.	Base grade on improvement	Perceived to be helpful; elementary (65%) teachers use this more than middle (48%) or high school (56%) teachers	Regular students tend to think this is "not fair," but students with learning disabilities tend to think this is "fair"
	Base grade on meeting IEP objectives	Perceived to be helpful but not used used much by teachers (14% elementary/middle, 10% high school)	(not asked)
	Grade effort and achievement separately	Perceived to be helpful; used by about 50% of teachers	Regular students are split on whether this is "fair," slightly more "not fair"; students with learning disabilities are split
	Adjust weights of grade components (e.g., count effort or projects more than tests)	Perceived to be helpful; used by about 50% of teachers	All students tend to see this as "not fair"
	Adjust grade for student ability	Perceived to be helpful; used more by elementary (54%) than middle (41%) or high school (25%) teachers	The student version of this question was about students "doing the best they can." Regular students are split on whether this is "fair," slightly more "not fair"; students with learning disabilities are split
	Base grade on academic or behavioral contracts	Perceived to be helpful; used by about 40% of teachers	(not asked)
	Base grade on learning less material than the rest of the class	Used more by elementary (31%) than middle (11%) or high school (13%) teachers	All students tend to see this as "not fair"
	Modify the grading scale (e.g., 90–100= A instead of 93–100 = A)	Used by about 30% of teachers	Regular students tend to think this is "not fair," but students with learning disabilities tend to think this is "fair"
	Pass students no matter what	Rarely used (11% elementary, 8% middle, 0% high school)	All students tend to to see this as "not fair"
	Pass students no matter how poorly they do as long as they try	Used by 43% elementary, 57% middle, and 35% high school teachers	All students tend to see this as "not fair"
	Use pass/fail grading	(not asked)	All students tend to see this as "not fair"

a list of 10 adaptations Bursuck and colleagues used in a series of studies, surveying teachers (Bursuck et al., 1996) and students (Bursuck et al., 1999) about their use of these methods and their perceptions of fairness. This is not a list of recommended practices, but a list that aims to represent the range of real practices. The list was developed from preliminary open-ended surveys of regular and special education teachers, a review of literature, consultation with experts, and a pilot study with teachers. Consistent with the philosophy of this book, these adaptations should be evaluated on the degree to which they reflect the principles of good grading or reporting. The adaptations should be about student achievement, and they should result in grades that communicate clear, interpretable information to students and parents.

ADAPTING METHODS OF ARRIVING AT REPORT CARD GRADES

Two practices are recommended for grading special education students in regular classes, to the extent possible within the district's grading policy.

- Use multiple grades to report separately on process (effort, promptness, etc.) and product (achievement of learning goals).
- Base achievement measures on IEP learning goals, preferably by modifying individual assignments to reflect these before combining them for report card grades and/or by specifying grading criteria in academic contracts.

Two practices are not recommended for special education students: grading on effort and grading on improvement.

Grading on effort, that is, assigning report card grades based on how hard a student worked, has several problems. First and foremost, the report card grade will be interpreted as a measure of achievement (see Chapter 2). Parents will assume a high grade means their children have performed well. Indeed, grades are supposed to reflect achievement of classroom learning goals (see Chapter 4). Second, measuring "effort" is very hard to do. Some children sit quietly and appear disengaged but are concentrating on their work. Others make a show of participation, waving their hands in the air and crying out, but are not really thinking about their lessons. More concrete measures of effort, such as turning in work done neatly and on time, are partly measures of behavior.

If not effort, then what about "progress," that is, grading students according to the amount of improvement they make from the start to the end of a report period. This method is about achievement, but it's on an uninterpretable scale. The information the teacher means to communicate doesn't survive the report card's trip home. Without the teacher to explain where the student started and ended, the grade can communicate only a general positive or negative—progress was made to some degree or it wasn't. The students and parents still don't have information that tells them about what the student actually learned.

Instead of grading on effort or improvement, specific adaptations that allow grading on achievement for special education students in regular classes are recommended (Bradley & Calvin, 1998; Jung, 2008). Grading adaptations should be made in consultation with all concerned: the students, parents, and special education teacher (Guskey & Bailey, 2001), or even a formal pupil evaluation team that will include these stakeholders in the creation of a written Personalized Grading Plan (PGP, Munk & Bursuck, 2003). Grading adaptations should be based on the student's IEP for students with identified special needs. For regular education students with special circumstances, teachers may adapt grading policies, as well. In fact, about 50% of teachers report that they use some grading adaptations for regular education students as well as those with identified special needs (Bursuck et al., 1996).

Jung (2008) recommends reporting three separate kinds of information, based on assessments of students' products (achievement), process (effort), and progress (growth), with separate criteria for each. In fact, Guskey (2001) recommends separating reports of product, process, and progress for all students. Jung and Guskey (2007, p. 5) point out that for special education students, when effort points and other grading adaptations are included in academic achievement grades, "Theoretically, these adaptations provide encouragement and opportunities for success to students for whom grade level standards may not be attainable. In reality, however, these adapted grades can lead such students to believe that their grades are not the result of what they do, but who they are." Jung (2008) also recommends that the product or achievement grades be based on the student's IEP, including any modifications made to state or regular curriculum standards for that student and any additional goals that were part of the IEP.

ADAPTING REPORTING MECHANISMS FOR STUDENTS WITH SPECIAL NEEDS

The use of multiple grades is recommended for students with special needs, as is the use of written comments and frequent personal communication with parents. If the district's report card structure does not allow teachers to report effort and achievement separately, the recommendation is to grade on achievement, preferably based on learning goals from the student's IEP. The best way to do that is to adapt individual assignments to match the IEP, and use grades on those assignments to calculate the final grade (see section below). It may be possible to augment the achievement information in the letter or number grade with written comments that convey information about student effort as well as achievement. This can sometimes be done in comment sections right on the report card. It can also be done by sending narrative comments home separately, by a phone call to the parents, and by parent conferences (see Chapter 10).

Some districts put information about special student services on the report card. This practice is controversial. Some feel it places a label on the report card, whereas others feel it provides information that will help parents interpret the grades. Figure 8-1 presents an example of an elementary report card from a district that does identify special services on the report card. Notice that this report card offers a version of multiple grading. The grading scale itself is set up to reflect achievement; the grade symbols are identified as levels of proficiency. The "Code of Remarks," from which teachers can select, functions like an "effort" grade; most of the teacher comments relate to student work habits. There is also space for additional written comments for each report period.

Some districts allow teachers to devise their own report cards with required adaptations for students with special needs. Figure 8-2 shows an example of a teacher-made report card for a first-grade student. The classroom teacher, the Title 1 reading teacher, and the learning support teacher all work together to assign the symbols describing the student's skill attainment. Such developmental/adaptive report cards should be matched to students' IEP learning objectives.

FIGURE 8-1 Example of an elementary report card with identification of special services

WASHINGTON SCHOOL DISTRICT
Washington Park Elementary School
Washington, Pennsylvania 15301

Name _____ Grade _____

Homeroom Teacher _____

Language Arts Teacher _____

SUBJECTS	1	Remark	2	Remark	3	Remark	4	Remark	Final
READING									
Vocabulary									
Comprehension									
Fluency									
Phonics/Skills									
LANGUAGE									
SPELLING									
HANDWRITING									
MATH									
SCIENCE									
SOCIAL STUDIES									
SOCIAL/SCIENCE (Gr. 1-2)									
HEALTH									
COMPUTER (Gr. 2-5)									
ART (Gr. 3-5)									
MUSIC									
PHYSICAL EDUCATION									
CONDUCT									
TARDIES									
ABSENCES									

1. TEACHER'S COMMENTS

2. TEACHER'S COMMENTS

3. TEACHER'S COMMENTS

4. TEACHER'S COMMENTS

GRADING SCALES/STUDENT PROFICIENCY LEVELS

A = 90% - 100% ...... Exemplary level of proficiency
B = 80% - 89.99% .... Highly acceptable level of proficiency
C = 70% - 79.99% .... Acceptable level of proficiency
D = 60% - 69.99% .... Lowest acceptable level of proficiency*
F = 0% - 59.99% ..... Unacceptable level of proficiency*

The letter grades may include + or – to further define the strengths and/or weaknesses in levels of proficiency.

In some K-5 Content areas, the following grading scale is used:

O ...... Exemplary level of proficiency
S+ .... Highly acceptable level of proficiency
S ...... Acceptable level of proficiency*
U ...... Unacceptable level of proficiency*

*Student assistance options recommended/required.

CODE OF REMARKS

1. Attendance is irregular
2. Need to improve class work
3. Lack of effort
4. Must study for tests
5. Must improve study habits
6. Must complete homework
7. Must pay attention
8. Excessive talking
9. Disruptive and uncooperative
10. Abusive to others
11. Work/grades adapted
12.
13.
14.

SPECIAL SERVICES YOUR CHILD RECEIVES:

1.____ **Speech**   3.____ **Learning Support**

2.____ **Hearing**   4.____ **Other** _____

Source: Courtesy of the Washington School District, Washington, Pennsylvania. Used by permission.

FIGURE 8-2 Example of a developmental/adaptive, teacher-made report card

Developmental / Adaptive First Grade Skills	4th Nine Weeks	Classroom Teacher: Ms. Title 1 Teacher: Mr. LS Teacher: Ms.	
Skill Evaluation Code: WA - with assistance I - inconsistent S - secure		Student's Name:	
READING	**CODE**	**MATH**	**CODE**
Can identify beginning letter(s) sounds/blends of unknown words		Number formation 1–25	
Can identify ending letter(s) sounds and parts of unknown words		Counts numbers 1–50	
Moves correctly across print (top to bottom/ left to right)		Identifies and writes numbers out of order 1–25	
Matches one to one (does not omit or insert words)		Addition of (2) numbers to sum of 10	
Checks own reading for errors and self-corrects		Recognizes + and − signs	
Solves new words using visual, meaning and structure cues		Subtraction from 10 using manipulatives	
Can read familiar books with minimal help and fluency		**DEVELOPMENTAL SKILLS**	
		Follows directions	
LANGUAGE ARTS		Works cooperatively in groups	
Letter formation - upper case/lower case		Cooperates with teachers	
Names letters and sounds		Completes tasks	
Writes 7–9 word sentence		Recognizes color words: purple, brown	
Uses capital letters and periods in sentences.		Fine motor skills	
Uses left-to-right directional movement		Uses appropriate pencil grip	
Recognizes vocabulary words outside of text		Speaks in full sentences	
		Plays cooperatively with others	
LISTENING		Copies from chalkboard	
Discriminating Sounds		Comments:	
Associating words with pictures and speech sounds with symbols			
Recall auditory stimuli			
Processing/understanding information presented auditorily			
		Promoted Assigned 1997–1998	

Source: Courtesy of the Washington School District, Washington, Pennsylvania. Used by permission.

ADAPTING GRADES FOR INDIVIDUAL ASSIGNMENTS

There are several ways to incorporate IEP learning goals in grading while still using the same report card for regular and special needs students. One way to do this is contract grading. The teacher, or the teacher and the student with special needs, work out a contract that specifies what grade a student will receive for specific accomplishments. For example, the contract might say that the student will get a B for the report period for doing a set of assignments at 80% correct and turning in all work on time. The set of assignments would be selected to match IEP learning objectives.

A second way to incorporate IEP goals while using the standard report card is to calculate the grade for the student with special needs in the same way as you calculate the grades for regular students, but to adapt each test and assignment to match IEP learning goals. IEP goals can be reflected in the length of the assignment, the substance of the assignment, or the criteria used to grade the assignment. Adapting the length of an assignment means requiring the student to study less content, for example, giving a student 10 spelling words instead of 20 or requiring a 3-page report instead of a 10-page report. Adapting the substance of the assignment means asking students to work on different content or a different level of content, for instance, allowing a book report on a chapter book instead of an adult novel. Adapting the criteria used to grade the assignment means using the IEP learning objectives to guide the grading itself (Bradley & Calvin, 1998, p. 28): "For example, if you require students to respond in complete sentences, you may accept partial sentences from a student who is currently working on writing in complete sentences as an IEP goal, without taking off points or lowering the grade. You may want to add a comment on the paper that encourages continued effort on that skill."

Tomlinson (2001) suggests individualized grading for all students as an extension of differentiated instruction. She recommends assigning achievement grades based on criteria for the tasks a student was assigned, and then noting on the report card whether the work was above, at, or below grade level.

PROVIDING FEEDBACK TO STUDENTS WITH SPECIAL NEEDS

As discussed in Chapter 6, the best written feedback to students when you grade their papers is descriptive, giving information that students can use to improve. The principle is the same when you provide feedback to students with special needs, but it may be harder to decide what sort of feedback is helpful. Students may get caught up in the "trees" of too many small corrections and never see the "forest" of information for constructing the way forward. The teacher has to find the balance between suggestion, correction, and information overload for each student. In order to illustrate the problem, I will present the case of Robert.

Robert was a fourth grader who had a mild learning disability. His teacher's approach to grading was "correcting papers." Figure 8-3 shows a corrected paper Robert brought home from school one day, in tears. It looks like the teacher was aiming for feedback in Tunstall and Gipps's (Table 6-1) category "Descriptive—Specifying Improvement." But Robert did not understand the descriptions, which were made in bold purple over his pencil writing. To him, the feedback felt like "Evaluative—Disapproving." No doubt the teacher meant well, but the effect on Robert was devastating. This paper was "the last straw" after 2 months in this classroom. Robert's parents took him out of that school and placed him in another school.

Figure 8-4 shows a writing paper Robert brought home the very next week. This was not a first draft; nevertheless, it is hard to believe that the same fourth grader who wrote

FIGURE 8-3 Robert's unsuccessful handwriting assignment

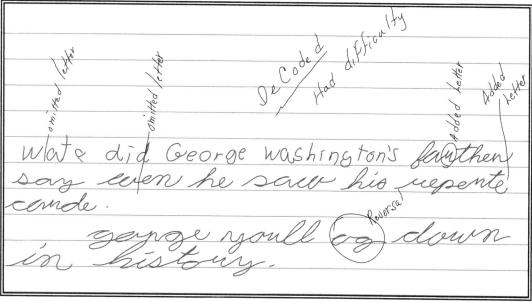

Source: Used by permission.

"George Washington" wrote "The Untrue Story" one week later! Descriptive feedback was given on rough drafts in class. On this final copy, you can see the teacher wrote an "Evaluative—Approving" comment at the bottom of the paper and gave Robert a sticker. Then she sent Robert to the principal to show her what good work he had done. The principal gave him the second sticker and said, "Robert, why don't you give yourself a grade for this paper? What do you think of your work?" So Robert drew the tiny star in the upper-right corner as his "grade" to himself. Then he took the paper home and gave it to his mother, who put it on the refrigerator door.

Not every story will be this dramatic. The point is that you will want to make sure that descriptive feedback to students with special needs communicates clearly and positively, and that it does not convey disapproval. Otherwise, students will get discouraged and not be able to use even good information you give them.

GRADING IN EARLY CHILDHOOD

As you saw in Chapter 7, kindergarten and early elementary report cards often list learning objectives and then use symbols to report categories of progress on objectives. In Chapter 9, we will consider in more detail how you as a teacher can arrive at the categorical symbols required for this kind of report card. But first, in this chapter we will consider the justification for this developmentally appropriate form of reporting in early childhood.

FIGURE 8-4 Robert's successful handwriting assignment

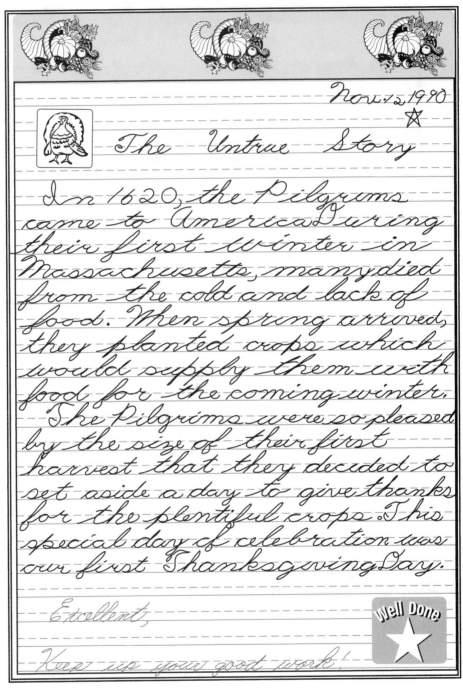

Nov. 2, 1990

The Untrue Story

In 1620, the Pilgrims came to America During their first winter in Massachusetts, many died from the cold and lack of food. When spring arrived, they planted crops which would supply them with food for the coming winter.

The Pilgrims were so pleased by the size of their first harvest that they decided to set aside a day to give thanks for the plentiful crops. This special day of celebration was our first Thanksgiving Day.

Excellent,

Keep up your good work!

Well Done

Source: Used by permission.

The National Association for the Education of Young Children (NAEYC) and the National Association of Early Childhood Specialists in State Departments of Education (NAECS/SDE) developed and adopted in 1990 Guidelines for Appropriate Curriculum Content and Assessment in Programs Serving Children Ages 3 Through 8 (NAEYC, 1990). The definition of "assessment" in that document goes well with the approach taken in this book (see Chapter 4). The NAEYC (1990, p. 1) writes:

> Assessment is the process of observing, recording, and otherwise documenting the work children do and how they do it, as a basis for a variety of educational decisions that affect the child, including planning for groups and individual children and communicating with parents.... Assessment in the service of curriculum and learning requires teachers to observe and analyze regularly what the children are doing in light of the content goals and the learning processes (p. 1).

Those 1990 guidelines recommended approaches to curriculum planning and assessment based on theories of learning and child development that emphasize that children grow and learn at different rates; that children's primary method of learning is interaction with people, objects, and other aspects of their environment; that observation of children engaged in real tasks is the most valid form of assessment of their capabilities; and that assessment over time is required for reliable conclusions about students' progress.

The early childhood period (ages 3 through 8) extends into regular schooling, from kindergarten through about the third grade. In 1990, the NAEYC grading and reporting recommendation for children in the early childhood years were (p. 15): "A regular process exists for periodic information sharing between teachers and parents about children's growth and development and performance. The method of reporting to parents does not rely on letter or numerical grades but rather provides more meaningful, descriptive information in narrative form."

In 2003, NAEYC and NAECS/SDE adopted a revised position statement for Early Childhood Curriculum, Assessment, and Program Evaluation. Perhaps not surprisingly for the post-NCLB era, more of that document relates to accountability than did the 1990 position statement. The new guidelines still emphasize using real activities as the context for assessment and multiple tools and processes assessing the whole child. These assessments should include teachers' observation records, collections of children's work, and results of performance assessment. The 2003 guidelines no longer admonish against letter or number grades. In fact, the position statement itself does not mention grading or report cards. Resources provided for use with the position statement (NAEYC & NAECS/SDE, 2003, p. 23) indicate that for Kindergarten/Primary students, "Assessment measures might include letter or numerical grades; when such grades are used, reports to parents also include narrative comments regarding children's learning across disciplines."

A comparison of the 1990 and 2003 statements shows that the meaning is nearly the same; however, the emphasis has shifted slightly. It is true that in this era of accountability, primary report cards might include letter or numerical grades. NAEYC and NAECS/SDE still advocate that descriptive comments that include information from teachers' observations of children and their work are the most valid basis for reporting young children's school achievement.

If the reporting system in place in the district in which you teach conforms to the NAEYC guidelines, you will have an easier time communicating valid information in recommended ways. But if you teach in a district where the report cards themselves do not conform to these guidelines, there are still things you can do. First, make sure you do assess young children by observation. Make sure, though, that these observations are systematic. Decide to observe something specific (e.g., using scissors), and then make a point to do it and to write down your observations. Make sure you observe all your children equally, not just when their behavior draws your attention to them. Decide ahead of time what criteria you are using in your observations, be able to describe them, and apply them consistently in all your observations.

Second, consider sharing narrative descriptions of your observations with parents on a more frequent basis than just at report card time. Early elementary children change quickly, and yet report cards go home only four to six times a year. Parents should welcome a narrative memo from the teacher on either an as-needed basis or on a regular basis, between report cards. See Chapter 10 for more suggestions about narrative reporting.

Third, if your early childhood report cards do not provide space for narrative comments, consider approaching your school administration with these guidelines and suggesting a revision. Many districts are revising report cards these days. If you are professional in your methods, and if you work with the other early elementary teachers in your district, you may find you are able to make needed changes. Be careful, though. Just because a report card lists learning objectives and developmentally appropriate categories or narrative comments doesn't mean it's a good report card! The contents of the report card must be carefully selected to match your curriculum, which should itself be developmentally appropriate. The contents of the report card must be carefully worded to communicate clearly with parents.

GRADING IN ELEMENTARY AND SECONDARY CLASSROOMS

As you may have concluded by now, the appropriateness of what is reported begins with the appropriateness of instructional goals, learning activities, and assessments that comprise the ongoing work in your classroom. This principle may be less evident for those students who do not have special needs or are early childhood students, but it is nonetheless true. All teachers, even in upper elementary, middle, and high school, need to pay attention to the developmental needs of their students. The way to build this into assessment and instruction is to plan developmentally appropriate learning goals and instructional activities and assess their achievement with valid and reliable measures. If an assessment matches an instructional goal (validity), and the instructional goal was developmentally appropriate, then the assessment should be, too.

As students reach the levels where subjects begin to be differentiated on report cards, typically late middle and high school, the subject listings themselves indicate developmental level. For example, an eighth grader whose report card has a line for Algebra I is clearly doing advanced work. The work of a senior in high school whose report card lists a "B" for Basic Math will be interpreted differently from that of a senior whose report card lists a "B" for Advanced Calculus.

CONCLUSION

Developmental appropriateness is built into assessments by starting with appropriate instructional goals, then following through with appropriate instruction and assessment. Reporting the results appropriately includes clearly communicating what students are expected to have learned and how well they have done so. Concern for appropriate assessment and communication is absolutely essential at all age and skill levels.

Two particular areas in which concern about the developmental appropriateness of assessment, grading, and reporting presents difficulties for teachers are grading students in special education and grading early childhood students. In special education, recommendations have been assembled from research about grading practices and recommendations of special educators. In early childhood, the professional organization has presented clear guidelines.

EXERCISES

1. Select an instructional objective for a subject and grade level with which you are familiar. Plan instructional activities and a test or performance assessment (whichever is appropriate; see Chapter 4) to assess students' achievement. Then describe how you would modify the instruction and assessment for a student with special needs. To do this, you will first need to describe the particular student's needs. If you are working in a field placement, work with your cooperating teacher to do this with a real assignment and a real student with special needs.
2. Interview a teacher in a regular classroom. Ask about his or her particular experiences modifying various assignments and/or grading policies for students with special needs. Since the teacher's experiences will depend very much on the instructional objective, the particular students' needs, and the school's grading policies, you will need to ask about these factors as well. Write a brief report about the context and the teacher's experiences.
3. In groups of three or four, share your interview results. What similarities did you find? What differences?
4. Obtain copies of the kindergarten, first-, second-, and third-grade report forms from the school district in which you live or work. What kind of grading system is used? Are there places for narrative comments?
5. Interview an early childhood teacher. Ask about his or her approach to grading and the system required. How does the teacher record observations of the children? How does he or she communicate with parents other than via report cards?

Note: These are intended as "short" exercises at the end of the chapter. See Part 3 Exercises on page 189 for additional exercises

Developing Skills at Combining Grades into Marks for Report Cards

KEY CONCEPTS

- Calculating one mark for a report card from a set of individual grades—constructing a *composite* grade—by definition masks the details that would be available if you could report everything. The challenge is to create the composite in such a way that it is as true as possible to the set of information on which it is based.
- The rules you use to put grades together into a composite mark for report cards should depend on two things: (a) the meaning you want the composite grade to convey, and (b) the type of scales or scores used for the various individual grades.
- To arrive at a categorical grade (e.g., Unsatisfactory/Satisfactory), you need decision rules about how to categorize student performance.
- One way to think about letter-grading scales is as "mega-rubrics." This system works best if most of your individual grades are also done with rubrics. An appropriate method for combining rubrics is to use the median.
- Another way to think about letter-grading scales is as cut points along the familiar "percentage" scale. This system works best if most of your individual grades are also done with percents. Two methods for combining these, using points or using percents, are mathematically equivalent.
- Plan ahead about how you will deal with failure—and with failure to try. Different methods of handling failure, Fs, and zeros can lead to very different final grades.
- Computers are helpful for recording and storing grade information and for calculating final grades. Gradebook software is sometimes provided for teachers by their school districts. Regular spreadsheet packages are useful as well.

At the end of a report period, typically every 6 or 9 weeks, teachers must report a "grade" or mark in whatever format the school's policies and procedures require. Most of the time there is one mark per subject. Some report card formats have spaces for both an achievement and an effort mark, and some even have separate subcategories for various skills or objectives. You can review the kinds of things that are likely to appear on report cards in Chapter 7.

Even when there are several different subheadings for one subject, however, chances are you will be combining several grades from various occasions into one mark for each subheading. Assessment in most classroom settings is based on a "summing up" rather than a "checking up" model (see Chapter 5). The reason for this is that in most cases, you will have taught (and students will have learned) a variety of instructional goals or learning targets. You will be called upon to furnish a report card grade that summarizes the students' achievement on the set of achievement targets for the report period. Assuming you're sure you have included all the right achievement targets, combining more grades will give you a more reliable picture of student achievement than would one or a few grades. This works up to a point; after about 10 grades you don't add much reliability to the mix.

The main goal of this chapter is for you to understand, and develop a repertoire, of different methods that you can use to put a set of individual grades together into one mark at the end of a report period. The principle is that the one mark should be the best representation it can be of your evaluation of student achievement in that area. It will not be perfect, and it will not be detailed, but it should be accurate, and it should lead parents and students to get an appropriate idea of the student's performance. You should give students and parents other sources of information in addition to report card grades (see Chapter 10).

A composite grade is a summary, and as with all summaries the object is to gloss over the details and provide a quick statement of the main point. So that is what you should ask yourself when you go about deciding how you will arrive at your report card grades: What is the main point about this student's level of achievement? The second question follows from the first: How can I best convey this main point?

The information you need to convey the main point about the student's achievement is a summary of the student's achievement on the set of learning goals for the report period. The key is that it be a meaningful whole. For example, suppose you meant for the students to learn a set of facts and concepts about plants, and also to demonstrate that they could grow a plant by making sure it had water, light, and nutrients. The Science grade for that report period should combine information about student knowledge of the facts and concepts with information about how the student could apply it by growing the plants. Each part of the grade should carry the amount of weight you intend it to carry. More important concepts should carry more weight in the final grade, and less important concepts should carry less weight.

In scoring terminology, individual grades that are combined into one mark (called a *composite*) for report cards are called *components*. How you combine and weight various components of a composite score depends in part on what kinds of scores the components are. Tests may have yielded percentages, whereas projects may have yielded either grades (A, B, C, D, F) or rubrics (4, 3, 2, 1). Observations may have yielded category descriptions (Satisfactory Progress, Needs Improvement).

It is very important to think about the nature of different scoring scales before you put them together. If the components are grades on projects that have been scored with rubrics, they are the kind of ordered categories (e.g., 4, 3, 2, 1) that don't lend themselves to percent-based scoring. A four-point rubric, for example, would yield A (100%), C (75%), F (50%), F (25%) if you made percentages out of the "points." Yet a 3 on a 4-point rubric may describe fairly good performance, and a 2 may describe minimal but still passing performance, so the percents don't communicate the appropriate message. Test scores and other point-based grades are on a different kind of scale, and often can be meaningfully combined as percents. Grades that are meaningful individually can still result in a report card grade that misrepresents student achievement if you do not combine them in ways that take into account the nature of the scale you used. You also need to think about the relative contribution each component should make to the final grade. Some of the individual grades may be more important than others for describing students' overall achievement for the report period.

ARRIVING AT A CATEGORICAL GRADE

In some cases, what is required is a categorical grade like Satisfactory/Unsatisfactory, or "Satisfactory/Making" "Progress/Unsatisfactory." Sometimes the words themselves are used, and sometimes a symbol system indicates the categories. Categorical grading is most often used for elementary school report cards (see Chapter 7 for some examples).

Such categorical systems almost always are ordered; that is, the categories are ranked. For example, "Satisfactory" is above "Unsatisfactory." If there is a "Making Progress" level, it is between Satisfactory and Unsatisfactory. So, these ordered categories are much like rubrics. We will discuss them separately in this text because this kind of elementary school categorical grading may rely more heavily on teacher observation than the rubric grading discussed in the next section. There may not be a set of assignments that were graded and need merely to be properly weighted and averaged.

Your task in assigning this kind of mark for a report card is actually an exercise in defining categories and specifying how you will know which one a student falls into. Your criteria for categorizing students should be based on learning goals for the report period. Let's use as an example the kindergarten report card in Figure 7-2. One of the Reading Comprehension subheadings reads, "Can orally retell a story in sequence." The choices are as follows:

* (commendable achievement in kindergarten)
+ (acceptable achievement in kindergarten)
√ (making progress toward acceptable achievement)
− (area of concern)

The points on this scale are not just evenly spaced divisions on a yardstick. In order to grade students on this scale, you need to define what counts as "acceptable" oral retelling of a story. How many times, how accurately, and with how complicated a story should the student retell a story for it to be acceptable? How much better than that before it's commendable?

Also notice that this scale has two different kinds of points below acceptable. "Making Progress" implies that kindergarten-level achievement is possible for the student. That must mean the student is "close" to acceptable. How close? How will you know? "Area of Concern" implies that the student has a long way to go before acceptable achievement. How long? Again, how will you know?

A subheading like this on a report card means that oral retelling of stories was a curricular goal, and should have been a classroom instructional goal, during the report period. One good way, then, to describe student achievement for each of the categories is to base it on classroom observation of performance. If you have asked each student to retell at least three stories over the course of the report period, perhaps "acceptable" performance might be that each one was retold mostly in order, with any omissions or misplaced events not significant to the meaning of the story. Is three enough? Do you need four? How about four with acceptable performance on at least three? The answer is that it depends on your students and the standards you want to set.

"Commendable" performance might be retelling the stories mostly in order, and in more complete detail, with any minor errors not significant to the meaning of the story. How detailed is "detailed"? You decide, based on your school's standards. "Making Progress" might be that a student can correctly retell some stories in sequence, but cannot be counted upon to do so. "Area of Concern" might mean that the student still does not seem to have a concept of sequence when retelling anything. The definitions might be more stringent than these, or more lenient. They might be based on a specified number of stories or they might be more open ended. It would be best to at least create an "at least" rule (e.g., at least three stories) for the sake of reliability. You don't want to give a grade based on too few observations—anything can happen once or twice!

My best advice is to write down your decision rules for defining categories. This will lend consistency to your grading, so that you are more likely to treat each student in a similar manner. It will also give you a ready answer for parents or students who ask about your grading, especially about achievement that is graded below "acceptable" levels.

I recently had a conversation with a kindergarten teacher who had assigned her grades using the scale of VG (Very Good), S (Satisfactory), and N (Needs Improvement) for a variety of skills listed on her district's kindergarten report card. She had used the report card in a holistic manner, rating each of her students VG, S, or N on the various skills based on her informal observations throughout the report period. Parents and even some other teachers had asked her how she decided on the grades, and she felt at a loss as to what to tell them. Yet, she was fairly confident that her yearlong observations had allowed her to accurately categorize her students' skills.

I asked her if she could tell me what she looked for in deciding whether a student was VG, S, or N on any particular skill, and she said yes, easily. I encouraged her to write down the decision rules she obviously had created, so that she could share them with parents and teachers if needed. This is a validity issue; the clearer the intended meaning, the more likely the grade is to be able to communicate. The teacher appreciated this idea; she envisioned it being useful for talking with parents and other teachers. Written, explicit descriptions have another advantage, too—it's easier to apply your criteria consistently from student to student when they are written down.

Be careful not to mistake the current interest in "high standards" for a need to hold out for perfection. A decision rule that a student will *always* do something perfectly, 100% of the time, is a decision rule that will not get much use! Think about what perfection means in your own life and work. You would be a "perfect" reteller of kindergarten stories, right? Are you sure? You'd never make a mistake? Better definitions of "perfection" for top-level grades are like those used in the previous example: "small omissions that don't impair demonstration of understanding of the main point of the story" instead of "no omissions."

I also suggested to the kindergarten teacher that she make some of the student observations on which she based her grades systematic. In other words, as she observes her students she would record her observations on paper. For example, she may observe each of her kindergartners counting to 10, or following directions, or whatever the skill is. There are two reasons for using a systematic approach. One, the human memory is notoriously faulty, and a teacher has millions of details to keep track of. It would be easy to misremember an observation of student performance. Two, keeping some written records makes it more likely that she'll observe each student equally, not just the ones who are calling for attention.

ARRIVING AT A LETTER GRADE VIA RUBRICS

If most of the grades in a report period are from rubrics, whether numerical (4, 3, 2, 1) or in the form of letter grades (A, B, C, D, F), just "averaging" the rubrics may not work very well. We have already seen that a 4, 3, 2, 1 rubric turned into "percents" and then grades is at best an A, C, F, F scale. "Percents" is in quotation marks because rubrics are ordinal (rank) scales that shouldn't be used with percents. But even if they were, the resulting grades would not give good information about student performance.

Some projects or other lengthy assignments are graded with a letter grade. For example, a student may get a B on a term paper. There may not be a point or percent scale; the B may be a judgment according to criteria for what a B paper should look like. In effect, this is using letter grades as rubric levels, only letters instead of numbers label the performance levels. One method of writing rubrics (admittedly a compromise because grades are needed) is to define the performance expected at each grade level. So instead of 4, 3, 2, 1 or 6, 5, 4, 3, 2, 1, or any other short scale of numbers, you write descriptions of the level of performance required for A, B, C, D, F (or whatever grading scale you need to use). Thus you describe, "What does A-level performance look like?", B-level, and so on.

THE MEDIAN METHOD FOR CALCULATING REPORT CARD GRADES

If most of your report period assignments have been graded with letters or other rubrics whose levels can be defined as grades, then one good way to put them together for a composite report card grade is to use the median of the set of individual grades. The median is simply the "middle" grade. It is the best way to calculate "typical" performance for a set of grades that are on short, ranked scales. It is also an excellent way to capture typical performance when there are few individual assignment grades from the report period (e.g., one test, one project, and one report).

Here's how it works. Decide what set of grades, taken together, represent achievement on all the important learning outcomes for the report period. Then decide whether each grade is worth the same amount, or whether some grades should count more heavily toward the final average. Line up each student's grades in order, from highest to lowest. If a grade for an individual assignment is to count double, list it twice; if it's to count triple, list it three times. Then count to the middle to find the median grade. If there is an odd number of grades, the median (middle) grade will be one of the grades on the list. If there is an even number of grades, the median will be between the middle two grades.

Table 9-1 gives an example of three students. Notice that there were five grades for the report period, but two of them—the test and the paper—count double. This decision should have been based on what learning goals the test and paper covered and how that fit with the learning goals for the whole report period. In this case, the test covered the main facts and concepts and the paper was the main vehicle for students to show they could apply the facts and concepts.

Let's work with Maria's grade first. Most of her grades were Bs, but she failed a quiz. Line up the grades for Maria (putting two Bs into the lineup for the test and two for the paper, to account for their double weights) and we have

B   B   B   B   B   F

The median (middle) grade is a B. With the median method, extreme scores (on both ends of the scale, extremely high or extremely low) impact the average to a lesser degree than with some other methods. This can be beneficial when you are calculating classroom grades, since a lone F in a set of otherwise good grades may not reflect genuine achievement level but rather some other issue. Using the median does take into account the low grade (unlike some methods that drop low grades and therefore don't count them at all); it's just that the median is not overly affected by extreme scores.

Let's try Ben next. He had As on his tests and quizzes, a B on his paper, and a C on his project. Listing the test and paper grades twice and lining them up in order, we have

A   A   A   A   B   B   C

				Paper		Report
TABLE 9-1		**Test (counts**		**(counts**		**Card**
Illustration of the	**Student**	**double)**	**Quiz #1**	**Quiz #2**	**double)**	**Project**	**Grade**
median method							
for calculating	Maria	B	B	F	B	B	B
report period	Ben	A	A	A	B	C	A
grades	Juan	C	B	D	C	A	C

Ben's median grade is A. Can you find the median of Juan's grades and justify that his report card grade should be a C?

There will not always be an odd number of grades. If there is an even number of grades, the median is the grade between the middle two. So the median of A, A, A, B is A, since it is the grade between the second and third grade, which are both As. The median of A, A, C, C is B, since it is the grade between the second and third grades, which are an A and a C. The median of A, A, B, B could be A– or B+ if plusses and minuses are part of the grading system. If not, make a rule about how you will round up or down and apply it consistently. I suggest rounding up, for reasons both mathematical and instructional.

COMBINING PERCENT SCORES AND RUBRICS OR GRADES

The median method is a good way to solve the "precision problem" some teachers encounter. Precision is a mathematical concept about the level of detail present in a measure. We measure height to the nearest inch, sometimes even to the nearest half inch. So I might say that my friend is 64 inches tall, or even 64.5 inches tall. I would not say that my friend is 64.5378 inches tall. We can't measure height that precisely!

The precision problem shows up in grading when some of the individual grades are on percentage scales and some are on rubric style scales. Percentage grades are more precise than rubrics because there are so many more levels (100, actually 101 if you count zero!) than there are for rubrics grades (e.g., there are five levels in the A, B, C, D, F scale).

Say you were trying to arrive at a report card grade for a student, and you had five individual grades for the student. Two were test scores of 86 and 92 on a percentage scale. You also had an A and two Bs for three short writing assignments. But what kind of A and Bs? Was the A equivalent to a 93? Or to a 98? You don't know. You can't go back and "add in" precision because you can't reinvent information (add precision) where there isn't any. But you can generalize from more precision to less. You could say that the test scores were a B (the 86%) and an A (the 92%), respectively. All together, then, you have an A and a B for the tests and an A and two more Bs for the writing assignments:

A   A   B   B   B

The middle grade is a B. If the tests and papers were all supposed to carry the same weight in the final grade, then the report card grade would be a B. Can you figure out what the final grade would be if both of the tests were worth twice what the writing assignments were? How about if the papers were worth twice as much as the tests?

ARRIVING AT A LETTER GRADE VIA POINTS

Sometimes district grading policies describe percent ranges for grades, as in the report card in Figure 7-3. This is more common at the middle and high school levels than for elementary schools. Districts with "percent" policies—knowingly or unknowingly—make it difficult for teachers to use rubrics in their work. Prescribing percent ranges for grades assumes that most of the individual component grades that are combined for the final grades will be recorded in the form of points or percentages. If only letter or rubric grades were recorded, there isn't enough precision or detail to identify 101 (0 to 100) different levels of achievement.

But often the precision in percentages is more apparent than real. Can you *realistically* distinguish 101 different levels of student accomplishment on most classroom tasks? Typically, the answer to this question will be no. Also more apparent than real is the appearance of rigor or higher standards. A scale of A = 94−100%, B = 87−93%, and so on, is not necessarily any more rigorous than a scale of A = 90−100%, B = 80−89%, and so on. The key question is, "Percent of *what?*" On a difficult assignment, 90% correct may represent a higher achievement level than 94% correct on an easy assignment.

Keep all of these cautions in mind, and one more. Strange but true, I spoke with the superintendent of a district that for several years had recorded both the letter grades its high school students received on their report cards (A, B, C, D, F) and the percentages on which they were based (95, 88, etc.). Over time, some of the averages became different! For example, the same student might have a B average in math from letter grades A, B, B, B over the four report periods in a year, but have received a 99, 89, 88, and 89, making her percentage average a 91. So, the same student would have a B average in math on one set of school records and a 91 (in the A range) on another! The point here is to decide what method you are going to use, justify why that is the method you chose, and then stick with it.

LETTER GRADES AS AVERAGES OF PERCENTAGE GRADES

One way to do percentage grading is to record each individual grade as a percent of 100 and then weight if necessary. If you record each assignment's grade as a percent and simply take the average of those percents, each assignment contributes equally to the final grade. Sometimes, that's what you want. If it's not, multiply grades you want to

				Paper		Report
Student	**Test (counts double)**	**Quiz #1**	**Quiz #2**	**(counts double)**	**Project**	**Card Grade**
Maria	87%	88%	52%	83%	81%	80% B
Ben	94%	96%	97%	83%	78%	89% B
Juan	76%	82%	64%	78%	96%	79% C

TABLE 9-2

Illustration of the percentage method for calculating report period grades

count more by the factor you decide should reflect their importance. For example, if you want project grades to count twice as much as test grades, multiply the project scores by 2 before averaging them with the test grades.

Table 9-2 illustrates using percentages to calculate grades. In this example, let's consider the grading scale A = 90−100%, B = 80−89%, C = 70−79%, D = 60−69%, F = 59% or less. We'll use the same three students, with the same general level of performance, as we did for the median method in Table 9-1. We'll also weight the assignments as in Table 9-1: The test and paper will count twice as much as the quizzes and the project in the final grade.

Notice that sometimes the various methods lead to the same final grade, and sometimes to a different one. Which is the "real" grade? Be careful how you answer that question. Remember that grades are not "natural" in the same way that a tree is natural. Grades are constructed by teachers (and sometimes students) based on rules of evidence *they invented* for measuring student achievement. The "real" grade is the one that most clearly conveys the kind of achievement information you intend it to. So, your scoring schemes or grading rubrics and your rules for combining individual grades into a report card summary grade are all part of your definition of achievement. This is why it's so important to be clear about what you are doing, both in your own mind and in communicating with students and parents.

Let's try the arithmetic. Multiply each of the "double" grades by two. Of course, do this for every student's test and paper. This amounts to multiplying each score in the test and paper columns, respectively, by 2, and leaving the others as is. A spreadsheet or gradebook program makes it easy to multiply all the figures in a given column by 2 (or 3, or whatever weight you have chosen). Divide by the maximum possible percentage points available, which is 700: 200 (the test) plus 100 (quiz #1) plus 100 (quiz #2) plus 200 (the paper) plus 100 (the project). So, here's Maria:

$$[(87 \times 2) + 88 + 52 + (83 \times 2) + 81] \div 700 =$$

$$561 \div 700 =$$

.8014 which rounds to

.80 or 80%

Let's try Ben:

$$[(94 \times 2) + 96 + 97 + (83 \times 2) + 78] \div 700 =$$

$625 \div 700 =$

.8928 which rounds to

.89 or 89%

This 89% translates to a B on the scale we are using. Remember that when we used the median method, Ben got an A. But notice that using percents in Table 9-2 added some precision that wasn't there when we just used letters in Table 9-1. Supposing Ben's B paper had been an 88 instead of an 83:

$$[(94 \times 2) + 96 + 97 + (88 \times 2) + 78] \div 700 = 635 \div 700 = .907$$

This rounds to .91 or 91%, an A on the scale we are using. So which is it? Should Ben get an A or a B on his report card? The answer depends on what the assignments were, and whether you really can make the fine distinctions that a percentage scale implies. These decisions should be made ahead of time and clearly communicated to students, too—not engineered after the fact to make grades "come out" a certain way.

It's your turn. Can you do the arithmetic for Juan's report card grade and show why he received a 79%?

LETTER GRADES AS PERCENTAGE OF TOTAL POSSIBLE POINTS

Another method for figuring grades when percentages are required is mathematically equivalent to the percentage method described above. If you consider each individual assignment to be worth a certain number of points, then record the number of points each student earned for that assignment, you can add up the total points each student earned for the report period, divide by the total possible points, and arrive at a percentage to use for the report card grade, either reported as a percent or converted to a letter by the district's or teacher's scale.

The relative contribution of assignments to the final average depends on the total number of possible points. For example, a test worth 100 points would count four times as much in a final grade as a quiz worth 25 points. A project worth 200 points would count twice as much as the test (and eight times as much as the quiz).

Table 9-3 illustrates what the grade book would look like using the point system for similar achievement to that in Table 9-2. The test and the paper are recorded as worth 100 points, whereas the quizzes and project are worth 50 points each. Since 100 is twice as many points as 50, the test and the paper count twice as heavily in the final grade as the quizzes and project, as before. Add up the total points and divide by the total possible points (350), and you get the same final grades as in Table 9-2.

Since the percentage method and the points method are mathematically equivalent, it wouldn't make any difference which one you chose if arithmetic were your only concern. However, there are some instructional and planning considerations that lead me to recommend using the percentage method rather than the point method. The most important of these is that a teacher might be tempted to "engineer" points that might compromise the validity of the information you get from an assessment. Suppose, for example, that you assign a term paper with a scoring scheme that reasonably allocates 45 points to various aspects of the research, content, organization, and writing, and

	Test (counts double)	Quiz #1	Quiz #2	Paper (counts double)	Project	Total Points	Report Card Grade (Total Points ÷ 350)
TABLE 9-3 Illustration of the point method for calculating report period grades							
Student							
Maria	87	44	26	83	41	281	80 B
Ben	94	48	49	83	39	313	89 B
Juan	76	41	32	78	48	275	79 C
Maximum	100	50	50	100	50		

that these points are in proper balance to one another (say, 30 for research and content and 15 for organization and writing, making the substance worth twice as much as the mechanics). Suppose, further, that you "needed" the assignment to be worth 50 points. You might be tempted to add 5 points for factors you didn't need to assess (like having a pretty cover), or to increase points for other factors and throw off the intended balance in the grade, just to get the number you needed. This would compromise validity, as we discussed in Chapters 4 and 5. It would be much better to allocate the 45 points according to the scoring scheme you could justify, and then record the student's score as a percentage of the 45 points.

THE INFLUENCE OF ZEROS IN POINT-BASED GRADING

One particularly sticky issue for point-based grading is the influence of zeros. This isn't an issue for the median method, but it is for any of the point-based methods because of the unequal size of the grading scale categories and the effect of that on averages. If the A, B, C, and D categories are all about the same number of percentage points wide, no matter whether that's 6 or 7 or 10, and the F category is 60 or 70 points wide, there is a much bigger difference between a "high F" and a "low F" than between high and low As, Bs, Cs, or Ds. So, variation in the Failure category can have devastating effects. A zero or any extremely low score will pull down an average dramatically.

Let's look again at the case of Juan, the third student in our running example. Table 9-4 reminds us that in the scenario so far, Juan got a C (76%) on his test. So his final grade is a C:

$$[(76 \times 2) + 82 + 64 + (78 \times 2) + 96] \div 700 = 550 \div 700 = .79 \text{ or } 79\%$$

Suppose he failed the test, receiving a grade of 58%, which is a "high" F:

$$[(58 \times 2) + 82 + 64 + (78 \times 2) + 96] \div 700 = 514 \div 700 = .73 \text{ or } 73\%$$

His grade is still a C. Although he failed the test, he did get a mixture of A, B, C, and D on the other assignments, so the C seems reasonable. But assume Juan's failing grade

TABLE 9-4

Illustration of the
effect of zeros
on report period
grades

Student	Test (counts double)	Quiz #1	Quiz #2	Paper (counts double)	Project	Report Card Grade
Juan (C on test)	76%	82%	64%	78%	96%	79% C
Juan ("high" F on test)	58%	82%	64%	78%	96%	73% C
Juan ("low" F on test)	30%	82%	64%	78%	96%	65% D
Juan (zero on test)	0%	82%	64%	78%	96%	57% F

was dramatically lower than that, say 30%. Now, although he still got the same mixture of letter grades (an F on the test and the same grades for the other assignments), his final grade is a D:

$$[(30 \times 2) + 82 + 64 + (78 \times 2) + 96] \div 700 = 458 \div 700 = .65 \text{ or } 65\%$$

If Juan had refused to take the test, or had missed the test as a result of an unexcused absence from school, perhaps he would have been assigned a zero. Two problems arise, one with the achievement measured by the test and then by extension a problem with the final grade. First, if the test was supposed to measure achievement on a set of instructional goals or objectives, zero sounds like Juan knew nothing. But, in actuality, we are unclear whether Juan knew anything or not. The zero doesn't represent a test score; rather, it indicates a possible behavior problem. What *looks* like achievement information in fact tells us nothing about Juan's actual achievement.

By extension, then, we have a problem with the meaning of the final grade. If this zero gets averaged in, Juan will fail for the report period, even though he got passing grades on everything but this one test, which is an F:

$$[(0 \times 2) + 82 + 64 + (78 \times 2) + 96] \div 700 = 398 \div 700 = .57 \text{ or } 57\%$$

This F will be interpreted to mean failure to achieve the set of learning goals for the report period.

Try substituting a zero for any of the individual assignment grades in Table 9-2, then recalculating. Note how one zero can cause the final grade to drop dramatically, even though other performance stays the same.

There are a couple of potential solutions to this problem; however, each solution raises other issues. One solution is to use the median method to grade, so the effects of an F are the same as the effects of any other grade. This solution makes the most sense *if* the grading policy and your instructional intentions support a rubric-based grading style. Another solution is to differentiate between "scoring failure and scoring failure to try" (Brookhart, 1999a). Use the percent for students who fail an assignment by getting a low grade (e.g., 58%), but instead of assigning a zero (0%) for missing achievement information—whatever the reason—calculate the final percentage grade without the missed assignment. Adjust the number you will use as the base (the denominator) of the percentage accordingly.

Some educators would not recommend this second method because it seems to condone skipping assignments. Others would object on the grounds that the grade was supposed to reflect a set of objectives, and information about some of those objectives is missing if a score is missing. Whether or not these considerations outweigh the practice of reporting only the actual achievement information you have depends on your grading purpose and policy and the policy of your school or district.

REVIEWING BORDERLINE GRADES

It should come as no surprise that educational measurement is not "perfect," not 100% accurate all the time. Test scores, rubric levels, or any other methods of judging student achievement are subject to error, even when both teacher and students are careful. Consider, for example, the tests you have taken as a student. Have you ever gotten a test back to go over in class and found you had chosen the wrong answer for a question when you actually knew the correct answer? Conversely, have you ever guessed on a test answer—a complete shot in the dark—and found that you were correct—that your test score gave you credit for more knowledge than you actually had? These are common examples of measurement error, when the score is a bit higher or lower than your true level of achievement.

Extend this principle to combining grades from individual assignments to make a composite report card grade. Any one of the individual grades might be a bit higher or lower than warranted by the student's true achievement level. Put them together and the report card grade can be expected to also include some measurement error.

This doesn't pose a problem if a student's grade is in the middle of the range for a letter grade. For example, if the student's final average is 96, but his true achievement should be 95, the student is still an A student. But what about borderline grades? Suppose a student has a report period average of 90: Is the student's true achievement level 90? 91? or 89—in which case the apparent A student is really a B student.

You can't remove measurement error; it's a fact of life. But you can approach it thoughtfully and put into place ahead of time policies to deal with it. There are several different approaches.

- **No borderline review.** One approach to removing measurement error is to acknowledge that, although a grade may not exactly pinpoint the level of student achievement, it is the best estimate available. It's an estimate that is as likely to be a little high as a little low. Realize that, in the long run, the grades will average out. The advantage to this method is that students know the final grade is "final," which may eliminate some disagreement.
- **Borderline review, "raises only" policy.** Some teachers review only borderline grades that are at the top of a grading category; for example, a student whose

average is 89 may be reviewed. A teacher who supports this method might comment, "I might raise a grade for a deserving student, but I would never lower one." Although this method is reasonable, there is one important principle to remember if you use it: review additional *achievement* information. If you raised the grade of a student whose achievement was a high B but who tried really hard, you are mixing achievement and effort and diluting the meaning of the grade. Find some additional information about achievement of the same learning goals the grade is intended to reflect. For example, look at the student's class work or other assignments not ordinarily counted in the final grade. Ask yourself, "Is this other work at the B level or the A level?," and adjust the final grade accordingly. If you do borderline review, make it a *real* review, not an automatic raise.

- **Borderline review.** A true borderline review would look at students who fell both just above and below a cutoff. For example, if the 89-Bs are reviewed as potential As, then the 91-As are reviewed as potential Bs, again using additional *achievement* information. Very few teachers use this method because of the potential difficulties it causes for the teacher's role as student advocate.

ELECTRONIC METHODS: GRADEBOOK PACKAGES, WEB-BASED SYSTEMS

Whichever method you use for combining individual assignment grades into report card marks or grades, a computer can make storing data and calculating final grades easier. Some teachers simply use the spreadsheet programs available as regular office software to do their grades.

A number of teachers use personal gradebook programs, which are typically a preprogrammed spreadsheet that is already set up to enter classes and student names, identify assignments and enter grades or scores, calculate various kinds of averages, and print reports. If you use a gradebook program, make sure you find out what kind of calculations it performs. You should be able to find out what the program does by default, and be able to change calculation methods to suit your needs. There are all sorts of methods for calculating final averages. Some of these methods take into account student standing in the class (for example, by considering the standard deviation of each assignment's scores), which is not the kind of grading recommended in this book. Each method suits some purposes well; the key is to make sure the method selected is really the method you want to use. Also make sure that the weighting method used matches your overall objectives.

Some districts supply gradebook programs for their teachers, or even require the use of a particular computer program. You will need to comply with district policies; nevertheless, you still should be able to adjust how the final grades are computed to match your learning targets and grading and communication intentions.

Some districts are exploring ways for parents to be able to check on their students' grades via the Internet. These Web-based methods have policies as to who has access to what information, typically requiring users to have an account and login information. Just as important, Web-based systems should have been subjected to some thoughtful reflection about any grading assumptions underlying them. For example, if the Web allows access to running averages during the semester, a "summing up" model is implied, and it also means it would be useful to know how many assignments with what weights are intended for the whole report period. This works better for some kinds of subjects and grade levels than others.

CONCLUSION

This chapter has given you some tools and options for combining various individual assignment grades into a composite mark or grade for the report period. Your task is to learn how to use each of these methods, and then consider how you will grade each different class that you teach. In general, it is recommended that you make a policy for each class and then stick with it. For example, if you teach tenth-grade World Cultures all year, your grading method should remain the same for each report period within that class. But you might use a different method for another class that you teach, even in the same semester. Or if you teach kindergarten, you might use a grading method based on descriptions of performance for various categories used on the kindergarten report card. You might use a different method if you teach another grade level the following year, especially if there is a different report card.

In any case, think about grading principles as you adopt your method:

- What are my students' learning goals?
- What evidence will best reflect student achievement of these goals?
- What is the best way to summarize that evidence for the grade I must supply?

Finally, although this will satisfy the need to supply a report card grade, ask yourself if there is any additional information about student achievement you would like to convey to students and parents. If there is, decide how you might communicate that information: letters to parents, phone calls, conferences with students and/or parents, sending work home, sending annotated work home.

All of the methods of arriving at final grades explored in this chapter may be described as criterion referenced. Student performance level is compared to a standard in order to assign grades. Each student's grade is calculated independently of his or her classmates' grades. Theoretically, it would be possible to have a class of all As, all Fs, or any distribution in between. These methods are recommended because they comport with the model of instruction (see Figure 4-1) that says assessment should reflect achievement of learning goals, not student standing in the class. Methods that reflect students' achievements relative to one another are called norm referenced and are not recommended for classroom grading. The purpose of grades should be to communicate how well students have met their learning goals, not whether they met them more or less well than others in their class. Readers who would like to learn how to calculate grades using norm-referenced methods can find information in Oosterhof (1987) and Ory and Ryan (1993).

EXERCISES

1. Imagine that you are a kindergarten teacher in the district that uses the report card in Figure 7-2.
   a. Select one of the Reading and Language Arts or Math categories. Describe what sort of evidence you would need to assign one of the symbols at the end of a semester. Invent information about three different students and tell how you would arrive at symbols for each. Explain how your process would result in valid and reliable information.
   b. Describe what sort of evidence you would need to assign one of the symbols at the end of a semester for each of the Work Habits categories. Explain how your process would result in valid and reliable information.

2. Imagine that you are a high school teacher in the district that uses the report card in Figure 7-4. You teach a course called American History to eleventh-grade students. You have used percentage grading on two quizzes, a test, a project, and homework. Use the gradebook that follows to answer questions 2a, 2b, and 2c.

Student	Quiz #1	Quiz #2	Home-work #1	Home-work #2	Home-work #3	Home-work #4	Test	Project
Albert	85	75	78	83	69	65	77	74
Rhonda	95	96	94	96	96	99	100	92
Devonna	78	83	78	79	76	45	82	90
Cory	64	66	78	80	85	75	69	73
Paul	87	89	93	92	97	98	95	92

   a. Based on the content of your instructional goals and your emphases in class, you wish to count the test and the project equally, and the homework all together as one "grade" that counts the same as the test. You wish to count the quizzes half as much as the test. Calculate the final grades for each student, using the scale 90–100% = A, 80–89% = B, 70–79% = C, 60–69% = D, 0–59% = F.
   b. Choose another set of relative weights for these assignments. Describe your weighting decisions and then calculate the final grades for each student.
   c. You consider the homework to be practice and do not wish to count it in the final grade. The test and the project count equally, and the quizzes count half as much as the test. Calculate the final grades for each student. Then do a borderline review for the student who falls just below a grade cutoff, using the homework grades as additional information about the student's achievement. What would you do for this student's final grade?

3. You are an English teacher, and it's time to calculate report period grades. This period, you have given: two tests, for which you have recorded percentage grades; two in-class writing assignments, which you graded according to a rubric with levels for A, B, C, D, and F; and a larger out-of-class paper that you also graded with letter grades. You wish the tests and in-class writing assignments to count equally,

and want the paper to count double. How can you combine marks that are on two different scales (percents and letters) in order to get a measure of students' achievement that reflects these emphases? Calculate final grades for the students in the gradebook below.

Student	Test #1	Test #2	Writing #1	Writing #2	Paper
Alice	64	74	C	B	C
Lin	92	88	B	A	A
Juanita	77	79	B	B	B
Carlisle	84	85	B	C	B
David	91	97	A	A	A

4. Figure the problems in Exercises 2 and 3 again, using a spreadsheet program on a computer.

Note: These are intended as "short" exercises at the end of the chapter. See Part 3 Exercises on page 189 for additional exercises.

Other Ways of Communicating About Student Achievement

KEY CONCEPTS

- A good communication and reporting system uses additional ways of communicating about student achievement besides a report card. Report cards are too infrequent, and too general, to give students and parents all the information they need about student achievement.
- Sending home student work can give parents some information about student achievement.
- Three systematic ways of communicating about student achievement—portfolios, narratives, and conferences—can each be accomplished through the following process: (a) set a purpose, (b) plan the logistics, (c) collect the evidence, (d) interpret the evidence, (e) communicate the information, and (f) listen to the response.
- Portfolios, or collections of student work over time with reflective comments, are an excellent method of communicating details about student achievement that are not well communicated through report cards.
- Narrative assessments allow teachers to describe students' learning. They can be sent as a companion to report cards or as separate assessments at other times. Teachers need skills at observing student work, summarizing, and writing in order to produce good narrative assessments, but the results are well worth the effort.
- Conferences are excellent ways of communicating with both students and parents. Student-teacher conferences are opportunities for instruction as well as assessment. Parent-teacher and student-parent-teacher conferences allow for two-way communication about student achievement.

Communicating about student achievement is too important to do only every 9 weeks or so, when report cards go home. As we saw in Chapter 3, students need regular feedback on specific learning tasks in order to continue to learn, and good teachers build those feedback opportunities into daily instruction and assessment. Parents want information about their children on a more regular basis than report cards give. Talking with parents can give teachers information they can use, as well. Parents have the opportunity to observe their children and can provide valuable insights into their learning, their thoughts, and their feelings.

Guskey and Bailey (2001) report that parents want information about their children that is frequent (available more often than every 9 weeks) and detailed. They want information that is easily interpretable and jargon-free. They want, in addition to evaluative information about their children's achievement, suggestions on how to help their children with specific learning needs. In addition, they want to know that their child's teacher is a competent professional who cares about their child individually (pp. 20–22).

The purpose of this chapter is to suggest how to fill some of these information needs using communication methods in addition to grades on report cards: portfolios, narratives, and conferences. In that perfect world where there are no grades, these methods and others like them would expand to fill all assessment and communication needs. Until that day comes, these are useful additions or alternatives to some grading functions. However, because this book is about grading, this chapter will not give you complete and detailed information about portfolios, narratives, or conferences. If you are interested in finding more detailed information about these methods, you are strongly encouraged to do further reading (see the resources listed in Exercise 2 at the end of this chapter).

SENDING WORK HOME

Communicating in detail about specific student accomplishments is by no means new. Many of us have discovered papers from our elementary school years in a parent's attic. How important these papers must have been to have been saved for decades, long forgotten by their juvenile authors, to reemerge decades later.

A common pattern for sending work home has been for teachers to allow students to take home corrected papers. Young children, at least young children who did well in school, would show these to their parents. Good work might end up on the family's refrigerator door. Bad work might end up on the sidewalk and never make it home from school. At some point in the child's development, different for each child and sometimes in a gradual progression, the student would stop showing work to the parents, keeping it or throwing it away, until high school when student would be considered responsible for his or her own work.

Another common practice aims to avoid having only some of the papers make it home. Teachers will send work home with students and require parents to sign it and return it. This solves the problem of making sure the parents do see the work, but it changes the nature of the communication. It can imply that the purpose of sending work home is for parents to acknowledge the grade. If the work must be returned the next day it cannot be useful for parents to review student problem areas, and it can change the communication from a largely informational function to that of reward and punishment. It does, however, work well to serve the accountability function. Parents cannot claim they did not see student work.

Elementary school teachers have long practiced another variation on sending work home: the weekly folder. A large piece of construction paper folded in half, and sometimes decorated by the student, makes a good file folder in which to store papers all week. For the trip home, typically on Friday afternoons, a staple can keep all the papers safe inside the folder and make it easy for little hands to carry. An additional benefit of this method is that the weekly collection of work can give a more complete picture of the child's achievements than one paper can give. This folder system stops short of being a "portfolio" because it is simply a collection of papers, without student reflection.

A COMMUNICATION PROCESS

Grading is the most common method of communicating about student achievement, but there are others. Three relatively common, systematic ways of communicating about student achievement are portfolios, narratives, and conferences. Each can be accomplished by following this basic process: (a) set a purpose, (b) plan the logistics, (c) collect the evidence, (d) interpret the evidence, (e) communicate the information, and (f) listen to the response. Table 10-1 describes this general process and shows how it also applies to report card grades.

It's important to note that these are *systematic* ways of communicating, which is what distinguishes them from simply sending work home. Like grading, all three of these alternative methods of communication require that you identify the kind of information you want to communicate and implement a system to base your information on sound evidence; for grading, we call this reliability and validity. These methods typically give teachers more room for individual planning than grading, where the procedures, such as the format and timing of report cards and the logistics for sending them home, are usually prescribed by the school district.

A systematic process for communicating about student achievement

Step	Description	Narratives	Portfolios	Conferences	Report Card Grades
Set purpose	Decide what you want to communicate.	Do you want to share information about student progress (change, improvement) or status (current achievement of goals)? One subject or several? Academics only or academics plus work habits, behavior, etc.?			The structure of the report card (the logistics) is usually in place already. The teacher sets purpose by identifying what learning goals will be reflected in each of the particular grades.
Plan logistics	Decide on method, format, timing, etc., for collection of evidence and communication of information.	Brief comments or longer narrative (letter or report)? To accompany report cards or instead of them? Timing?	What kind of work to save? Who selects? How should students reflect on their work? Format, storage, how to share with parents?		
Collect evidence	Gather samples of student work and/or observational notes that will support your purpose.	Start several weeks before writing to gather student work and make systematic observational notes.	Gather and select work samples and student reflections.		Record grades for selected assessments.
Interpret evidence	Draw the conclusions you can make about your intended purpose based on the evidence.	Write generalizations based on the evidence, and support with examples.	Reflect on the portfolio in a narrative or assign a grade(s) to the work.	Decide what you'll say at the conference, based on the evidence and supported with examples.	Assign grades, weighting appropriately according to your plans.
Communicate information	Send information home or talk with parents and students.	Send home or mail narratives.	Send home portfolio itself, or use as basis for conference, narrative, or grade?	Conferences allow for two-way communication on the spot.	Send home report cards.
Listen to response	Ascertain what parents and students heard and how they respond. Plan together for the future.	Require response or not (e.g., require signature?). Schedule conference if needed.		Teachers can gather additional information about the student from parents, as well as listen to parent responses to teacher or student reports on progress.	School district policy often requires report cards to be signed and returned.

PORTFOLIOS

A *portfolio* is a collection of student work, often with student reflections on that work, selected to serve a particular purpose. Arter, Spandel, and Culham (1995) defined a portfolio as "a purposeful collection of student work that tells the story of student achievement or growth" (p. 3). There are those who define portfolios as simply a collection of student work, and others who say that without reflections, a collection of student work is just a file.

Different authors list different "types" of portfolios, but they fall into two general categories: growth portfolios and "showcase" or best-work portfolios. Growth portfolios contain evidence of student progress over time and are excellent for formative evaluation, demonstrating change over time, and supporting self-referenced feedback students can use for their own further development, and therefore for instruction. A classic example of a growth portfolio is a writing portfolio that includes evidence of the writing process, from brainstorming through various drafts to the final copy, for successive writing assignments over a period of time.

Best-work portfolios contain evidence of what students have achieved and are useful for criterion-referenced feedback. Best-work portfolios are typically the kind of collections of student work used in parent-teacher or student-parent-teacher conferences. Student reflections explain why the various pieces of work were selected for inclusion in the portfolio and what they show about student learning.

Portfolios are an excellent method of communicating details about student achievement that are not well communicated with report cards. Use the systematic process for communicating about student achievement to make sure your portfolios convey meaningful, accurate information.

SET A PURPOSE

The first thing to consider is what purpose you want the portfolio to serve. Decide what learning goals it will address, whether the portfolio will be formative or summative in nature, and what you—and the student—intend to learn from the portfolio. These decisions will help you determine the structure of the portfolio, including what evidence to collect and how to collect it, what sort of reflections should be included, how much student choice should be involved, what topic(s) should be included, what time period(s) should be specified, and so on. Ensuring that all of these factors are consistent with the purpose you want the portfolio to serve helps make the portfolio a valid indicator of student achievement. Making sure that the portfolio contains enough evidence of the student's achievement helps confirm the portfolio's reliability.

PLAN THE LOGISTICS

The task of planning portfolio logistics falls between that of assessment and instruction. Typically, students construct their portfolios during class time. Portfolio construction can be a good use of instructional time, because students have the opportunity to reflect on their work and learn from that reflection. You will need to decide what kind of work to save, who gets to select the work that goes into the portfolio, and how students should reflect on their work. Will students write captions on sticky notes for every assignment? Will they write general reflections about all their work once a week? Consider when you will fit portfolio time into your class time.

Format and storage are important decisions for portfolios, too. Portfolios can be constructed in a variety of formats, including folders of various kinds, notebooks, boxes, electronic files, or combinations of these. Each of these formats requires different types of storage space and access.

Finally, part of your plan from the beginning should be about how you will use the portfolios. Will they be mainly part of instruction, and thus formative assessment? For example, a writing portfolio that contains drafts of various kinds of work and student reflections on their progress as writers might be an integral part of an English class. Or will they be mostly summative, as in the example on page 186 where students at Center Middle School in Kansas City used best-work portfolios as part of parent conferences?

COLLECT THE EVIDENCE

Gathering and selecting the work to put into the portfolio should be partly or mostly done by the student, who should also reflect on what the work shows about his or her achievement. Both students and teachers should understand the plan for what work to select; for instance, two examples each for solving four different kinds of math problems covered in a report period may be included.

INTERPRET THE EVIDENCE

The way you choose to interpret the evidence of student work presented in the portfolio should depend on the purpose you meant to serve. If you want the evidence to point to a student's grade on the particular learning goals demonstrated in the portfolio work, then you might use rubrics for each assignment separately, or you might use an overall rubric for the collection. Selection or development of these rubrics should be based on the same considerations discussed in Chapter 5, as rubrics for any kind of performance assessment. If you want the evidence to inform a student-teacher conference intended to be formative, to help the student with the next set of assignments, you might instead draw a narrative conclusion, writing a sentence or two giving some generalizations about the student's work and then showing what evidence in the portfolio supported that conclusion. You could sit down with the student and share this information, perhaps together setting goals for the student's next steps.

COMMUNICATE THE INFORMATION AND LISTEN TO THE RESPONSE

However you plan to share the information about student achievement evidenced in the portfolio, the next steps are to communicate the information and then listen to the response. Whether you send home a portfolio and require written parent responses, or use the portfolio for student or parent conferences—or whatever your communication method is—the communication process should be consistent with your original intention or objective.

This is perhaps best illustrated in the negative. It would *not* be consistent, for example, to decide you want to use growth portfolios to help students learn to write essays, to require them to put drafts and other unfinished pieces in the portfolio, and to require them to reflect honestly about their goals for improvement, and then later to decide to use the quality of all the essays in the portfolio as part of the final grade. You deliberately included work, and reflections on the work, that was not "done" yet, so it is inconsistent (and not valid) to turn around later and treat the essays as if they were finished products.

STRENGTHS AND WEAKNESSES

Portfolios are particularly good for formative assessment, when you want to integrate assessments with instruction. Some growth-type portfolios become the major vehicle for instruction, especially in areas like writing. Portfolios are particularly good at helping students to organize information about their achievement, to see it as a body of work instead of isolated assignments, and to see the way their assignments fit together. Portfolios are helpful in supporting student self-reflection because the evidence is concrete and right in front of them. This is especially important for younger students, who can reflect only in concrete terms. Portfolios can be a way of complementing other modes of communication about student achievement—narratives or conferences.

Portfolios are not particularly good at summarizing broad, overall achievement in a large domain, however. A portfolio more easily shows student achievement of a more limited, specific learning goal or set of related goals than it documents "math" for instance (referring to everything the student learned all year in math). Portfolios can present some logistical problems (for example, of space or even expense), depending on what sort of folders or containers are required, how large they are, and how many are needed. Finally, portfolios can backfire and turn into a "Mickey Mouse" activity if they are not thoroughly integrated with instruction; for example, turning the last 15 minutes of class every Friday into "portfolio" time as if it were an unrelated subject.

NARRATIVES

Narrative assessments are descriptions of student work that include details about student accomplishments, and sometimes goals for future learning. They come in all sizes and shapes, however. One can envision a continuum of narrative assessment from the most prescribed to the most open and comprehensive (see Figure 10-1). Some report cards have spaces for written teacher comments (see, for example, Figures 7-2, 7-3, 8-1, and 8-2). I make a distinction between spaces for open-ended narrative comments and report cards that allow teachers to select from a menu of prepared comments (see, for example, Figures 7-4 and 8-1).

FIGURE 10-1 Continuum of narrative assessment types

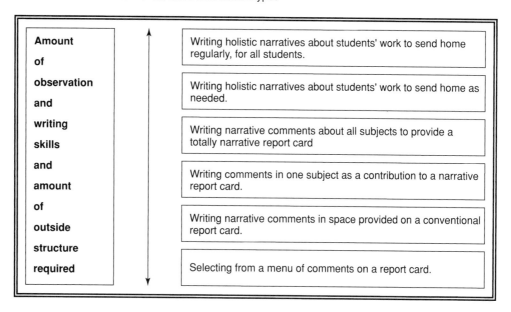

Amount of observation and writing skills and amount of outside structure required	Writing holistic narratives about students' work to send home regularly, for all students.
	Writing holistic narratives about students' work to send home as needed.
	Writing narrative comments about all subjects to provide a totally narrative report card
	Writing comments in one subject as a contribution to a narrative report card.
	Writing narrative comments in space provided on a conventional report card.
	Selecting from a menu of comments on a report card.

Skills required for narrative assessment include effectively observing student work, identifying strengths and areas for further practice, summarizing those observations in descriptive language free of educational jargon, and writing clear sentences and paragraphs. The drawback is that these are not skills that are often taught in teacher education classes or English composition classes, but skills that nevertheless must be developed for effective narrative assessment. The second format, selecting from a menu of comments, does not call into play the teacher's own writing skills. These comments are useful for more normal circumstances (e.g., "Puts forth best effort," see Figure 7-4), but are not specific enough to suggest particular actions if change is needed.

SET A PURPOSE

As for all methods of assessing and communicating about student achievement, you should begin with purpose. What information about the students would you like to communicate through your narratives? Do you want to share information about student progress (change, improvement) or status (current achievement of goals)? about one subject or several? about academics only, or academics plus work habits or behavior? Narratives can address these if you are careful and clear about what you write and the evidence you use.

Power and Chandler (1998) make several suggestions for teachers who would like to develop their skills at writing narrative assessments. They suggest that you start with a single subject area if you are an elementary teacher, or with a single class if you are a secondary subject teacher, so that the amount of work is not overwhelming. Often, it is possible to write a common introductory paragraph that can be repeated for all students. Narrative assessments often start with a description of class goals or class work for the report period, so that individual students' achievements can be described in context. Individual students then each receive a second paragraph or section describing their particular strengths, weaknesses, moments of learning, personal goals, and anything else the teacher wishes to report. Your learning objectives for the period, or even a checklist or review sheet, can be a useful starting place from which to make your comments.

PLAN THE LOGISTICS AND COLLECT THE EVIDENCE

Narrative writing requires preparation. Starting the night before you want to send letters home to parents will not work! Of course you are continually observing your students over time, but preparation for narrative reports requires systematic and recorded observations. This not only enhances the validity of your observations, but it also ensures that you have something to say. Power and Chandler (1998) suggest that 2 or 3 weeks before you write narrative comments you begin to jot down observations about students, in the style of anecdotal records but using a class list to make sure you pay attention to everyone. They suggest one way to frame your observations is to try to think of three adjectives that describe each student, and then note from your observations specific evidence or examples of what you mean. Another version of this method is to use prompts. Ask yourself how you would finish a sentence like, "Stewart's best work is in__" and then use your notes to provide examples.

Another requirement for producing high-quality narrative assessments is developing a system to save student work for your reflection and summary at the time you write the narrative. If your students already keep portfolios, you have a mechanism for this. If not, you will want some sort of filing system so that you can save the examples you will talk about in your narratives. The more students you have to write about, the more necessary it becomes to have the actual work in front of you when you write.

INTERPRET THE EVIDENCE AND COMMUNICATE THE INFORMATION

The simplest way to think about writing narrative comments based on evidence is to remember what your English teachers told you when you learned to write paragraphs using topic sentences and supporting details. For longer narratives, it's more like writing essays using thesis sentences and supporting paragraphs, but the principle is the same. Your topic sentence or theme is a generalization or assertion about the student's achievement. Then, just like a student writing an essay, you need to use examples from student work or from your observations of the student to support that generalization. The examples will serve both to warrant your conclusion about the student and to illustrate what it means.

Power and Chandler (1998) give several suggestions for teachers who are starting to build the habits and routines necessary to produce sound narratives on a regular basis. First, focus on the positive and build from student strengths. Parents and students know "what's wrong" and don't need a special note to remind them. Cast difficulties as challenges, and suggest ways to meet them that the student can do realistically, with your help and the parents' help. Second, ask for help from colleagues; for example, ask another teacher who has the same student to assist in providing additional observations.

The third suggestion is to write the easy comments first, building your skills to work up to the more difficult ones. Finally, base your comments about students on classroom-based information and follow through with recommendations for home activities. Consider starting your recommendations by referring to the student's own goals.

LISTEN TO THE RESPONSE

Parents can respond in a variety of ways to narratives. If the comments were on a report card, a district-wide response process is probably in place. You can require that narratives be signed and returned to school. You can follow up narratives with phone calls or conferences. If you have suggested ways in which parents might assist their children in the narrative, you can base your follow-up on assistance and support for parents as they carry out your suggestions.

STRENGTHS AND WEAKNESSES

Narratives are usually welcome because parents enjoy descriptions of their children's accomplishments. They can give a detailed picture of student achievement not possible in more summary-type measures such as grades. Narratives also can describe other aspects of the student's work in school besides achievement: behavior, work habits, attitudes, and interests. Make sure that such descriptions are carefully written so that, for example, a description about a positive attitude does not come across as a description of outstanding achievement. Narratives are also flexible. They can be done at various times, regularly or as need arises. Narratives can be written at any level, about one assignment or several, one subject or many, and include a short time period or a long one.

Probably the biggest drawback for using narratives is that they require good writing skills, as already mentioned. Descriptions need to be clear, concise, based on sound evidence, and convey the information and the tone that you intend. Narratives can easily degenerate into comments that are either too vague to be helpful or too judgmental rather than descriptive. We have all read comments like, "Sally is an excellent student and a pleasure to have in class," which don't mean much. Positive comments of this nature might not do any real harm, but they do waste a precious communication opportunity where something more helpful could be said. Of course, negative comments of this nature can be hurtful without providing any means for change.

PARENT-TEACHER, STUDENT-TEACHER, OR STUDENT-PARENT-TEACHER CONFERENCES

Narratives are only one way to share comments about student work. Even better, when the opportunity arises, is to talk *with* the students and parents about student achievement because then you can listen and have a dialogue. Parent conferences require that teachers use the same observational, summarizing, and goal-setting skills as do narrative assessments. In this case, however, oral communication skills and relationship skills are the vehicle for working with parents instead of writing skills. Student conferences can be a regular part of some classes, typically concerning individual assignments before students turn in the final product.

SET A PURPOSE

In some cases you won't have much choice about whether or not to hold parent conferences. Many school districts require one or two parent conferences be offered each year, especially for younger students. Decide what evidence you'll need to collect, and in what form, to show to parents at the conference. It may sound silly now, but I remember doing parent conferences with middle school students years ago prepared only with the gradebook. It never occurred to me that systematically saved pieces of evidence would give me a good conversation starter or focusing tool. Even if you are just doing individual student conferences about one assignment in your classroom, set a purpose. Don't start talking with students until you know what you want to accomplish with the conference.

PLAN THE LOGISTICS

For conferences, planning the logistics can be complicated. Schedules and appointments must be made, and appropriate space reserved. The space needs to provide privacy. You shouldn't, for instance, conduct conferences in your classroom with one family while another waits for their turn in the same room.

COLLECT THE EVIDENCE

There are several different ways you can prepare the evidence for conferences. Portfolios can be shared at conferences, as can checklists, anecdotal records, narratives, or grades. You can collect individual pieces of evidence to show as illustrations of the general level of student work, and reasons students received the kind of grades they did. Students can assist in the selection of evidence. How exactly you should do this depends on the purpose of the conference.

INTERPRET THE EVIDENCE, COMMUNICATE THE INFORMATION, AND LISTEN TO THE RESPONSE

The interpretation and communication process for conferences is similar to that for narratives and portfolios, with one important difference: You will be talking directly with students or parents; therefore, it is extremely important that you actively listen to what they have to say. Involve them in interpreting the evidence from student work or from your observations of students in class.

STRENGTHS AND WEAKNESSES

The major advantage of conferences is the opportunity for dialogue. This, of course, requires good listening and interpersonal skills. Another strength of conferences is that they help develop home-school relationships. Face-to-face communication allows for better understanding between parents and teachers, the two most important sets of adults in the child's life, and among parents, teachers, and the student.

Weaknesses of conferences include the time-consuming and difficult nature of scheduling and other logistics, and the related problem that you can't hold conferences very frequently. Dysfunctional or antagonistic parents can be a problem. When confronted with these situations, respond professionally. Your job as the child's teacher is to understand the child's environment as best you can, not to become the family's counselor, and certainly not to become afraid or anxious.

I once had a conference with the father of a seventh grader who refused to do anything in my Language Arts class; instead, he played with a toy truck on his desk. When I took the truck from him, instead of stopping, he would make a "Vroom-vroom" noise and pretend his hand was the truck, steering around the top of his desk. Roy's reading and writing were very poor and not getting any better. At my conference with his father, I met a very angry, unemployed man. He yelled at me, saying that teachers made too much money and that his son didn't have to do what I asked in class. Apparently, the father's response to his troubles was to withdraw and become belligerent—just as his son did in class. I did not try to argue with Roy's dad. Instead I tried, not entirely successfully, to stick to a discussion of Roy's work and behavior. I did not fall into the trap of talking about teachers' salaries or personalize the attack and get upset because he was yelling at me.

PARENT-TEACHER CONFERENCES

Relationship skills required for parent conferences include communicating genuine caring, building rapport, listening, empathizing, reflecting parents' feelings, and clarifying (Perl, 1995). Perl's list of relationship skills for parent conferences about students with disabilities applies as well to parent conferences about all students.

Often, schools will have a school-wide parent conference day set up during the fall, typically sometime in October after the school year has started and the teachers have had a chance to get to know their students. Another conference day may be scheduled in the spring. Make sure not to confuse these with "open house" times, which are not times to share specific information about individual students. Parent conferences should be scheduled individually, and information should be kept confidential.

STUDENT-TEACHER CONFERENCES

Typically, student-teacher conferences are about smaller "chunks" of work, specific assignments or groups of assignments, than are conferences with parents involved. Students can receive specific feedback from teachers, and students can help teachers understand their particular needs or points of confusion and the accomplishments of which they are particularly proud. One good way to integrate assessment with instruction is to engage in student-teacher conferences during the course of independent work. A classic version of this is student-teacher conferences about students' writing. Teachers meet with students about drafts of specific work, and together size up the effort to date and set goals for improvement.

If your school does not permit students to attend parent-teacher conferences, Stiggins (2005) recommends using student-teacher conferences as preparation for parent-teacher conferences. Go over with the student the evidence that you will present to the parents. Make sure the student understands what you will be telling his or her parents, to eliminate a sense of "they're talking about me behind my back."

STUDENT-PARENT-TEACHER CONFERENCES

An idea gaining some momentum at the present time is a version of parent conferences that has the student not only present, but also taking a leading role (Stiggins, 2005). These conferences require preparation both in terms of the meeting itself and in the work students do in their daily classwork. Two scenarios follow. You will notice that in both examples the students are responsible for understanding and describing their work as a whole, for describing their strengths and weaknesses, and for setting goals. Response to this kind of conference is generally positive, although some parents still prefer teacher conferences without their child present.

Elementary School Example Elementary school teachers in Coronado Unified School District, California, devised a student-led conference for first graders (Bennett & Kovac, 1995). Students "share a portfolio of their work as they explain personal and academic strengths and discuss academic goals for improvement. They are given the opportunity to take control of their own learning while practicing confidence building skills and leadership abilities" (p. 1). The conference itself functions as a performance assessment, with students, parents, and teachers jointly evaluating what the students demonstrate and together setting goals for the future. Teachers facilitate, but the schedule is arranged in an overlapping fashion so that teachers do not attend the entire conference with each student and parent. Students work through a format of demonstrating their accomplishments in literacy, numeracy, social development, and psychomotor development. They read to their parents, share writing and math portfolios, solve a math story problem, reflect on their own social and emotional strengths, and demonstrate skills like hopping, jumping, throwing, and catching. Parents listen and then help students with goal setting. Teachers facilitate the discussion and help with goal setting as well. Parents then complete pre- and post-conference questionnaires.

Middle School Example At Center Middle School in Kansas City, Missouri, faculty developed a student-led parent conference model to serve the following purposes (Hackmann, Kenworthy, & Nibbelink, 1995, pp. 4–5): "to encourage students to accept responsibility for their academic progress; to encourage parents, students, and teachers to openly communicate as equal partners; to facilitate the development of students' oral communication skills and increase self-confidence; and to increase parent participation in the conferences." Students participated in a special course called Seminar that included study skills, career exploration, and interdisciplinary work. Students developed Individualized Student Plans with the help of their homeroom teachers, identifying goals in five areas: academic, personal responsibility, leadership, community service, and physical/wellness. They also developed action plans for their goals. In Seminar classes, students role-played student-led parent conferences based on their individual goals and a packet of materials they had accumulated.

The actual conferences were held in 20-minute time blocks. The teacher advisor served as the facilitator. Students shared with parents items they had prepared: their "Goals for Growth" folder, including their Individualized Student Plan and an activity log documenting progress; a "Coat of Arms" they created depicting their skills, successes, and influential people; an assignment notebook documenting completion of assignments, tests, and other academic work; a grade sheet including expected and actual grades for each course and ways to improve or maintain their grades; and two portfolios, a best-work portfolio and a career exploration portfolio. Students made thank-you cards for their parents for coming to the conference. After the student presentations, parents had the opportunity to question student and teacher. Student, parent, and teacher each had an opportunity to make concluding or summary remarks. Parents were able to schedule follow-up conferences with the teacher alone, if they wished.

CONCLUSION

Communicating about student achievement is one of the most important parts of a teacher's job. The purpose of this book has been to prepare you to do the most common kind of communicating about student achievement—grading. The purpose of this last chapter is to remind you that grading is only *one* way of communicating about student achievement, and to introduce you briefly to three other methods: narratives, portfolios, and conferences. Although the communication process is analogous for all three methods, some work better than others for specific circumstances. Report card grades fulfill administrative, community, and student-parent needs for quick quantification of levels of achievement. They have the advantage of being a conventional, culturally important medium with which everyone is familiar. Narratives, if well written, can describe particular achievements in more detail than grades can. Portfolios can describe particular achievements in detail and serve as a repository of the evidence and a vehicle for reflection. Conferences can describe particular achievements and behaviors in detail and have the added benefit of being two-way communication. The quality of all of these methods depends on the soundness of the purpose, the appropriateness of the evidence to the purpose, the reliability and validity of the conclusions based on the evidence, and the clarity of communication and attention to student and parent responses. Important work!

EXERCISES

1. Discuss why it is important to think of communicating about student achievement as a process, and why it is important to start with setting a purpose.
2. Choose one or more of the three methods of communication discussed in this chapter for further reading. Write a report on the method you have chosen, and share it with your class.

a. For narratives, you might start with this book:
   Power, B. M., & Chandler, K. (1998). *Well-chosen words: Narrative assessments and report card comments.* York, ME: Stenhouse.
b. For portfolios, you might start with either this article or this book, respectively:
   Arter, J., & Spandel, V. (1992). Using portfolios of student work in instruction and assessment. *Educational Measurement: Issues and Practice, 11*(1), 36–44.
   Hebert, E. A. (2001). *The power of portfolios: What children can teach us about learning and assessment.* San Francisco: Jossey-Bass.
c. For conferences, you might start with this book:
   Bailey, J. M., & Guskey, T. R. (2001). *Implementing student-led conferences.* Thousand Oaks, CA: Corwin Press.

Note: These are intended as "short" exercises at the end of the chapter. See Part 3 Exercises on the next page for additional exercises.

Part 3 Exercises

1. Request copies of report cards and grading policies from a school district(s). Describe the grading purpose(s) and policies and discuss them in light of the key principles from Part 3. Describe the format and symbols of the report cards and the type of grading methods that would be appropriate.

The following grading scenarios* present problems regarding effort, improvement, or missing work. Use them for exercises 2 and 3.

2. Read each scenario. For each one, identify the grading issues or principles involved in addressing the problem. Note that for some of these scenarios there may be no right answer but rather a choice among various kinds of compromises. For others, one solution may be clearly preferable. For each of the choices given, discuss the advantages and disadvantages of each, referring to the key concepts you learned in Part 3. Can you suggest any changes the teacher might make to his or her grading policies for the future? If so, explain what they are and why you suggest them.

3. Ask several teachers to read the scenarios, choose the answer they prefer, and tell you their reasons. Report your findings and discuss them in light of the key concepts you learned in Part 3.

You are a sixth-grade teacher of a class that is grouped heterogeneously. Chris, one of the students in your class, has high academic ability, as shown by her previous work, test results, reports from other teachers, and your own observations. As you look over her work for the grading period, you realize two things: the quality of her work is above average for the class, but the work does not represent the best that she could do. The effort she has shown has been minimal, but, because of her high ability, her work has been reasonably good. In this situation, you would
   a. grade Chris on the quality of her work in comparison to the class, without being concerned about the amount of work that she could have done.
   b. lower Chris's grade because she did not make a serious effort in your class; she could have done better work.
   c. assign Chris a higher grade to encourage her to work harder.

You are a seventh-grade science teacher of a class that is grouped heterogeneously. Barbara is one of your students who has low ability based on previous performance and observation of her former science teachers. Throughout this

*The scenarios presented in these exercises are from Loyd, 1991. Used by permission.

grading period, you notice that she has worked very hard. She has turned in her assignments on time and has often come to you for extra help before tests. Her average for this grading period is 2 points below what is needed for a D on the grading scale you use. In this situation, you would

a. raise Barbara's grade and assign her a D for the effort she has shown.

b. grade Barbara according to the work she has done and assign her an F.

You are a fifth-grade teacher of a class of mixed ability levels. Sandy, a student in your class, appears to have average ability to do the required work. In evaluating her work for this grading period, you observe that she did not do the work she is capable of; she could have done better. She, however, managed to meet what is required for her to get a C. In this situation, you would

a. assign Sandy a lower grade because she could have put in more effort in your class and could have done better.

b. assign Sandy a grade based on the quality of her work, without taking into account the amount of work that she could possibly have done.

c. assign Sandy a higher grade to encourage her to try harder.

In your seventh-grade social studies class, report card grades were based on quizzes, tests, and an out-of-class project that counted as 25% of the grade. Terry obtained an A average on his quizzes and tests but has not turned in the project despite frequent reminders. In this situation, you would

a. exclude the missing project and assign Terry an A.

b. assign Terry a zero for the project and an F on his report card because his average would be 68%.

c. assign Terry a C, counting off some points for not turning in the project.

You are the English teacher of a class of ninth graders with varying ability levels. During this grading period, the students' grades are based on quizzes, tests, and homework assignments that involve working out exercises. Kelly has not turned in any homework assignments despite your frequent reminders. His grades on the quizzes have ranged from 65% to 75%, and he received a D on each of the tests. In this situation, you would

a. assign Kelly a grade of zero for the homework assignments and include this in the grade, thus giving him an average of F for the grading period.

b. ignore the missing homework assignments and assign Kelly a D.

c. ignore the missing homework and assign Kelly a C.

You are a high school algebra teacher. In your class of general and academic track students, you give two tests in each grading period. David's score on the first test was an F. On the second test, he obtained a low D. In this situation, you would

a. assign David an overall grade of F based on the average of his performance in the two exams.

b. assign David an overall grade of D because he showed improvement in his performance.

You are a biology teacher of a high school class that consists of students with varying ability levels. For this class you give two exams in each term. As you compute Bernie's grade for this term, you see that on the first exam, he obtained a score equivalent to a B and on the second exam, a low A. In this situation, you would
a. assign Bernie an overall grade of B, which is the average of his scores on the two exams.
b. assign Bernie an overall grade of A, noting that there was improvement in his performance.

You are a mathematics teacher of a sixth-grade class that is heterogeneous. Frank is one of the students in the class who has average ability, as seen from his past grades and as viewed by his other math teachers. During the term, he has exerted a lot of effort; he submitted seat work and assignments on time, has asked a classmate to help him after school, and has seen you for consultation on questions. In computing his grade for this period, you find that his average is 2 points below what is needed for a C on the grading scale you use. In this situation, you would
a. grade Frank based on the work that he has done and assign a D.
b. raise Frank's grade and assign him a C, taking into consideration his effort and hard work.

In the ninth-grade geography class that you teach, grades were based on quizzes and tests and an out-of-class project (25% of the final grade). Jesse's scores on the quizzes and tests average to a D, but he did not submit a final project. In this situation, you would
a. assign Jesse a zero for the project and include this in computing his grade, thus giving him an F.
b. ignore the missing project in the grading and assign Jesse a D.

You are teaching American history to a high school class in which Karen is a student. The students in this class have varying ability levels. In computing the grade for each term, you include two tests. Karen's score on the first test was a D; on the second test, her score was a low C. In this situation, you would
a. assign Karen an overall grade of C to recognize the improvement in her performance.
b. assign Karen an overall grade of D, which is the average of her performance on the two exams.

You are an eighth-grade teacher of a class composed of students with mixed ability levels. She is a student with high ability. You observe that during this grading period Leslie has put much effort into her work for this particular class. Her out-of-class writing assignments were on time, and she has come to see you many times after class to discuss her work. Her average for this grading period is 2 points below what is needed for an A on the grading scale you use. In this situation, you would
a. raise Leslie's grade and give her an A for the amount of effort she has put forth.
b. grade Leslie on the basis of the work that she has done regardless of her effort.

You are the teacher of a seventh-grade class that is heterogeneously grouped. Lee, a student in your class, is one of the students who is considered of low ability, gauging from his test results and work in the past. As you compute his grade for this term, you see that the amount of effort he put in is far less than what he is capable of but that his work is equivalent to that which is required to get a D. In this situation, you would

a. assign Lee a higher grade to encourage him to work harder.
b. assign Lee a grade based on the quality of his work, not taking into consideration the amount of work that he was capable of putting in.
c. assign Lee a lower grade because he could have exerted more effort and could have done better work.

You teach social studies to seventh-grade students with varying ability levels. For this term, grades are based on quizzes, tests, and homework assignments that consist of answering review questions found at the end of each section in the textbook. The records show that Sara has not turned in any of the homework, although you have repeatedly given her reminders. Her grades on the quizzes have ranged from 89% to 97%, and she received an A on each of the tests. In this situation, you would

a. ignore the missing homework and assign Sara an A.
b. average the homework assignments as zeros, then assign Sara an F for the grading period.
c. assign Sara a B or a C, to penalize her to some extent for not turning in the assignments even though she understood the content.

You are a high school algebra teacher. In your class of general and academic track students, you give a midterm and a final test in each grading period. Shane scored 35% on the first test, which is a grade of F. On the final test, he scored 57%, which is also an F. In this situation, you would

a. give Shane an F overall. Both of his grades were Fs.
b. give Shane a D overall. He showed substantial improvement which should be recognized.

To make a two-way Table of Specifications or Test Blueprint for a test on a unit of instruction in the classroom:

1. Identify and set aside those unit objectives (learning goals) that will be evaluated with performance assessment.
2. For the remaining objectives, list the content down the side of a table, defining rows.
3. List the cognitive level at which performance is desired (usually also from the unit's objectives) across the top of the table, defining columns. Use any applicable cognitive taxonomy. A simplified version of a cognitive taxonomy may also work well. For example, some tests will not have extended analysis or evaluation, especially if you have papers or other assignments that require this level of cognitive functioning that will also go into the report card grade. Thus the test might use only the Knowledge, Comprehension, and Application levels of Bloom's taxonomy.
4. Determine what portion of the score should be devoted to each content area and each level. Blank cells are fine if it's intentional.
5. *After you have completed the blueprint,* write items that match the point distribution you have planned.

EXAMPLE:

Objectives from an eighth-grade science unit on plate tectonics:

- Explain Wegener's theory of continental drift and supporting evidence.
- Explain seafloor spreading and give evidence.
- Define: plate tectonics, mid-ocean ridges, rift valleys, trenches, and convection currents.
- Name seven major plates.
- Name three types of plate boundaries.
- Explain relationships among plate boundaries, earthquakes, and volcanoes.
- Construct a world map with major plates and related characteristics labeled.

First, set aside the last objective and use a map project assignment to assess it.

Next, construct a blueprint like the following. Check to see that the distribution of weight matches your instructional intentions, both for the content and for the cognitive levels. You can check this by using the "Total" and "Percent" columns.

Finally, write test items to the point specifications on the blueprint. The "define terms-recall" cell might be 5 separate one-point objective test items. The "continental drift-explain" cell might be 15 one-point items, or 3 five-point items, or some combination. For each multiple-point question, you will need a scoring scheme or rubric.

	Recall	Explain	Apply	Total	Percent
Continental drift		15		15	30%
Seafloor spreading		5	5	10	20%
Define terms	5			5	10%
Name plates	7			7	14%
Types of boundaries	3			3	6%
Quakes and volcanoes		5	5	10	20%
Total	15	25	10	50	
Percent	30%	50%	20%		100%

APPENDIX B: DO'S AND DON'TS FOR WRITING GOOD TEST ITEMS*

DO'S AND DON'TS FOR WRITING OBJECTIVE TEST ITEMS

General

1. Use clear and concise language.
2. Prepare a draft and edit it.
3. Proofread the draft from a student's point of view.
4. Test important ideas, not trivial points.
5. Write short, clear directions for all sections of the test.
6. Don't copy statements from the textbook.

True/False items

1. Make statements definitely true or definitely false.

   Not: The advent of the computer was the strongest force for social change in the 20th century.

   Better: Some authors have compared the social impact of the advent of the computer with that of the printing press.
2. Keep statements short.
3. Have only one idea per statement.

   Not: Captain Ahab was not afraid of death, whereas Ishmael wanted very much to live.

   Better: Captain Ahab was not afraid of death.
4. Use positive statements; if the statement contains a "not," highlight it.

   Not: The issue of the Emancipation Proclamation in 1863 did not result in immediate freedom for any slaves.

   Better: The issue of the Emancipation Proclamation in 1863 did *not* result in immediate freedom for any slaves.
5. Make "trues" and "falses" about the same length.
6. Avoid patterns of answers (e.g., TTFF or TFTF).

Matching items

1. Number the items in the first column; letter the response choices in the second column.

*From Brookhart, 1999b.

2. Make items and response choices homogeneous.
   Not: Match the word with its definition.

1.	Solid bodies bounded by planar surfaces.	a.	Absolute zero
2.	At a constant temperature, the volume of a given amount of gas varies inversely with pressure.	b.	Boyle's law
		c.	Crystal
3.	Temperature at which the kinetic energy of molecules is zero.	d.	Enthalpy of fusion
4.	Process of passing from solid to gas without going through the liquid state, or vice versa.	e.	Ionic radii
		f.	Sublimation
5.	Heat required to melt 1 mole of a substance.		

   Better: Match each gas law with the name of the scientist associated with it.

1.	The volume of a certain mass of gas is inversely proportional to the pressure, at constant temperature.	a.	Avogadro
		b.	Boyle
2.	The total pressure in a mixture of gases is the sum of the individual partial pressures.	c.	Charles
		d.	Dalton
3.	The rates of diffusion of two gases are inversely proportional to the square roots of their densities.	e.	Graham
		f.	Kelvin
4.	Equal numbers of molecules are contained in equal volumes of different gases if the temperature and pressure are the same.		
5.	The volume of a given mass of gas is directly proportional to the absolute temperature, at constant pressure.		

3. Each response choice should look like a plausible answer for any item in the set. If not, the list is not similar enough to be a set of matching items.
4. Keep the lists short (5 to 10 items).
5. Separate longer lists into two or more shorter ones, using the principle of homogeneity.
6. Avoid having the same number of items and response choices so that the last answer is not really a choice.
7. Put the longer phrases in the left column and the shorter phrases in the right column.
8. Avoid using incomplete sentences as items.
9. Keep all items and response choices in a set on the same page of the test.

Completion/fill-in-the-blank items

1. Don't put too many blanks together.
   Not: The _____ left _____ over issues of _____.
   Better: The Puritans left England over issues of _____.
2. Make the answer a single word if possible.
3. Make sure there is only one way to interpret the blank.
   Not: Abraham Lincoln was born in _____. (A log cabin? Poverty? Kentucky? 1809? A bed?)
   Better: Abraham Lincoln was born in the year _____.
   Or: In what year was Abraham Lincoln born? _____.

4. A word bank (a set of choices in a box or list) is often helpful, depending on whether total recall is important or not and whether spelling counts.

Multiple-choice items

1. The stem (the numbered section) should ask or imply a question.
2. If the stem is an incomplete sentence, the alternatives should be at the end and should be the answer to an implied question.
3. If "not" is used, underline it.
4. Avoid statements of opinion.
5. Don't link two items together so that getting the second one correct depends on getting the first one correct.

> **Not:** 1. What is the next number in the series 1, 5, 13, 29, . . . ?
>   a. 43   b. 57   c. 61   d. 64
>   2. What is the following number in the series in question #1?
>   a. 122   b. 125   c. 127   d. 129
> **Better:** 1. What is the next number in the series 1, 5, 13, 29, . . . ?
>   a. 43   b. 57   c. 61   d. 64
>   2. What is the next number in the series 1, 4, 16, 64, . . . ?
>   a. 128   b. 256   c. 372   d. 448

6. Don't give away the answer to one item with information or clues in other items.
7. Use three to five functional alternatives (response choices). Silly alternatives (e.g., "Mickey Mouse") do not draw serious consideration and should not be used. To inject humor into a test, use a whole silly item, not part of a serious one.
8. All alternatives should be plausible answers for those who are truly guessing.
9. Repeated words go in the stem, not the alternatives.

> **Not:** Computer-based tutorials are called "adaptive" if they change based on information
>   a. about the student.
>   b. about the content material.
>   c. about the computer.
> **Better:** Computer-based tutorials are called "adaptive" if they change based on information about the
>   a. student.
>   b. content material.
>   c. computer.

10. Punctuate all alternatives correctly, given the stem.
11. Put the alternatives in logical order, if there is one.
12. Avoid overlapping alternatives.

> **Not:** Which of the following possibilities enabling communication over the Internet is the best choice for a class discussion in a distance-learning course?
>   a. E-mail
>   b. Usenet news
>   c. Chat systems
>   d. Conferencing software

Better: Which of the following possibilities enabling communication over the Internet is the best choice for a class discussion in a distance-learning course?

    a. E-mail

    b. Usenet news

    c. Chat systems

13. Avoid "all of the above" as an alternative.
14. Use "none of the above" sparingly.
15. Adjust the difficulty of an item by making the alternatives more or less alike. The more similar the alternatives, the more difficult the item.

DO'S AND DON'TS FOR WRITING ESSAY TEST ITEMS

Restricted range essay items (usually one to three paragraphs per answer)

1. For most purposes, use several restricted essays rather than one extended essay.
2. Ask for a focused response to one point; state the question so the student can tell what kind of response is required.
3. Do not ask a question that requires merely extended recall. Questions should require some critical thinking; for example:
   * explain causes and effects
   * identify assumptions
   * draw valid conclusions
   * present relevant arguments
   * state and defend a position
   * explain a procedure
   * describe limitations
   * apply a principle
   * compare and contrast ideas
4. Use clear scoring criteria.
5. Don't use optional questions.

Extended range essay items (answer will be a true "essay" form)

1. Use to test in-depth understanding of a small range of content.
2. Call for students to express ideas in an organized fashion. Specify both what should be discussed and how it should be discussed.
3. Allow enough time for students to think and write.
4. Assign the essay as a paper or theme if out-of-class time is needed or if students' choice and resources are required.

The following evaluation form is a checklist for designing or selecting alternative assessments.

Alternative Assessment Evaluation Form

	Yes	Somewhat	No
1. Content/Skill Coverage and Correct Method	3	2	1

The assessment
- Clearly states skills and content to be covered.
- Correctly uses alternative assessment to measure these skills and content.
- Avoids irrelevant and/or unimportant content.
- Deals with enduring themes or significant knowledge.
- Matches statements of coverage to task content and performance criteria.

2. Performance Criteria	3	2	1

- Include everything of importance and omit irrelevant features of performance.
- State criteria clearly and provide samples of student work to illustrate them.
- Are stated generally, especially if the intent is use as an instructional tool.
- Are analytical trait, especially if the intent is use as an instructional tool.

3. Performance Tasks	3	2	1

General:
- Elicit the desired performances or work;
- Recreate an "authentic" context for performance.
- Exemplify good instruction.
- Are reviewed by others (students, peers, experts).

Sampling/Representativeness/Generalizability:
- Cover the content or skill area well; results can be generalized.
- Sample performance in a way that is representative of what a student can do.

Bias and Distortion:
- Avoid factors that might get in the way of student ability to demonstrate what they know and can do.

Handout A3.6, H1, p.1

(Continued)

	Yes	Somewhat	No
4. Fairness and Rater Bias	3	2	1

Performance Tasks
- Have content and context that are equally familiar, acceptable, and appropriate for students in all group.
- Tap knowledge and skills all students have had adequate time to acquire in class.
- Are as free as possible of cultural, ethnic, or gender stereotypes.
- Are as free as possible of language barriers.

Performance Criteria and Rater Training:
- Ensure that irrelevant features of performance do not influence how other, supposedly independent, features are judged.
- Ensure that knowledge of the type of student does not influence judgments about performance quality.
- Ensure that knowledge of individual students does not affect judgments about performance quality.

	Yes	Somewhat	No
5. Consequences	3	2	1

The assessment
- Communicates appropriate messages.
- Results in acceptable effects on students, teachers, and others.
- Is worth the instructional time devoted to it; students learn something from doing the assessment and/or using the performance criteria.
- Provides information relevant to the decisions being made.
- Is perceived by students and teachers as valid.

	Yes	Somewhat	No
6. Cost and Efficiency	3	2	1

The assessment
- Is cost efficient—the results are worth the investment.
- Is practical/"do-able".

Handout 3.6, H1, p. 2

Source: From "How to Critique an Assessment" by Northwest Regional Educational Laboratory, in *Toolkit 98*. Available at: http://www.nwrel.org/assessment/toolkit98/A36H1.pdf. Used by permission.

Figure Number	Rating*
6–2	1
6–3	2
6–4	3
6–5	1
6–6	2
6–7	2
6–8	1
6–9	3
6–10	2
6–11	1
6–12	2
6–13	2

*Rating scale from Chapter 6

3—A variety of relevant details are organized to support the topic sentence.

2—Some details are present; they are related to the topic sentence.

1—Minimal details are present, or unrelated details do not support the topic sentence.

REFERENCES

Airasian, P., & Russell, M. (2008). *Classroom assessment: Concepts and applications* (6th ed.). Columbus, OH: McGraw-Hill.

Ames, C., & Archer, J. (1988). Achievement goals in the classroom: Students' learning strategies and motivation processes. *Journal of Educational Psychology, 80,* 260–267.

Anderson, L. W., & Bourke, S. F. (2000). *Assessing affective characteristics in schools* (2nd ed.). Mahwah, NJ: Lawrence Erlbaum.

Arter, J., & Spandel, V. (1992). Using portfolios of student work in instruction and assessment. *Educational Measurement: Issues and Practice, 11*(1), 36–44.

Arter, J., Spandel, V., & Culham, R. (1995). *Portfolios for assessment and instruction.* ERIC Digest EDO-CG-95-10. (ERIC Document Reproduction Service No. ED388890)

Austin, S., & McCann, R. (1992, April). *"Here's another arbitrary grade for your collection": A statewide study of grading policies.* Paper presented at the annual meeting of the American Educational Research Association, San Francisco.

Bailey, J. M., & Guskey, T. R. (2001). *Implementing student-led conferences.* Thousand Oaks, CA: Corwin Press.

Barnes, S. (1985). A study of classroom pupil evaluation: The missing link in teacher education. *Journal of Teacher Education, 36*(4), 46–49.

Bennett, B., & Kovac, K. (1995, April). *The student led conference.* Poster session presented at the annual meeting of the National Council on Measurement in Education as part of the Teacher Awards in Classroom Assessment session.

Bennett, D. T., & Collins, E. (1994, April). *Scoring packet for secondary school science assessment.* Paper presented at the annual meeting of the American Educational Research Association, New Orleans.

Bergin, D. A. (1999). Influences on classroom interest. *Educational Psychologist, 34,* 87–98.

Biggs, J. (1998). Assessment and classroom learning: A role for summative assessment? *Assessment in Education, 5,* 103–110.

Black, P., & Wiliam, D. (1998). Assessment and classroom learning. *Assessment in Education, 5,* 7–74.

Bloom, B., Hastings, J. T., & Madaus, G. F. (1971). *Handbook on formative and summative evaluation of student learning.* New York: McGraw-Hill.

Bradley, D. F., & Calvin, M. B. (1998). Grading modified assignments: Equity or compromise? *TEACHING Exceptional Children, 31*(2), 24–29.

Brookhart, S. M. (1993a). Assessing student achievement with term papers and written reports. *Educational Measurement: Issues and Practice, 12*(1), 40–47.

Brookhart, S. M. (1993b). Teachers' grading practices: Meaning and values. *Journal of Educational Measurement, 30,* 123–142.

Brookhart, S. M. (1994). Teachers' grading: Practice and theory. *Applied Measurement in Education, 7,* 279–301.

Brookhart, S. M. (1999a). Teaching about communicating assessment results and grading. *Educational Measurement: Issues and Practice, 18*(1), 5–13.

Brookhart, S. M. (1999b). *The art and science of classroom assessment: The missing part of pedagogy.* ASHE-ERIC Higher Education Report (Vol. 27, No. 1). Washington, DC: George Washington University.

Brookhart, S. M. (2001). Successful students' formative and summative uses of assessment information. *Assessment in Education, 8,* 153–169.

Brophy, J. (1999). Toward a model of the value aspects of motivation in education: Developing an appreciation for particular learning domains and activities. *Educational Psychologist, 34,* 75–85.

Bruner, J. S. (1966). *Toward a theory of instruction.* Cambridge, MA: Harvard University Press.

Bursuck, W. D., Munk, D. D., & Olson, M. M. (1999). The fairness of report card grading adaptations. *Remedial and Special Education, 20,* 84–92, 105.

Bursuck, W., Polloway, E. A., Plante, L., Epstein, M. H., Jayanthi, M., & McConeghy, J. (1996). Report card grading and adaptations: A national survey of classroom practices. *Exceptional Children, 62,* 301–318.

Butler, D. L., & Winne, P. H. (1995). Feedback and self-regulated learning: A theoretical synthesis. *Review of Educational Research, 65,* 245–281.

Butler, R. (1987). Task-involving and ego-involving properties of evaluation: Effects of different feedback conditions on motivational perceptions, interest, and performance. *Journal of Educational Psychology, 79,* 474–482.

Butler, R., & Nisan, M. (1986). Effects of no feedback, task-related comments, and grades on intrinsic motivation and performance. *Journal of Educational Psychology, 78,* 210–216.

California Assessment Collaborative. (1993, September). *Charting the course: Toward instructionally sound assessment.* San Francisco: Far West Laboratory.

Cochran-Smith, M., & Lytle, S. L. (1999). Relationships of knowledge and practice: Teacher learning in communities. *Review of Research in Education, 24,* 249–305.

Covington, M. V. (1992). *Making the grade: A self-worth perspective on motivation and school reform.* Cambridge: Cambridge University Press.

Covington, M. V., & Müeller, K. J. (2001). Intrinsic versus extrinsic motivation: An approach/avoidance reformulation. *Educational Psychology Review, 13,* 157–176.

Crooks, A. D. (1933). Marks and marking systems: A digest. *Journal of Educational Research, 27,* 259–272.

Crooks, T. J. (1988). The impact of classroom evaluation practices on students. *Review of Educational Research, 58,* 438–481.

Cuban, L. (1993). *How teachers taught: Constancy and change in American classrooms 1890–1990* (2nd ed.). New York: Teachers College Press.

Cureton, L. W. (1971). The history of grading practices. *Measurement in Education, 2*(4), 1–8.

Deci, E. L., & Ryan, R. M. (1985). *Intrinsic motivation and self-determination in human behavior.* New York: Plenum.

DePencier, I. B. (1951). Trends in reporting pupil progress in the elementary grades, 1938–1949. *Elementary School Journal, 51,* 519–528.

Donahoe, K., & Zigmond, N. (1990). Academic grades of ninth-grade urban learning-disabled students and low-achieving peers. *Exceptionality, 1,* 17–27.

Eccles, J. (1983). Expectancies, values, and academic behaviors. In J. T. Spence (Ed.), *Achievement and achievement motives* (pp. 75–146). San Francisco: Freeman.

Elawar, M. C., & Corno, L. (1985). A factorial experiment in teachers' written feedback on student homework: Changing teacher behavior a little rather than a lot. *Journal of Educational Psychology, 77,* 162–173.

Elliot, A. J., & Covington, M. V. (2001). Approach and avoidance motivation. *Educational Psychology Review, 13,* 73–92.

Elliot, A. J., & Thrash, T. M. (2001). Achievement goals and the hierarchical model of achievement motivation. *Educational Psychology Review, 13,* 139–156.

Evans, E. D., & Engelberg, R. A. (1988). Student perceptions of school grading. *Journal of Research and Development in Education, 21*(2), 45–54.

Friedman, S. J., & Frisbie, D. A. (1995). The influence of report cards on the validity of grades reported to parents. *Educational and Psychological Measurement, 55,* 5–26.

Gallagher, P. K. (n.d.) *Grading.* Unpublished materials, Resources for the Education of All Children with Handicaps (REACH), Intermediate Unit III, PA.

Gipps, C. (1994). *Beyond testing: Towards a theory of educational assessment.* London: Falmer Press.

Glaser, R. (1963). Instructional technology and the measurement of learning outcomes: Some questions. *American Psychologist, 18,* 519–521.

Greenhouse, L. (2002, February 20). Practice of students' grading papers doesn't violate privacy laws, Supreme Court says. *New York Times.*

Guskey, T. R. (2001). Helping standards make the grade. *Educational Leadership, 59*(1), 20–27.

Guskey, T. R. (2004). The communication challenge of standards-based grading. *Phi Delta Kappan, 86,* 326–329.

Guskey, T. R. (Ed.) (2008). *Practical solutions for serious problems in standards-based grading.* Thousand Oaks, CA: Corwin Press.

Guskey, T. R., & Bailey, J. M. (2001). *Developing grading and reporting systems for student learning.* Thousand Oaks, CA: Corwin Press.

Hackmann, D. G., Kenworthy, J., & Nibbelink, S. (1995, November). *Student-led conferences: Encouraging student-parent academic discussions.* Paper presented at the annual meeting of the National Middle School Association, New Orleans. (ERIC Document Reproduction Service No. ED388449)

Hall, W. S. (1906). A guide to the equitable grading of students. *School Science and Mathematics 6,* 501–510. Reprinted in Laska, J. A., & Juarez, T. (1992). *Grading and marking in American schools: Two centuries of debate* (pp. 15–19). Springfield, IL: Charles C. Thomas.

Hattie, J., & Timperley, H. (2007). The power of feedback. *Review of Educational Research, 77,* 81–112.

Haydel, J. B., Oescher, J., & Kirby, P. C. (1999, March). *Relationships between evaluative culture of classrooms, teacher efficacy, and student efficacy.* Paper presented at the annual meeting of the American Educational Research Association, Montreal.

Hidi, S., & Harackiewicz, J. M. (2000). Motivating the academically unmotivated: A critical issue for the 21st century. *Review of Educational Research, 70,* 151–179.

Jung, L. A. (2008). The challenges of grading and reporting in special education: An inclusive grading model. In T. R. Guskey (Ed.), *Practical solutions for serious problems in standards-based grading.* Thousand Oaks, CA: Corwin Press.

Jung, L. A., & Guskey, T. R. (2007). *Determining fair grades for students with special needs: A standards-based model.* Paper presented at the annual meeting of the American Educational Research Association, Chicago.

Kirschenbaum, H., Napier, R., & Simon, S. B. (1971). *Wad-ja-get? The grading game in American education.* New York: Hart Publishing.

Lantos, G. (1992). Evaluating written work: You get what you expect. *Issues and Inquiry in College Teaching and Learning, 15*(3), 79–86.

Loyd, B. H. (1991). Unpublished survey instruments.

Loyd, B. H., Nava, F. J. G., & Hearn, D. L. (1991, April). *High school students' perceptions of the grading process.* Paper presented at the annual meeting of the National Council on Measurement in Education, Chicago.

Marzano, R. J. (2000). *Transforming classroom grading.* Alexandria, VA: Association for Supervision and Curriculum Development (ASCD).

McClymer, J. F., & Knoles, L. Z. (1992). Ersatz learning, inauthentic testing. *Journal on Excellence in College Teaching, 3,* 33–50.

McElligott, J., & Brookhart, S. (2008). Legal issues of grading in the era of high stakes accountability. In T. R.

Guskey (Ed.), *Practical solutions for serious problems in standards-based grading*. Thousand Oaks, CA: Corwin Press.

McEllistrem, S., Grzywacz, P., & Roth, J. A., Eds. (2000). *2001 Deskbook encyclopedia of American school law.* Birmingham, AL: Oakstone.

Meyer, M. (1908). The grading of students. *Science 28,* 243–250. Reprinted in Laska, J. A., & Juarez, T. (1992). *Grading and marking in American schools: Two centuries of debate* (pp. 20–27). Springfield, IL: Charles C. Thomas.

Morrison, H. C. (1926). *The practice of teaching in the secondary school.* Chicago: University of Chicago Press, pp. 35–40, 74–75, 79–81. Reprinted in Laska, J. A., & Juarez, T. (1992). *Grading and marking in American schools: Two centuries of debate* (pp. 45–52). Springfield, IL: Charles C. Thomas.

Munk, D. D., & Bursuck, W. D. (2003). Grading students with disabilities. *Educational Leadership, 61*(2), 38–43.

National Association for the Education of Young Children. (1990). *Guidelines for appropriate curriculum and assessment in programs serving children ages 3 through 8.* Washington, DC: Author.

National Association for the Education of Young Children & National Association of Early Childhood Specialists in State Departments of Education. (2003). *Position statement with expanded resources: Early childhood curriculum, assessment, and program evaluation.* Available at: http://www.naeyc.org/about/positions/pdf/CAPEexpand.pdf

Natriello, G. (1987). The impact of evaluation processes on students. *Educational Psychologist, 22,* 155–175.

Nitko, A. J., & Brookhart, S. M. (2007). *Educational assessment of students* (5th ed.). Upper Saddle River, NJ: Merrill/Prentice Hall.

Northwest Regional Educational Laboratory. (2001). Assessment. Available at: http://www.nwrel.org/assessment/

Oosterhof, A. J. (1987). Obtaining intended weights when combining student scores. *Educational Measurement: Issues and Practice, 6*(4), 29–37.

Ory, J., & Ryan, K. (1993). *Tips for improving testing and grading.* Newbury Park, CA: Sage.

Pajares, F. (1996). Self-efficacy beliefs in academic settings. *Review of Educational Research, 66,* 543–578.

Perl, J. (1995). Improving relationship skills for parent conferences. *TEACHING Exceptional Children, 28*(1), 29–31.

Pilcher-Carlton, J., & Oosterhof, A. C. (1993, April). *A case study analysis of parents', teachers', and students' perceptions of the meaning of grades: Identification of discrepancies, their consequences, and obstacles to their resolution.* Paper presented at the annual meeting of the American Educational Research Association, Atlanta.

Polloway, E. A., Epstein, M. H., Bursuck, W. D., Roderique, T. W., McConeghy, J. L, & Jayanthi, M. (1994). Classroom grading: A national survey of policies. *Remedial and Special Education, 15,* 162–170.

Power, B. M., & Chandler, K. (1998). *Well-chosen words: Narrative assessments and report card comments.* York, ME: Stenhouse.

Ross, J. A., Rolheiser, C., & Hogaboam-Gray, A. (2002). Influences on student cognitions about evaluation. *Assessment in Education, 9,* 81–95.

Ryan, R. M., Connell, J. P., & Deci, E. L. (1985). A motivational analysis of self-determination and self-regulation in education. In C. Ames & R. Ames (Eds.), *Research on motivation in education: The classroom milieu* (Vol. 2, pp. 13–51). Orlando, FL: Academic.

Sadler, D. R. (1989). Formative assessment and the design of instructional systems. *Instructional Science, 18,* 119–144.

Schuster, C., Lynch, T., Polson-Lorczak, M., & Nadeau, K. (1996, April). *A study of kindergarten and first grade report cards: What are young children expected to learn?* Paper presented at the annual meeting of the American Educational Research Association, New York.

S.G.B. (1840). Weekly reports in schools. *The Common School Journal, 2,* 185–187. Reprinted in Laska, J. A., & Juarez, T. (1992). *Grading and marking in American schools: Two centuries of debate* (pp. 11–14). Springfield, IL: Charles C. Thomas.

Smallwood, M. L. (1935). *An historical study of examinations and grading systems in early American universities.* Harvard Studies in Education #24. Cambridge, MA: Harvard University Press.

Smith, A. Z., & Dobbin, J. E. (1960). Marks and marking systems. In C. W. Harris (Ed.), *Encyclopedia of Educational Research* (3rd ed., pp. 783–791). New York: Macmillan.

Starch, D. (1918). *Educational measurements.* New York: Macmillan.

Starch, D., & Elliott, E. C. (1912). Reliability of the grading of high-school work in English. *School Review, 20,* 442–457.

Starch, D., & Elliott, E. C. (1913a). Reliability of grading work in mathematics. *School Review, 21,* 254–259.

Starch, D., & Elliott, E. C. (1913b). Reliability of grading work in history. *School Review, 21,* 676–681.

Stiggins, R. J. (2005). *Student-involved assessment FOR learning.* (4th ed.). Upper Saddle River, NJ: Merrill/Prentice Hall.

Stiggins, R. J., & Conklin, N. F. (1992). *In teachers' hands: Investigating the practices of classroom assessment.* Albany, NY: SUNY Press.

Stiggins, R. J., Frisbie, D. A., & Griswold, P. A. (1989). Inside high school grading practices: Building a research agenda. *Educational Measurement: Issues and Practice, 8*(2), 5–14.

Talley, N. R. (1989). Weighted averages and college admission. *Journal of College Admissions, 125,* 19–21.

Talley, N. R., & Mohr, J. I. (1991). Weighted averages, computer screening, and college admission in public colleges and universities. *Journal of College Admissions, 132,* 9–11.

Talley, N. R., & Mohr, J. I. (1993). The case for a national standard of grade weighting. *Journal of College Admissions, 139,* 9–13.

Thomas, S., & Oldfather, P. (1997). Intrinsic motivations, literacy, and assessment practices: "That's my grade. That's me." *Educational Psychologist, 32,* 107–123.

Tomlinson, C. A. (2001). Grading for success. *Educational Leadership, 58*(6), 12–15.

Tunstall, P., & Gipps, C. (1996). Teacher feedback to young children in formative assessment: a typology. *British Educational Research Journal, 22,* 389–404.

Waltman, K. K., & Frisbie, D. A. (1994). Parents' understanding of their children's report card grades. *Applied Measurement in Education, 7,* 223–240.

Washburne, C. W. (1932). *Adjusting the school to the child.* Yonkers-on-Hudson, New York: World Book Company.

Weiner, B. (1979). A theory of motivation for some classroom experiences. *Journal of Educational Psychology, 71,* 3–25.

Welsh, M., & D'Agostino, J. (2008). Fostering consistency between standards-based grades and large scale assessment results. In T. R. Guskey, (Ed.), *Practical solutions for serious problems in standards-based grading.* Thousand Oaks, CA: Corwin Press.

Wiggins, G. (1998). *Educative assessment.* San Francisco: Jossey-Bass.

Winger, T. (2005). Grading to communicate. *Educational Leadership, 63*(3), 12–15.

Wise, S. L. (Ed.). (1993). *Teacher training in measurement and assessment skills.* Lincoln, NE: Buros Institute of Mental Measurements, University of Nebraska-Lincoln.

Wolf, D. P. (1993). Assessment as an episode of learning. In R. E. Bennet & W. C. Ward (Eds.), *Construction versus choice in cognitive measurement* (pp. 213–240). Hillsdale, NJ: Lawrence Erlbaum.

Young, J. W. (1993). Grade adjustment methods. *Review of Educational Research, 63,* 151–165.

Zirkel, P. W. (2000). A D-grading experience? *Phi Delta Kappan, 82,* 243–254.